CRASH COURSE

The American Automobile Industry's

Road from Glory to Disaster

CRASH COURSE

PAUL INGRASSIA

I.C.C. LIBRARY

RANDOM HOUSE
NEW YORK

Published in the United States by Random House,
an imprint of The Random House Publishing Group,
a division of Random House, Inc., New York.

RANDOM HOUSE and colophon are
registered trademarks of Random House, Inc.

LIBRARY OF CONGRESS CATALOGING-IN-PUBLICATION DATA

Ingrassia, Paul.
Crash course : the American automobile industry's
road from glory to disaster / Paul Ingrassia.
p. cm.
ISBN 978-1-4000-6863-0
eBook ISBN 978-1-58836-891-1
1. Automobile industry and trade—United States—History.   I. Title.
HD9710.U52I55 2010
338.4'76292220973—dc22   2009033152

Printed in the United States of America on acid-free paper

www.atrandom.com

9 8 7 6 5 4 3 2 1

FIRST EDITION

Book design by Fritz Metsch

Title page photograph by iStock

For my parents, Regina and Angelo Ingrassia, who left too soon.

Contents

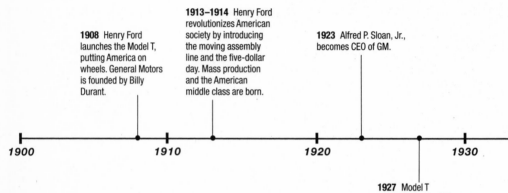

1913–1914 Henry Ford revolutionizes American society by introducing the moving assembly line and the five-dollar day. Mass production and the American middle class are born.

1908 Henry Ford launches the Model T, putting America on wheels. General Motors is founded by Billy Durant.

1923 Alfred P. Sloan, Jr., becomes CEO of GM.

1900 1910 1920 1930

1927 Model T production ends. GM passes Ford as the largest U.S. car company.

Timeline

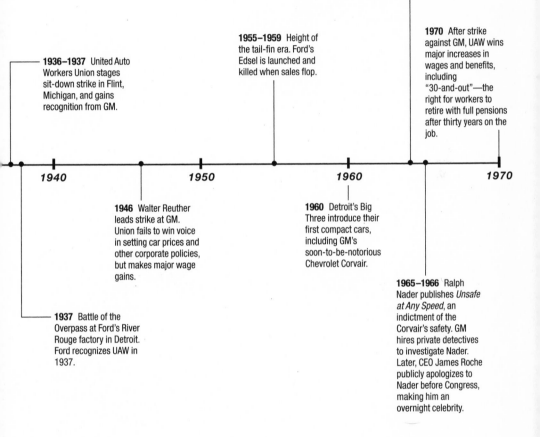

1964 Ford introduces the Mustang, catching GM off guard and smashing all sales records for a new model. But GM launches the Pontiac GTO and ushers in the era of "muscle cars," high-horsepower vehicles beloved by boy racers and celebrated in rock music.

1955–1959 Height of the tail-fin era. Ford's Edsel is launched and killed when sales flop.

1970 After strike against GM, UAW wins major increases in wages and benefits, including "30-and-out"—the right for workers to retire with full pensions after thirty years on the job.

1936–1937 United Auto Workers Union stages sit-down strike in Flint, Michigan, and gains recognition from GM.

1940　　*1950*　　*1960*　　*1970*

1946 Walter Reuther leads strike at GM. Union fails to win voice in setting car prices and other corporate policies, but makes major wage gains.

1960 Detroit's Big Three introduce their first compact cars, including GM's soon-to-be-notorious Chevrolet Corvair.

1937 Battle of the Overpass at Ford's River Rouge factory in Detroit. Ford recognizes UAW in 1937.

1965–1966 Ralph Nader publishes *Unsafe at Any Speed*, an indictment of the Corvair's safety. GM hires private detectives to investigate Nader. Later, CEO James Roche publicly apologizes to Nader before Congress, making him an overnight celebrity.

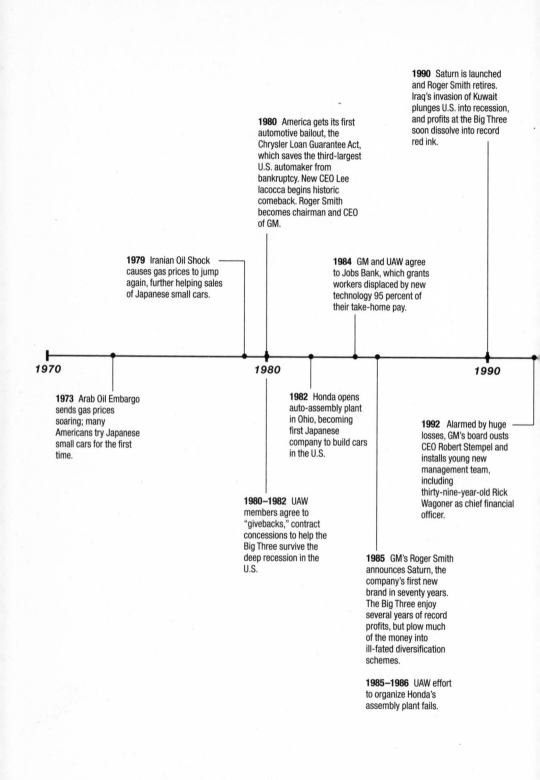

1990 Saturn is launched and Roger Smith retires. Iraq's invasion of Kuwait plunges U.S. into recession, and profits at the Big Three soon dissolve into record red ink.

1980 America gets its first automotive bailout, the Chrysler Loan Guarantee Act, which saves the third-largest U.S. automaker from bankruptcy. New CEO Lee Iacocca begins historic comeback. Roger Smith becomes chairman and CEO of GM.

1979 Iranian Oil Shock causes gas prices to jump again, further helping sales of Japanese small cars.

1984 GM and UAW agree to Jobs Bank, which grants workers displaced by new technology 95 percent of their take-home pay.

1970   1980   1990

1973 Arab Oil Embargo sends gas prices soaring; many Americans try Japanese small cars for the first time.

1982 Honda opens auto-assembly plant in Ohio, becoming first Japanese company to build cars in the U.S.

1992 Alarmed by huge losses, GM's board ousts CEO Robert Stempel and installs young new management team, including thirty-nine-year-old Rick Wagoner as chief financial officer.

1980–1982 UAW members agree to "givebacks," contract concessions to help the Big Three survive the deep recession in the U.S.

1985 GM's Roger Smith announces Saturn, the company's first new brand in seventy years. The Big Three enjoy several years of record profits, but plow much of the money into ill-fated diversification schemes.

1985–1986 UAW effort to organize Honda's assembly plant fails.

2007 Daimler sells Chrysler to Cerberus for $7.4 billion, just 20 percent of the price that it paid nine years earlier. GM takes $38.6 billion write-off, acknowledging that it doesn't expect an early return to profitability.

1998 Germany's Daimler-Benz acquires Chrysler for $38 billion. UAW members in Flint, Michigan, stage strikes that saddle GM with more than $2 billion in losses.

September 2008 Losses mount at all three Detroit car companies. The collapse of Lehman Brothers crashes the stock market, and auto sales plunge.

2005 GM posts loss of $10.6 billion, despite near-record industry-wide car sales.

1994 The SUV boom begins, catching Japanese car companies off guard.

2002–2004 GM's Wagoner expands commitment to pickup trucks and SUVs; home-mortgage lending accounts for growing share of company profits.

November–December 2008 GM and Chrysler say they will run out of money without government aid. After Congress refuses to appropriate funds, President George W. Bush diverts bank-bailout funds to keep the two companies afloat.

2000 Rick Wagoner becomes CEO of GM.

2000

2010

1995 Stephen Yokich elected president of the UAW and pursues campaign to unravel innovative labor contract at Saturn.

2001 Ford posts major losses; Nasser is replaced as CEO by William Clay Ford, Jr.

2003 Saturn workers vote to scrap their innovative labor contract and revert to the standard contract between GM and the UAW.

1999 Ford and GM earn record profits. Jacques Nasser becomes CEO of Ford. Mike Bennett, an advocate of union-management cooperation, is defeated as head of UAW Local 1853 at Saturn.

2006 Ford posts loss of $12.6 billion; Alan Mulally from Boeing succeeds Bill Ford, Jr., as CEO. Soon afterward, Ford borrows $23.6 billion to fund a corporate turnaround effort.

February–March 2009 President Obama's Automotive Task Force takes shape.

March 2009 The task force forces the resignation of GM CEO Rick Wagoner. President Obama gives Chrysler thirty days to form a partnership with Fiat or face liquidation, and gives GM sixty days to restructure outside of bankruptcy.

April 2009 Chrysler seeks Chapter 11 bankruptcy protection, as part of a government-sponsored "fast track" bankruptcy that will result in operational control of the company by Fiat.

June 2009 GM files the second-largest industrial bankruptcy in U.S. history. In July, the "new GM" emerges from bankruptcy majority-owned by the U.S. government.

CRASH COURSE

ONE

WHERE THE WEAK ARE KILLED AND EATEN

It really wasn't intended to be a prophecy. It was just a smart-alecky T-shirt worn for years by local teenagers to annoy their parents and show their perverse pride in the Motor City's tough-town image. It said: DETROIT: WHERE THE WEAK ARE KILLED AND EATEN. But the menacing message seemed all too appropriate in the bleak winter of 2008–2009, when signs of weakness—indeed, desperation—erupted everywhere in Detroit.

One bankrupt car-components company economized by servicing the bathrooms in its suburban headquarters only every other day. Some of the bathrooms ran out of toilet paper, prompting employees to hoard it or bring their own from home. In the city itself employment prospects were so bleak that some prisoners begged to stay in jail to get food and shelter—"three hots and a cot," in the local parlance.

The city's battered economy was reflected on the football field, where the University of Michigan was enduring its first losing season in forty years, and the Detroit Lions were plummeting to pro football's first 0–16 season. During their 47–10 drubbing on Thanksgiving Day 2008, fans unfurled a banner reading BAIL OUT THE LIONS. It was a gallows-humor reference not only to the football team but also to the weakest teams in town—General Motors, Ford, and Chrysler.

Since the beginning of the century America's Big Three car companies, bleeding from more than $100 billion in losses in four years, had shed more than 333,000 employees, enough to populate the city of Cincinnati. In November 2008 GM's stock closed below $3 a share for the first time since 1946, when Harry Truman was president. To conserve cash, the company ended its nine-year endorsement deal with golfer Tiger Woods, who was making more money than GM anyway. That same month Detroit's automakers went to Washington to beg Congress for a bailout—in a last-ditch effort to avoid another b-word, *bankruptcy.*

Their potential demise marked a shocking reversal of fortune for companies that had been defining forces in shaping America and indeed the world. Detroit's manufacturing muscle had helped win World War II and underpinned U.S. economic hegemony in the postwar Pax Americana. The companies had made Detroit the Silicon Valley of the mid-twentieth century, a place of economic opportunity, where hillbillies from Appalachia and sharecroppers from the South could break out of poverty and grab a piece of America's bounty.

Ford had invented mass manufacturing and, with it, the car that had put the country on wheels, bringing mobility to the masses and freeing multitudes of American farmers from the drudgery of rural peasantry. Henry Ford's Model T had been the first people's car and had indirectly inspired the development of another people's car: the Volkswagen Beetle.

General Motors, in turn, had pioneered mass marketing, with a hierarchy of brands ranging from the practical Chevrolet to the prestigious Cadillac that fit Americans on all rungs of the socioeconomic ladder. GM also had developed the organizational principles—decentralized operations subject to central financial control—that would underpin virtually every corporation in America and the world. GM scientists had invented the room air conditioner and the mechanical heart pump. And in 1955 GM had become the world's first company to earn more than $1 billion in a single year.

That General Motors could go bankrupt seemed as unlikely as, say, America's banks going broke or a black man being elected president of the United States. But in fact all three of those things—one a historic breakthrough, the other two historic breakdowns—would happen in the mind-numbing months between late 2008 and mid-2009. In the end the bailout of America's banks would cost seven or eight times as much as rescuing Detroit, but the emotional impact would be nowhere near as deep.

It was cars, after all, not banks, that Americans celebrated in books, movies, and music. The Beach Boys' memorable 1963 song was "Little Deuce Coupe," not "Little Deuce Coupon," and Wilson Pickett's hit three years later was "Mustang Sally," not "Mustang Sallie Mae."

Millions of Americans cherished the memories of the 1950s tail fins, the 1960s muscle cars, and their own sexual and other escapades in the automobiles of their youth. A typical episode occurred in Kalamazoo, Michigan, in 1969, when two boys driving a hot new Ford Mustang pulled out of a local Chicken Charlie's drive-in, tailed by girls driving a Plymouth Barracuda. It was showtime. When the Mustang's driver hit the accelerator, the car literally flew over a blind hill and momentarily went airborne—just as it was passing a parked policeman. The cop must have been startled, because when he pulled the boys over, he had hot coffee spilled on his uniform. Thousands of such incidents, all across America, would inspire Hollywood a few years later to make a movie called *American Graffiti*.

By the end of the twentieth century America's love affair with the automobile had evolved into an infatuation with the sport-utility vehicle, or SUV, designed for traversing off-road terrain, although few people actually took it there. The vehicle's unlikely popularity made it fitting that on December 7, 2008, Detroit's greatest hour of need, three gleaming white ones—a Chevrolet Tahoe, a Ford Escape, and a Dodge Aspen—were parked like sacred icons at the altar for a special service at the Greater Grace Temple Pentecostal Church on Detroit's northwest side.

It happened to be the sixty-seventh anniversary of Pearl Harbor, but the service wasn't to pray for deliverance from Japanese dive-bombers or torpedo planes. Instead it was to beseech relief from Toyota Camrys and Honda Accords, whose wide popularity—on top of America's financial crisis—was a critical cause of Detroit's affliction. A vice president of the United Auto Workers led prayers for a congressional bailout and gave the worshipers a benediction for the occasion. "We have done all we can do in this union," he said, "so I'm going to turn it over to the Lord."

The presiding prelate at the service intoned: "We have never seen as midnight an hour as we face this week. Lives are hanging above an abyss of uncertainty as both houses of Congress decide whether to extend a helping hand."

.   .   .

Uncertainty was hanging heavily in many places across America that were far from Detroit. One was the "sparrow fart" town of South Paris, Maine, as Gene Benner affectionately put it. There he owned Bessey Motor Sales, the Chrysler-Jeep-Dodge dealership that served the town of 2,200 people, some ninety minutes northwest of Portland. Benner was the quintessential small-town car dealer. His road to that occupation, while less than direct, was a real-life version of the American dream.

He had been a star wide receiver, and holder of a host of school records, on the University of Maine football team. After graduating in 1970, Benner was drafted by the Cleveland Browns and hoped for a pro football career. But after being cut in the team's tryouts, he played semipro football in Connecticut for a while, then returned to Maine to become a high school teacher and coach.

In 1984 he wanted to change careers and started selling cars at Bessey Motors. A decade later he scraped together all the money he could find, including borrowing some from his mother, and bought the dealership. In his twenty-five years in the car business he had seen a lot: Chrysler's incredible comeback under Lee Iacocca in the 1980s, the smash-hit successes of the company's minivans and Jeeps, Chrysler's 1998 merger with Daimler-Benz to form the first postnational car company, and the sale of Chrysler in 2007 to a private equity firm after the Germans had given up on the deal.

In 2008 Benner's dealership was losing money, and he faced difficult decisions on how to save it. Nothing he could do would matter, however, if Chrysler just collapsed. That calamity, if it happened, would throw his thirty employees out of work and wipe out everything he had worked for in the last quarter-century. Detroit's crisis, in a very real sense, was Gene Benner's crisis too.

The same was true for Fred Young and his son, Gene, in another small town far from South Paris. They were autoworkers—Fred retired, Gene still active—at the Chrysler assembly plant in Belvidere, Illinois, a town of about 22,000 people some seventy miles northwest of Chicago. America's automotive history ran deep in Belvidere, where the first car had been built in 1904: the Eldredge Runabout, an open-air two-seater produced by the local National Sewing Machine Company. Like the Zenkmobile, the Orient Buckboard, and most cars that appeared in the auto industry's early years, the Eldredge Runabout soon flopped.

Not for another sixty years would cars again be made in Belvidere. In 1965 Chrysler built a spanking-new assembly plant just outside the town, and Fred Young started working there. He toiled in the factory for thirty-six years before retiring in 2001 with a comfortable pension and free medical care for life—or so he thought. In 2008 he was seventy years old, and with Chrysler's survival in doubt, Young was worried about his future too.

Gene Young had followed his father's footsteps onto the factory floor in 1999. Over the next nine years he had spent only half of his assigned working hours actually building cars, but he had gotten paid for the other half anyway. That was thanks to the Jobs Bank, a program that was started by the car companies and the UAW in the 1980s.

The original intent of the Jobs Bank was to provide temporary security for hourly workers on layoff. But like a lot of other things in Detroit, it had evolved into something else altogether. By the 1990s laid-off workers could remain "bankers," as they were nicknamed with knowing irony, for an unlimited time, making 95 percent of their wages while not working. Thus an arrangement begun to protect workers had helped plunge the automakers into red ink—and was threatening the survival of the companies that provided their jobs.

In a perverse but predictable twist, the Jobs Bank led to something called "inverse layoffs," which occurred when senior workers volunteered to be laid off and thus bumped junior workers back onto the assembly line. After all, why should a worker with high seniority slave away building cars when workers with lower seniority collected virtually full pay just for sitting around? Such was the logic of Detroit's dysfunction.

Even Gene Young, who regularly bounced to and from the assembly line between his cycle of layoffs and inverse layoffs, thought the system was crazy—though, understandably, he didn't want to walk away from such a sweet deal. But if Chrysler should succumb to the crisis of 2008–2009, the latest one in the company's roller-coaster eighty-year history, he wouldn't have a choice.

As the two Youngs, father and son, watched Detroit's meltdown and contemplated their uncertain futures, Fred couldn't believe it was happening. "How did it get this way?" he asked plaintively. "It happened so slowly that nobody noticed it. Not till it hit us right between the eyes."

In late 2008 millions of other Americans were asking that very same question, but the answer really wasn't complicated. Detroit's auto industry was built on a corporate oligopoly and a union monopoly—a combination that had produced decades of astounding success but also sowed the seeds of failure. For seventy years the two sides had expended so much effort trying to outwit each other that they had precious little energy left to take care of their customers—or to comprehend the threat of new competitors from beyond America's shores.

The relationship between Detroit's car companies and the UAW had been born in violence in the 1930s and 1940s, with incidents that were celebrated in union lore: the Sit-down Strike, the Battle of the Running Bulls, and the Battle of the Overpass. These romantic names continued to infuse the ethos of the UAW and made confrontation instead of cooperation its default mode, long after the union had gained the upper hand over the companies in the 1970s.

During that time the union won contracts that allowed many workers to collect pensions and enjoy free healthcare for more years in retirement than they actually would spend on the job. Contracts that originally had been the size of little pamphlets grew, as time went on, to become as thick as phone books. The complex rules governing seniority (and thus layoffs and inverse layoffs) ran sixteen pages alone.

In addition, the contracts established dozens of distinct job classifications for hourly workers. Each worker was assigned a classification and was strictly prevented from doing work reserved for members of another. The increasingly intricate "work rules" were administered by big (and expensive) bureaucracies of corporate labor-relations staffs and their counterparts in union "desk jobs"— who were paid by the car companies.

It was difficult to place sole blame for all this on the UAW, however; the companies' managements had sometimes seemed determined to alienate their workers at every turn. In the recession of the early 1980s, on the very day that workers approved pay cuts to help tide the company through tough times, General Motors sweetened the bonus formula for its executives. The workers, of course, were outraged.

Even late in that decade, GM's factories had bathrooms that were segregated—not by race, but by rank. The "salaried men's rest room" and the "hourly men's rest room" usually sat side by side, but psychologically they were worlds apart. They were part of an apartheid system in which the behavior of white-collar managers constantly sent humiliating reminders to blue-collar workers that said, in effect, "I'm better than you are."

Over the years such dysfunction came to be accepted as normal by corporate bureaucracies focused on managerial minutiae. General Motors had a Bulletin Board Study Committee (no kidding), which in 1988 recommended that new bulletin boards be installed at company headquarters for the GM Women's Club and the GM Men's Club. The committee could have been the punch line in a corporate comedy skit. As for separate women's and men's clubs, they were relics from the days of tail fins—and evidence of a corporate culture frozen in time.

In this insular world, a GM executive returned to his suburban Detroit home one evening to be shocked by the sight of an unfamiliar car sitting in the family driveway. It was a used Toyota, which his son had bought at college and driven home for the weekend. A father-and-son talk ensued, during which it was agreed that the offending vehicle couldn't be parked in the driveway or even in front of the house—but on a street around the corner instead.

In his retirement a quarter-century later, with GM hovering near bankruptcy, the executive recalled the incident ruefully. "Maybe instead of getting mad about the Toyota," he said, "I should have asked him what he liked about the car."

.　　.　　.

The answer would have been fuel economy, for starters. For fifteen years Toyota, Nissan, and other Japanese car companies had struggled in the United States with only mixed success. Then in 1973 the Arab Oil Embargo sent fuel prices soaring and prompted many Americans to try fuel-efficient Japanese cars, as opposed to the Detroit leviathans they had bought in years past.

After trying the cars for gas mileage, Americans found they liked their reliability. By 1980, with Japanese cars gaining popularity and America entering a deep recession, Chrysler was on the brink of bankruptcy, and Ford and General Motors were posting record losses—record, at least, for their day.

Then in 1982 Honda opened an assembly plant in Ohio, a daring and risky move because Honda was only a second-tier automaker at the time. But it became, improbably, the first Japanese company to build cars in the United States. Honda didn't have to worry about UAW work rules or convoluted contracts because there wasn't any union. The UAW's leaders had been on the verge of cutting a deal with Honda's executives in Japan to gain recognition for the union. But their secret negotiations were undermined by Honda's managers and workers in Ohio, neither of whom wanted the UAW around. Virtually every other Japanese car company followed Honda in building nonunion plants in America—more than two dozen in the next twenty-five years.

The bottom line was that Japanese car companies broke Detroit's corporate oligopoly in the 1970s, and then broke the UAW's labor monopoly in car factories in the 1980s. But when all seemed lost, unexpected things began to happen.

The Big Three and the UAW began a painful process of introspection and self-reform. Their efforts produced a new company called Saturn, launched by GM with its own streamlined union contract, and several joint-venture factories with Japanese car companies, so the Detroiters could learn their methods.

As the reform efforts took hold, the Detroit companies began to narrow the quality and productivity gaps with their Japanese competitors. They also proved adept at innovation. Chrysler's minivan was a new kind of vehicle that made the family station wagon obsolete. Ford revolutionized automotive styling with the aerodynamic Taurus sedan.

"We didn't undergo fundamental change *by our own choice*," wrote Bob Lutz, who would become the only person to hold senior executive jobs at Ford, Chrysler, and GM. "It was *forced* on us. The wisest of people or institutions seldom can deduce, on their own, that change is needed. And if they do, they never muster the courage to act on that need." His words later would prove prophetic.

Just as unexpectedly, in the mid- and late 1990s the Japanese themselves skidded off course. Japan's automakers missed the SUV boom, Honda was reeling from a corporate kickback scandal, and Nissan almost went bankrupt. At the end of that decade, Detroit was raking in record profits and had a sterling opportunity to surge ahead for good.

But what might have ended as an admirable—indeed, heroic—chronicle of comeback wasn't to last. Throughout the 1980s and 1990s, every time the Big Three and the UAW returned to prosperity, they would succumb to hubris and lapse back into their old bad habits. It was like a Biblical cycle of repentance, reform, and going astray, again and again, as Detroit was repeatedly lured by the golden calves of corporate excess and union overreach.

The cycle reached its peak at the beginning of the new millennium, when the Big Three plunged from record profits to breathtaking losses in just five years. By then the UAW too was reeling, having dropped to just 655,000 members from 1.5 million a quarter-century earlier. Neither the companies nor the union could muster the will to change without a crisis; that would make them both desperately vulnerable when events spun out of control.

Detroit's final descent into disaster began on September 15, 2008—just one day before General Motors, ironically, would celebrate the hundredth anniversary of its founding. The fifteenth happened to be the day that bank failures on Wall Street sparked another historic event—the collapse of the U.S. stock market. Almost immediately car sales collapsed too.

Two months later the Big Three CEOs swooped into Washington on their private jets to ask for money. They came away, instead, with

Detroit's worst PR drubbing in forty years. After Congress said no, President George W. Bush opened the public purse anyway—just enough so he could pass the presidency, along with Detroit's crisis, to Barack Obama.

In late March, just two months after taking office, the new young president himself launched a last-ditch effort to save Chrysler, even though many of his own advisers opposed the idea as foolhardy. And he defrocked the CEO of General Motors—a onetime boy wonder just like the president himself—prompting GM's directors to mount an angry rebellion. But it collapsed when they realized who held the purse strings and thus the power. Those steps, and all the behind-the-scenes maneuvering that preceded them, were just the beginning.

In April the president's people slapped down Chrysler's creditors, which included some of the nation's biggest and most powerful banks. They forced the UAW to swallow things it had fought successfully for years. In the process they pushed Chrysler into bankruptcy and into the orbit of an unlikely savior—an Italian company that had fled the United States more than thirty years earlier because its cars were shoddier than even the worst of Detroit's.

Then in May, while Gene Benner and Gene Young were wondering how Chrysler's bankruptcy would affect their fates, attention turned to General Motors. The only way to save the company, the president's aides concluded, was to do what GM had stoutly and stubbornly resisted—dismantle much of the industrial empire that the company had built over the previous hundred years. But doing that would force the company that once had been the biggest and most powerful on earth into bankruptcy court—albeit lubricated by billions of dollars of additional government bailout money.

The bankruptcy filing on June 1, 2009, began with rhetorical flourishes that evoked General Motors' glorious history. "For over one hundred years," the filing began, "GM has been a major component of the U.S. manufacturing and industrial base, as well as the market leader in the automotive industry . . . General Motors' highly-skilled engineering and development personnel designed and manufactured the first lunar roving vehicle driven on the moon." In addition, the company noted, it had made 450 million earth-bound vehicles during its century of existence.

But the company's new CEO, Fritz Henderson, soon dispensed with lofty language and described GM's grim reality. The company would sell or shutter half of its brands, eliminate hundreds of dealers, and cut thousands more employees on top of those already shown the door. "There is simply no other alternative" to bankruptcy, he said in his own court affidavit. "There is no other sale, or even other potential purchasers, present or on the horizon. . . . There is no other source for financing. The only alternative available is liquidation."

Actually, had General Motors come to grips with reality earlier, there would have been another alternative. It was evident in plain view, right across town: Ford, the only American car company that had steered clear of bankruptcy. In the nick of time Ford had made tough and painful decisions. It had changed the CEO, even though his name was on the building. It had dumped money-losing brands. And it had mortgaged every asset it had—including its iconic blue-oval logo—to fund a turnaround effort without government help.

The measures Ford took were all things that General Motors could have, and should have, done. But even some retired GM executives had taken to calling the company's inept board of directors the "board of bystanders." The consequences of GM's denial and delay would be paid by the company's stockholders, employees, and dealers—and by every American taxpayer as well.

None of this was inevitable, as Ford proved by its just-in-time awakening. Hubris and sclerosis had been building for years in Detroit, in a heedless union and feckless managements. The signs included inverse layoffs, bulletin board committees, segregated bathrooms, corporate recoveries followed by repeated relapses, and the success of American workers led by Japanese management. Everything that happened to Detroit's auto industry in 2009 was so avoidable and so incredibly sad, especially when measured against the brilliant promise of the early years of America's automotive age.

TWO

DYNASTY AND DESTINY

*M*odern *America's love affair* with the automobile began in a run-down red brick building on Woodward Avenue in Highland Park, Michigan, a little municipality surrounded by the city of Detroit. The four-story building, which today stands near the Model T Plaza shopping center and has a shoe-outlet store in the rear parking lot, was built nearly a century ago by Henry Ford. It's still owned by the Ford Motor Company, which uses it to store old documents. A dark-green historical marker, largely obscured in spring and summer by overgrown shrubbery, explains the building's more illustrious past: "At this plant, Ford instituted the 'five dollar day,' a generous wage for the time. In factory 'H,' located directly east of here, he began mass producing automobiles on moving assembly lines." It was 1913, and the automobiles produced here were Model T Fords, the car that changed the world.

Surveying the faded glory of Highland Park, and the desperate state of Detroit's auto industry, in the winter of 2008–09, the wealth and power of America's car companies during most of the twentieth century seemed incomprehensible. They had reshaped America's landscape and its society with suburbs, interstate highways, fast-food restaurants, shopping malls, and drive-in everything: banks, movies, churches, and more.

They created an industrial base with supporting industries—steel, oil, glass, rubber, advertising, electronics—that made America the world's wartime "Arsenal of Democracy." And they fostered personal mobility that changed movies, music, books, status symbols, and sexual mores. "Most of the babies of the period were conceived in Model T Fords," wrote John Steinbeck in *Cannery Row* in 1945, "and not a few were born in them."

In 1923, a decade after Henry Ford invented mass production in

Highland Park, another automobile magnate, Alfred P. Sloan, Jr., invented mass marketing. Sloan's vision of automobiles was radically different from Ford's. To him, cars were vehicles for aspiration as well as transportation. Under Sloan, General Motors created a social ladder of brands, with Chevrolet at the bottom and Cadillac at the top and several rungs in between. Each brand, and each model within the brand, signaled its owner's social status to any onlooker.

Ford and Sloan were the two giants of the American auto industry's formative years. A mathematician might express the collective result of their work with this equation:

Mass production + mass marketing = mass consumption = modern America

That's at least as true as, say, $E = mc^2$, and it's probably better for the economy.

Henry Ford was born less than a month after the Battle of Gettysburg, on July 30, 1863, on a farm about a dozen miles west of Detroit, in what today is Dearborn, Michigan. As a boy he preferred tinkering with machines to doing farm chores, and at sixteen he departed for Detroit to work in the city's machine shops. At thirty he was chief engineer at Detroit's Edison Electric Company. As a sideline, he built his first car, the Quadricycle, so called because it basically was a motorized platform carried on four bicycle tires. So focused was Ford on getting the device to work that he didn't measure the door of his workshop and had to knock down a wall to drive the car onto the street. Henry's first two attempts to start car companies with help from local investors ended in failure, because he had a way of clashing with his backers.

Detroit was a mecca for automotive entrepeneurs back then, just as San Jose is for Internet innovators today, and then as now most of the inventions failed. But in 1901 Henry Ford cemented his reputation and won a $1,000 prize by scoring an upset victory in a race on a dirt track in what is now Grosse Pointe. So in 1903 Ford found new investors to start a third company, the Ford Motor Company. With himself as vice president and chief engineer, it turned out a few hand-built cars a day. His engines came from the Dodge brothers, Horace and John, who accepted 10 percent of Ford stock in lieu of cash. "I will build a car for the great multitude," Ford said, describing his ambition. "No man making a good salary will be unable to own one, and enjoy with his family the blessing of hours of pleasure in God's great open spaces."

By 1908 Ford had located his company in a brick building on Detroit's Piquette Street, which is now filled with abandoned buildings and lots but then was home to a hive of fledgling factories. He walled off an area on the third floor of his factory to develop his dream car. Like his previous cars, this one was named for a letter of the alphabet and was called the Model T. In September of that year Henry, along with aides, took the car on an extended test drive around Lake Michigan. Heading north from Detroit, traversing Michigan's Upper Peninsula, driving through Wisconsin and Chicago, then heading home, they covered nearly fourteen hundred miles. On October 1, 1908, the Model T Ford went on sale.

Henry Ford was like Steve Jobs a century later; as word spread that Ford was up to something special, his new car was greeted with the sort of hoopla now reserved for iPhones. Before the Model T went on sale, Ford dealers ordered fifteen thousand of them—nearly twice the number of cars that Ford had sold the year before. The initial price was $850, about two-thirds that of competing Buicks and Chevrolets, but price wasn't the only appeal.

The Model T had parts that were readily interchangeable, making repairs easy. Its frame used a new steel from Europe called vanadium that was strong but light, so the Model T weighed about 25 percent less than a comparable Buick. Most cars of the day, including the Buick, used ultra-heavy frames to cope with America's rough and rutted roads, which made them prone to getting stuck. But Ford's car flexed with the road, which allowed it to go places that other cars couldn't.

The Model T's four-cylinder, 20-horsepower engine—less horsepower than some of today's John Deere lawn tractors—could go nearly forty miles an hour and get almost twenty miles a gallon. In 1909 a Model T won a transcontinental race from New York to Seattle. Later it emerged that Ford had cheated by replacing the car's engine en route. But he had already reaped a publicity bonanza from the victory.

In 1913, after moving to the Highland Park plant, Ford got the idea for a moving assembly line by studying the meat-packing plants of Chicago, which were basically dis-assembly lines. Ford tried the assembly line in the "sub-assembly" of components such as engines and transmissions and soon spread the concept—with its enormous gains in productivity—to his entire operation. To simplify the production process further, he decreed that instead of making the Model T available in red, green, and blue, customers henceforth could have "any color they wanted, as long as it's black." Ironically, the actual color was called "Japan black enamel." Had Henry known what the Japanese would do to Detroit a century later, he might have chosen a different color.

Thanks to the moving assembly line, production time dropped from thirteen hours a car to about ninety minutes. Early the next year, on January 5, 1914, Ford made a stunning announcement. The company would immediately start paying its factory workers $5 a day, more than double their previous wages. Ford started a new Sociological Department to ensure, as *Time* magazine later would explain, that "the extra pay went only for better homes, milk, fruit, vegetables and Ford cars—not for liquor and riotous living."

The $5 day generated enormous publicity and powerful marketing momentum for Ford Motor, just as Henry and his aides had foreseen. Model T sales soared, and Ford was besieged with letters from grateful workers who no longer had to hire out their children as servants. Other industrialists were outraged, however, and *The Wall Street Journal* ranted on January 7, two days after the announcement, that Ford "has in his social endeavor committed economic blunders, if not crimes."

But Ford stuck to his guns, explaining that his employees should be able to afford to buy his cars. "If an employer does not share prosperity with those who make him prosperous," he wrote (with collaborator Samuel Crowther) in his 1926 book *Today and Tomorrow,* "then pretty soon there will be no prosperity to share." What began at least partly as a commercial move, in short, quickly took on sweeping social significance and planted the seeds for America's middle class.

In the six years between 1908 and 1914 Henry Ford unleashed more creativity than most men exhibit in a lifetime. He developed an innovative car, introduced a revolutionary production method, and instituted a wage level that would change America forever. New companies grew up to make Model T accessories, including an attachment that converted the hot engine manifold into a handy griddle, forming a mini-industry.

New competitors sprang up, including the Dodge brothers, who started their own car company even while they remained the third-largest shareholders in Ford. Meanwhile, success was changing Henry Ford himself, and not for the better. His personality, always cantankerous, took a turn toward erratic venality. In 1918 he ran for the U.S. Senate, believing he could cruise to victory without campaigning. But he lost. Stung by defeat, he became a publisher by buying his hometown newspaper, the *Dearborn Independent*. He used it to write anti-Semitic diatribes, asserting that the Jews had started the Great War so the Gentiles would kill each other.

In 1919 Henry and his son Edsel, whom he had installed as president of Ford Motor, announced they would quit and start another car company, of which they would be the only owners. It was a brazen attempt to scare Ford Motor's minority shareholders into selling, and it worked. Henry paid $105.8 million to buy them all out, including the Dodge brothers.

None of Ford's erratic and imperious behavior seemed to matter, however, as the 1920s began. In 1923 Model T sales peaked at 1.8 million cars, and Ford was outselling all his competitors combined. In 1925 the company cut the Model T's base price to an all-time low of $260. But by then the buying public was no longer responding to Ford's price cuts. The Roaring Twenties were under way, and Americans wanted more from their cars than basic, no-frills transportation. Henry Ford's singular success had made him unwilling to change, and that in turn was making Ford Motor vulnerable. Smug self-confidence was a force that would play out again and again in the annals of the automobile industry. The path lay open for men with newer, more modern ideas about cars to leave Henry Ford in the dust.

One of the upstart challengers was Billy Durant, whose remarkable life was a corporate soap opera, sort of a cross between *Barbarians at the Gate* and *As the World Turns*. Durant created General Motors, lost it, founded Chevrolet, regained control of GM, lost it again, and ended his career running a bowling alley in Flint, Michigan— convinced that bowling would be the Next Big Thing of the 1940s. Along the way he amassed an enormous personal fortune and then went bankrupt.

Durant hired many of the formative figures of the American auto industry, including Walter Chrysler, who would start his own successful car company, and Alfred P. Sloan, Jr., who would make Durant's dream for General Motors a reality. Durant used the stock market as his personal playground, creating stock in his companies that he used, in turn, to buy more companies. But his uncanny ability to buy and sell companies was matched only by his utter inability to run them.

William Crapo Durant was born in Boston in 1861 and raised in Flint. He found the new horseless carriages appearing on Flint's streets noisy and annoying until, in 1904, he drove a smoother, quieter machine made by a local contractor named David Buick. Durant went to work for Buick as general manager, bought out the founder, and took control of the company.

In 1908 he incorporated General Motors in New Jersey (after rejecting the name "International Motor Car Company," suggested by Wall Street bankers) and moved to consolidate the fledgling auto industry. Armed with $12 million he reaped from a GM stock offering, Durant bought Oldsmobile from Ransom E. Olds, acquired the struggling Oakland Company of Pontiac, Michigan (later renamed Pontiac), and Cadillac. Within eighteen months of launching General Motors, Durant acquired nearly thirty companies that made cars and components. The one that got away was Ford Motor, which Henry Ford had agreed to sell for $8 million as long as the money came in cash. But Durant wanted to pay with GM stock, which Henry declined. A deal that would have changed the auto industry forever didn't get done.

Which was just as well, because by 1910 GM had issued too much stock and too much debt and wasn't selling enough cars to support it all. The company had ten different brands offering nearly two dozen models, many nearly alike, and the needless duplication greatly increased GM's complexity and costs. (The same issues, ironically, would bring General Motors down nearly a century later.)

The New York banks rode to the rescue by lending GM money and installing a new five-man management committee and an executive team headed by GM up-and-comer Walter Chrysler. Durant remained on the management committee but was semidisgraced and sidelined. He soon sought new horizons, gaining control of Chevrolet Motor Company and using its profits to start secretly accumulating General Motors stock. GM was Durant's baby, and he wanted it back.

On September 16, 1915, when he showed up for a General Motors board meeting, he was treated as a gate-crasher at a family gathering. A GM official took him aside beforehand and said, "Let's not have any trouble." Durant replied, "There won't be any trouble. It just so happens that I own General Motors."

Indeed, Durant had amassed more than half of GM's shares, or so he claimed. Months of proxy-counting and maneuvering followed, but on December 23 a *New York Times* headline proclaimed: "Durant Again Holds Control of General Motors." Chevrolet was just one-fifth the size of GM, which made Durant's feat the equivalent of a corporate minnow swallowing a whale.

Durant installed the blue-blooded Pierre S. du Pont as board chairman, giving comfort both to GM's bankers and to the du Ponts, who were plowing their munitions profits from the war in Europe into buying GM shares. Durant took the post of president (and CEO) for himself and convinced Walter Chrysler to stay.

Over the next couple of years Durant folded Chevrolet into GM along with other companies, including Hyatt Roller Bearing Company of Newark, New Jersey, which he had bought from Alfred Sloan, Jr.

The polar opposite of Billy Durant in almost every respect, Sloan was born in May 1875 to upper-middle-class respectability in New Haven, Connecticut, the oldest child of a wholesaler of coffee, tea, and cigars. His father moved the family and the business to Brooklyn when Alfred was ten and at seventeen he was admitted to the Massachusetts Institute of Technology. Sloan graduated in just three years, in 1895, with an engineering degree and a Phi Beta Kappa key.

Through a friend of his father's Sloan landed a job at Hyatt Roller Bearing, a New Jersey company that made bearings for sugarcane-crushing machines and was teetering on failure. But Sloan believed Hyatt's product—a proprietary ball bearing flexible enough to adjust to its housing, a capability that made machinery run better—had broad potential. In 1899 his father and a partner put up $2,500 each to buy the little company and installed Alfred Jr. at the helm. He quickly reorganized production, fixed the record-keeping, and produced a profit of $12,500 in his first six months. A year later, in the summer of 1900, he landed an order for roller bearings from a Michigan company called Olds Motor Works (later to become Oldsmobile).

The new motorcar industry proved a boon to Sloan's company. After a decade his single largest customer was Ford Motor, which was a blessing but also a potential threat. While Ford was America's biggest and fastest-growing car company, Henry Ford was mercurial; Sloan feared Ford would start making its own ball bearings instead of relying on outside suppliers. When Durant came along in 1916 and offered to buy Hyatt Roller Bearing for $13.5 million, Sloan accepted and agreed to stay on to run a group of GM's car-components companies.

Predictably, their styles clashed. Sloan was low-key, methodical, and prudent, making decisions with his head instead of his heart. Durant was just the opposite: intuitive, undisciplined, and frenetic, always charging off in several directions at once. He would summon Sloan, Chrysler, and other executives to meetings, only to leave them cooling their heels outside for hours—sometimes days—while he handled other matters, juggling half a dozen phones on his desk in an all-too-real parody of a corporate tycoon. Ego and excess staked out an early claim on the Detroit executive mind, and it would stay entrenched for decades.

By the summer of 1919 Chrysler had had enough. Sloan, one of Chrysler's best friends, tried to talk him out of quitting, but to no avail. A few months later Sloan sent Durant a corporate reorganization plan that would streamline GM's structure and give Durant more time to think about long-term corporate strategy. True to form, Durant never even found time to consider the plan. He was too busy borrowing more money and issuing new shares of stock to finance GM's headlong expansion. Sloan was on the verge of leaving too.

In 1920 America's postwar economic boom collapsed. That spring GM had been selling more than 40,000 cars a month, but by fall monthly sales volume dropped below 15,000 cars. GM's stock price plunged as well, from more than $400 a share to under $15. One of the biggest losers was Durant himself, who had been buying GM stock heavily with borrowed money and was $38 million in debt.

It was 1910 all over again. On November 20, 1920, just weeks before his fifty-ninth birthday, Billy Durant left GM for good, and board chairman Pierre du Pont became president and CEO of General Motors.

An overextended and failing company. A financial rescue from people who insisted, in return, that the CEO resign. Was this GM in 1920 or GM in 2009? It was both, actually, though in 2009 the money would come from the government, and the CEO would be named Rick instead of Billy. But the similarities are more striking than the differences.

In 1920, meanwhile, Pierre du Pont's mission was to stablize GM and find a long-term leader for the company. Thirty months later, on May 10, 1923, Alfred Sloan was elected president and CEO of General Motors.

Sloan started touring the country in a private railcar (the corporate jet of its day) to visit GM's dealers, factories, and far-flung offices. Wherever he went, the slightly built Sloan "dressed just as he did in New York City," wrote one biographer. "He wore custom suits, beautifully tailored, usually double-breasted and made of the finest wools, and starched hand-tailored white dress shirts with high, stiff white collars." The clothes, indeed, defined the man. Sloan quickly concluded that GM couldn't beat Henry Ford at his own game— constantly cutting costs, boosting efficiency, and passing the benefits on to consumers in the form of ever-lower prices. Besides, he figured that strategy had about run its course as America's transformation from a rural nation to an urban one accelerated. Farmers might be satisfied with basic transportation, but city dwellers wanted comfort, status, and style.

Sloan laid out his strategy in a letter to shareholders in GM's 1924 annual report, writing that General Motors would "build a car for every purse and purpose." Instead of competing directly against each other, GM's different divisions—Chevrolet, Oakland, Oldsmobile, Buick, and Cadillac—would constitute a hierarchical product portfolio, in which more costly cars would have more and better features, all the way up the line.

Sloan envisioned a "mass-class" market, as he put it, and an organization governed by "decentralized operations, central control." Division managers would be given wide latitude to run their business within the financial parameters established by headquarters. The concept basically invented the modern corporation and would underlie the structure of companies for decades to come. To create the designs that would make each GM brand different, Sloan retained a consultant named Harley Earl, whose father had owned a Los Angeles "carriage" shop that built custom car bodies for Hollywood movie stars. Seeking an alternative to the stolid, upright shapes on most GM cars, Sloan asked Earl to design a different look for a new marque called LaSalle, intended as a lower-priced "companion brand" to Cadillac.

The six LaSalle models were unveiled on March 4, 1927, with a lower, sleeker shape than other cars of the day. Thanks partly to their success, 1927 was the year everything came together for Alfred Sloan and General Motors. By then the Model T looked hopelessly outdated and sales were collapsing. On May 25 Ford announced it would discontinue the car after a twenty-year run, during which 15 million had been made. Henry Ford had stuck to his beloved Model T so tenaciously that Ford Motor wasn't ready to launch its successor, the Model A, for another six months.

That summer, meanwhile, Sloan hired Harley Earl full-time to head GM's new Art and Colour Section, the auto industry's first design staff. And at year end, for the first time ever, General Motors seized sales leadership from Ford. It would hold the top spot for more than eighty years.

To create social acceptance for GM, Sloan used corporate advertising to portray the company as an institution that provided tangible benefits to society. Typical was an advertisement in the *Oakland Tribune* on January 27, 1929. "Every year has offered you *more* for your automobile dollar—in performance, in comfort, in safety, in beauty and in style," Sloan wrote in an open letter to the public. "Such progress, born of the inherent ambition of an organization of active minds to do better and to give more, is of benefit to all."

During the late 1920s Alfred Sloan's new, more modern vision of the automobile industry had trumped that of Henry Ford. Sloan transformed cars into dream machines, with help from a man he imported from Hollywood, America's foremost city of dreams. But though he catered to Americans' emotions, Sloan ruled GM with strict business discipline. In 1940 he killed the LaSalle brand because sales were slumping and hurting profits. Killing brands to boost profits was a concept that his successors, unfortunately, would forget. They also would forget something else Sloan proved: that a dominant and seemingly invincible company—in his day, Ford Motor—could fall behind if it failed to adopt better ideas. It would have been a useful lesson to remember.

In the dozen years following the ascendancy of Alfred Sloan and General Motors, two more men emerged to shape the American automobile industry. Walter Chrysler had grown up in Kansas City as the son of a railroad engineer. After he quit General Motors in 1919 in disgust with Billy Durant, Chrysler went into the car business for himself.

He purchased control of several small car companies, including Maxwell and Chalmers, and folded them into Chrysler, which he incorporated in 1925. In 1928 he launched a couple of new brands, Plymouth and DeSoto. His biggest breakthrough that year was the purchase of Dodge from New York bankers, who had gained control of the company after the deaths of Horace and John Dodge.

After the Dodge deal, General Motors, Ford, and Chrysler collectively controlled 75 percent of the U.S. car market. A trade publication, *Automotive News,* started calling the companies the "Big Three," a term that would be valid for another eight decades. Walter Chrysler himself, meanwhile, was making a personal impact as big as his company.

In 1928 he broke ground on the Chrysler Building at East 42nd Street and Lexington Avenue in New York; its distinctive art deco spire briefly made it the tallest building in the world. The building was his personal, private venture, separate from the car company, though it would contain Chrysler Corporation's New York offices and an office for Walter himself. The announcement of the building capped a year of activity that made Chrysler *Time*'s 1928 Man of the Year.

During the 1930s, as the power of the Big Three solidified, the Depression brought an end to many of their would-be rivals. Among them were Peerless, Marmon, Pierce-Arrow, Stutz, and Duesenberg—the last of which had made cars so esteemed that it fostered a lasting approbation: "It's a Duesie." A few other smaller companies soldiered on, but General Motors, Ford, and Chrysler settled into a comfortable oligopoly, of which GM was the undisputed leader. The only real challenge to their power came, not from another company, but from a union.

The United Automobile Workers was formed in 1935 after the passage of the federal Wagner Act, which guaranteed workers the right to organize. Its first elected president was Homer Martin, a former Baptist preacher, but the union's keenest intellectual and ideological energy came from the three Reuther brothers—Victor, Roy, and especially Walter, the oldest. Their father, Valentine Reuther, was a German immigrant and a trade union leader in Wheeling, West Virginia, where family dinners typically were devoted to discussion and debate about social justice and the central role of unions in achieving it. After coming to Detroit in 1926, Walter Reuther completed high school and three years of college before landing a job at Ford, only to be fired in 1932 for union activity.

Reuther's response was to take a road trip. He and Victor—eager to see the world and to examine firsthand the experiences of workers in other countries—took their $900 in savings and bicycled through Europe, often sleeping in youth hostels. In Berlin they witnessed the Reichstag fire on February 27, 1933, and moved on to the Soviet Union, where they worked in an American-built auto factory in Gorky.

While the Reuthers admired Russia's rapid march to modernity, they were repulsed by the brutality of Communism—an attitude that would later earn them enemies in the U.S. labor movement. When the brothers departed Gorky, they headed east, traversing the Soviet Union and landing in Japan before returning to the United States, eighteen thousand miles later. In 1935, at age twenty-eight, Walter Reuther helped organize the UAW's West Side Local 174 in Detroit, which elected him president.

In late 1936 UAW members at two General Motors plants in Flint, frustrated by their inability to gain recognition from the company, took matters into their own hands. On December 30 they simply sat down at their posts, occupying the plants and refusing to leave. The union "served a new demand on GM," reported International News Service, "for a national conference on collective bargaining for all GM plants." Alfred Sloan wanted no such thing. What followed was the tense forty-four-day standoff known ever after as the Sit-down Strike.

GM guards turned off the heat in the factories, but the workers stayed put anyway, warmed by homemade fires. On January 11, 1937, local police—"bulls" in the derogatory slang of the day—stormed the Chevrolet No. 2 plant with tear gas and billy clubs. Workers hurling car parts repulsed them, in a victory that the union labeled the "Battle of the Running Bulls." Had the incident occurred on a college campus thirty years later, it would have been called the "Battle of the Running Pigs."

On February 11, after the Michigan National Guard had failed to expel the strikers, the company caved. GM executives signed a short agreement that pledged, "The corporation hereby recognizes the union as the collective bargaining agency for those employees of the corporation who are members of the union." Within months Chrysler signed a similar agreement.

Ford, however, proved difficult to crack. On May 26 a group of UAW organizers in Dearborn decided to distribute organizing leaflets at Ford's massive Rouge manufacturing complex. Among the leaders was Walter Reuther. He neither drank nor smoked, and his red hair and pink complexion gave him a cherubic look that belied his toughness. Shortly before the march Ford's thuggish personnel chief, Harry Bennett, said his security guards wouldn't try to stop the leafleting, but added, "Of course, we can't say what the men will do." Actually, it was predictable.

As they walked across a pedestrian overpass and neared the plant, the UAW men were assaulted by the Ford security guards and beaten. The guards' brutality was matched only by their stupidity, because the assault occurred right in front of press photographers. The incident made front-page news around the country, along with pictures of Reuther nursing a bloody nose alongside other wounded colleagues. The young union leader became an overnight celebrity.

Just three months after the Battle of the Running Bulls, the UAW added the Battle of the Overpass to its lore. Not until 1941, four years later, would the union win recognition from Ford, thereby achieving a labor monopoly in the nation's auto plants that matched the corporate oligopoly in the new-car showrooms. The oligopoly-monopoly combination would rule the American auto industry for decades, propelling it to prosperity, then sowing the seeds of its undoing.

The UAW's early battles fostered an antipathy toward the car companies that would stay with the union forever. Even in the 1960s and 1970s, after the UAW had won remarkable middle-class prosperity for its members, autoworkers' emotions would run high when they gathered in union halls to lock arms and sing labor's unofficial anthem, "Solidarity Forever." Written early in the century by an organizer for the Industrial Workers of the World, or Wobblies, it was sung to the stirring tune of the "Battle Hymn of the Republic." Among the verses:

> *They have taken untold millions that they never toiled to earn,*
> *But without our brain and muscle not a single wheel can turn.*
> *We can break their haughty power, gain our freedom when we learn*
> *That the union makes us strong.*

During World War II Detroit served as the Arsenal of Democracy, producing planes and tanks instead of cars. But the victory over Germany and Japan, when it came, brought no peace to Detroit. In November 1945 Walter Reuther led a strike against General Motors. He demanded that GM hold the line on car prices while granting a 30 percent increase in wages, or else open its books to the union to prove that it couldn't afford to pay.

Sloan regarded the demands as an outrageous usurpation of management's right to run the business, and the battle lines were drawn. The strike lasted 113 days, after which GM still refused to open its books or discuss its pricing with the union, but it did grant workers a hefty raise and better vacation pay. It was an enormous victory for Reuther, and a month later, in April 1946, he took the next step. In a tightly fought election he ousted UAW president R. J. Thomas and became, at thirty-eight, president of the United Auto Workers. For the next quarter-century he would win better and better contracts for his members and help shape Detroit's destiny.

The other young man who consolidated his power in Detroit in the mid-1940s was Henry Ford II, grandson of the founder.

In 1945, at age twenty-eight, Henry II was elected president of Ford Motor and inherited an empire in such disarray that bills were paid simply by weighing them on a scale, on the assumption that every pound of paper equaled a certain amount of money that the company owed. A few months later the young heir hired a group of former military officers who offered to deploy the organizational skills they had learned at the Department of Defense to fix Ford Motor. The ten included a brainy young analyst named Robert Mc-Namara, later to run both Ford and the Pentagon. They quickly became known as the Whiz Kids. By the time Henry I died in 1947, at age eighty-three, the Whiz Kids were pushing Ford toward recovery.

None of them were on hand, though, in March 1948, when Henry II met with British army officials in Germany. The British occupation zone contained a partially destroyed factory that turned out small numbers of an odd-looking beetle-shaped car that the British thought had commercial potential. They offered to give Volkswagen to Ford Motor, free of charge. Henry II turned to one of his vice presidents, Ernest Breech, who said, "Mr. Ford, I don't think what we are being offered here is worth a damn."

Sixty years later Volkswagen would be worth more than General Motors, Ford, and Chrysler combined. Ford's historic missed opportunity wasn't evident then, however, and in any case it didn't seem to matter. The shape of the American auto industry had been determined by forty-five years of inventing, maneuvering, building, fighting, and growing.

The eighty-eight American car companies that existed in 1921 would shrink to just five by 1958—American Motors and Studebaker in addition to the Big Three. Of the five, GM, Ford, and Chrysler accounted for 90 percent of sales. Power in the auto industry had been concentrated, as if by natural selection and survival of the fittest, in the hands of three companies and one union. The model of corporate oligopoly and union monopoly seemed poised to stay in place forever. Meanwhile America was enjoying an historic postwar economic boom, with Detroit leading the way.

THREE

GLORY DAYS OF PONIES AND GOATS

It was remarkable that a straitlaced, stiff-collared guy like Alfred P. Sloan, Jr., would conceive of cars as personal me-mobiles—rolling advertisements, as it were, for the sensibilities and aspirations of their owners, however ostentatious or frivolous. But Sloan probably never figured that his insight would evolve into cars with designs, styling cues, and names inspired by women's breasts, men's genitals, Flash Gordon spaceships, and wild animals. That's exactly what was happening to automobiles by the 1950s, when Sloan was ending his career with acclaim as the greatest manager of the twentieth century.

Whatever Detroit built, America bought, partly because it didn't have much choice. But during these years General Motors, Ford, and Chrysler really did seem to know exactly what people wanted. And what Americans wanted was often pretty outlandish. Tail fins that pointed to the sky. Sporty cars that exuded the exuberance of the country's youth culture. Muscle cars with 350-horsepower engines driven by testosterone-fueled boy racers whose driver's licenses were barely two weeks old.

Cars were celebrated in song: "Fun, Fun, Fun," "Little Deuce Coupe," and "409" by the Beach Boys, "GTO" by Ronny and the Daytonas, "Dead Man's Curve" by Jan and Dean, and more. The 1960 hit television series *Route 66* starred two hot young actors, Martin Milner and George Maharis, and one very hot car—the Chevrolet Corvette. In 1968 Steve McQueen, as detective Frank Bullitt, drove his Ford Mustang fastback through the streets of San Francisco, pursuing the bad guys driving a Dodge Charger. It was Hollywood's first iconic car chase, and such chases would be a staple of action movies happily ever after.

Throughout the 1950s and 1960s, America's love affair with the automobile deepened and intensified. In the late 1950s Gene Benner (unaware, of course, that half a century later he would be a car dealer scrambling to cope with Detroit's greatest crisis) played car-watching games with his twin brother, Tom. They would sit on the front steps of their home in Auburn, Maine, and call out the make and model years of the different cars that passed by. In those days each model had its own distinct style, which wouldn't always be the case later.

Boys across America played similar games and dreamed of buying their first car. Benner's came in 1967, when he was a college sophomore: he bought a well-used, seven-year-old Ford for $500. But his joy was deflated not long afterward when a windstorm blew a huge branch off a tree and onto his car's roof, wrecking it entirely. With cars, Benner learned, things could go from good to bad in a hurry.

In the 1950s and 1960s, television brought cars and all they represented—freedom, status, style, and sex—into millions of American living rooms nightly. Cars were the perfect appliances for a society that was physically and upwardly mobile. And new institutions were being built around the automobile by people who didn't even work for the car companies.

One was Abraham Levitt, who built tract housing in Long Island in the late 1940s and early 1950s, creating Levittown, suburban sprawl, and the attendant daily commute to work by car. Another was Kemmons Wilson, who opened his first Holiday Inn on the road between Memphis and Nashville in 1952, launching a national motel chain that made car travel more reliably comfortable than the no-name dives then dotting the highways.

Then there was Ray Kroc, who bought a little drive-in hamburger stand in San Bernardino and built it into a nationwide chain called McDonald's, turning cars into portable dining rooms. Knitting all these things together was the new interstate highway system, which President Dwight Eisenhower developed to move troops quickly from one place to another as part of America's national defense during the Cold War. Thus it might be said, with some poetic license, that Detroit boomed in the 1950s and 1960s because of the "4-H Club": hamburgers, highways, houses, and hotels.

Who knew then that Detroit's sky's-the-limit success was fostering the insularity and arrogance that would bring the American auto industry to its knees half a century later? America was preoccupied with its remarkable postwar economic prosperity, underpinned by Detroit. In January 1953, during his confirmation hearings as Eisenhower's secretary of defense, GM president "Engine Charlie" Wilson responded to a question by declaring, "I thought that what was good for our country was good for General Motors, and vice versa."

Wilson's remark would be famously quoted—and far more often misquoted—over the years, but it contained a great deal of truth. In the early 1950s two-car families and even women drivers were rarities in the United States. By 1970 they had become the norm. The 1950s also saw the development of automotive creature comforts—notably air-conditioning and electrically powered windows—that would become increasingly common.

In the early 1950s, new leaders burst onto the scene in Detroit. In 1955 Edward N. Cole, Chevrolet's hard-charging chief engineer, had developed a hot new engine that put some zip into everyday driving and put zest into Chevy's sales. Cole's landmark "small-block" 265-cubic-inch V8 was only as powerful as some four-cylinder engines forty years on, but it was a marvel in its day. What's more, the '55 Chevy could be purchased with coral and charcoal paint, two-tone coloring that gave the car a memorable art deco look.

Cole was also a key figure behind the Chevrolet Corvette, a two-seat sports car destined for a place in boyhood fantasies. It was launched in late 1953, a seminal year that brought the end of the Korean War, the debut of *Playboy* magazine (with more boyhood fantasies), and the beginning of Elvis Presley's career. The two-seat sports car looked great but had a weak six-cylinder engine, a mushy suspension, and an ill-fitting convertible top.

Those flaws made the Corvette's early sales so disappointing that GM was ready to drop the car. But a mid-level Chevy engineer named Zora Arkus-Duntov argued that killing the Corvette was precisely the wrong move, because Ford was preparing a sporty two-seater of its own, the Thunderbird. "If Ford makes success where we failed, it may hurt," wrote Duntov, a Russian refugee, in a 1954 memo that was awkwardly worded but clear. "In the bare-fisted fight we are in now, I would hit at any opening I could find, and the situation where Ford enters and where Chevrolet retreats, it is not an opening, it is a hole!"

The prospect of humiliation at the hands of Ford persuaded Cole to let Duntov reengineer the Corvette with a V8 engine, a better transmission, and other upgrades. The Corvette-versus-Thunderbird battle seemed destined to run for decades, but in 1958 the 'Bird took a radical detour. Ford's Robert McNamara decided the Thunderbird would appeal to a broader market if a backseat was added.

Thus the Thunderbird became a four-passenger boulevard cruiser designed more for show than for go, surging ahead of the Corvette in sales. In 1964 (the year that U.S. car sales passed 8 million vehicles for the first time) the Thunderbird was immortalized in the Beach Boys lyric song "Fun, Fun, Fun," about a teenage girl's adventures and misadventures while cruising in her car. GM, however, heeded its heart instead of its head, keeping the Corvette a true sports car with a smaller sales volume but an intensely devoted following.

The Thunderbird was a rare commercial victory for Ford over GM, which U.S. antitrust authorities warned "to settle for no more than 50% of the market and keep out of trouble." But Sloan, still GM's chairman (though not CEO) at eighty, would have none of that. "If you stand still," he said, "you go behind." GM's market share climbed past 50 percent in the early 1960s, though the company would escape antitrust action. Four decades later GM's market share would plunge below 25 percent, as competitors did to the company what the trust busters didn't.

If the Corvette and the Thunderbird embodied exuberance in Detroit's postwar automobiles, the Cadillacs of the 1950s exuded garishness that made them icons. The credit, such as it was, went to GM's Harley Earl, who believed that cars should provide "visual entertainment."

During World War II Earl noticed the stabilizer fins that shot upward from the twin tails of the Lockheed P-38 fighter and decided to deploy smaller versions of them on cars. The result was small but distinct "finlets" that sprouted on the tails of the 1948 Cadillacs. Their popularity prompted Earl to turn his attention to the front of the car. Like the fins, the chrome protrusions he added to the front bumpers of Cadillacs started out small. But in 1953 they gained a prominent conical shape that was supposed to resemble artillery shells and thus project a sense of power. They also resembled female breasts, invoking a different sort of power. The chrome protrusions were quickly nicknamed "dagmars," after a generously endowed starlet in a television variety show. To accentuate the obvious, in 1957 the chrome dagmars got black rubber tips that added an unmistakable nipplesque accent. Meanwhile, as the dagmars entered, well, full bloom, the great Tail Fin War of the late 1950s was getting under way.

The war started not with Cadillac but with Chrysler, whose reputation for engineering excellence was often undermined by its dull designs. To change that, the company put exceptionally tall fins on the tails of its 1955 cars and labeled the new styling "The Forward Look."

Chrysler's rocketlike fins proved an instant hit in a country that was becoming enamored of the space age. In the first five months of 1955 the company's market share jumped to more than 18 percent, up from just 13 percent the prior year. Much of the increase came at the expense of General Motors.

Chrysler put even bigger fins on its 1956 and 1957 cars, causing GM executives even more worry about the unlikely success of their smaller competitor. Cadillac designers rushed back to their drawing boards, and in the fall of 1958 GM unveiled the most outlandish cars the world has ever seen.

The 1959 Cadillacs had tail fins that reached almost as high as the car's roof. The fins were so big that Cadillac's Series 75 model was three feet longer than GM's massive Hummer H2 would be fifty years later. Astride each fin sat two prominent red taillights, placed side by side, resembling a particular part of the male anatomy. Nicknamed "gonads," they briefly supplanted hub caps as the theft item of choice for greasy-haired juvenile delinquents. Cadillac reasserted its supremacy, and each different GM marque got its own distinctively shaped fins, including angled "delta wing" fins for Buick and horizontal "bat-wing" fins for Chevrolet.

The booming crop of variously shaped fins would be little more than an amusing historical curiosity, except for one thing. It showed that the Big Three had taken to competing on styling instead of on technology or engineering. The obsession with styling eventually would catch up with Detroit when foreign car companies took a different tack. But in the 1950s Americans seemed enamored of styling, the more outlandish the better. The exception that would prove the rule was taking shape—literally—at Ford.

In January 1956 big events were under way at Ford. It became the last of the Big Three to go public, though the Fords retained control with supervoting shares that only family members could own. At the same time plans were unfolding for a new premium brand.

The Edsel brand was introduced on September 4, 1957, with four models. Instead of tall tail fins, their distinctive styling cue was an enormous, oval-shaped front grille. Before long it was being compared to a horse collar, a toilet seat, and, inevitably, a vagina.

The grille was just one of the Edsel's problems. Besides being aesthetically ridiculous, the car was technically pedestrian, and its quality—especially the jerky suspension system—was suspect. In the first year, Ford sold only 200,000 Edsels, less than one-third the number planned. In November 1959, after two years of futility and nearly $400 million in losses, Ford killed the Edsel before further losses could kill Ford.

Five years into the tail fin craze, it was becoming clear that not everyone was buying Detroit's definition of the American dream. The dissenters ranged from counterculture bohemians to college professors and students to sober-minded people who valued practicality over style. Some of them were turning to the little car made by the German company that Ford had brushed off a decade earlier.

The Volkswagen Beetle was developed in the early 1930s by Ferdinand Porsche, a talented but stubborn engineer who had worn out his welcome at established car companies such as Mercedes-Benz. The car got its first name—Kraft durch Freude—from another guy who eventually wore out his welcome everywhere, Adolf Hitler. He wanted a people's car for Germans, as the Model T had been for Americans. Kraft durch Freude, which means Strength Through Joy, was the name of the Nazi labor movement.

The car was saved from that name by the outbreak of World War II, when the factory at Wolfsburg in north-central Germany switched from making the car to producing military vehicles. After the war the British occupied Wolfsburg and hired a former executive from Opel,

GM's German subsidiary, to run the partially bombed factory. Heinz Nordhoff didn't really want the job, but in the wreckage of postwar Germany he was desperate.

Nordhoff, like the British, saw possibilities for the car, which had a quirky design. Besides its buglike shape, it had an air-cooled engine mounted in the rear, quite the opposite of the front-mounted, water-cooled engines on virtually every other car in the world. But the result was terrific traction in rain and snow, because the engine's weight sat squarely over the rear-drive wheels.

To boost production, however, Nordhoff had to get modern machine tools, and the best place to buy them was the United States. For that he needed dollars, and that basic need—more than any grand strategy—prompted him to start shipping Beetles to America. The first year's export, in 1949, totaled two cars. In 1952, the number topped 1,000, beginning nearly two decades of rapid growth.

Early buyers included returning GIs who had seen, and often driven, the cars in Europe and liked them. At first the cars had just 25 horsepower, not much more than Henry Ford's Model T. And they were strictly no-frills, lacking even a gas gauge until 1962. But no-frills meant low price: $1,548 in 1958 compared to more than $2,400 for a Ford Fairlane. That year Volkswagen sold more than 100,000 cars in the United States for the first time, including 25,000 Microbuses, a Beetle derivative that had been developed after the war. By 1959 Volkswagen's success was prompting Detroit to enter the market for small cars. As a result, VW reluctantly started advertising.

The Volkswagen ads, created by an upstart agency named Doyle, Dane and Bernbach, were as quirky as the cars. One of the first, in late 1959, showed a Beetle sitting in front of a prosperous suburban house and a headline that asked: "What year car do the Jones drive?" Readers couldn't tell, of course, because the Beetle looked the same year after year. The ad took direct aim at annual styling changes, which lay at the very heart of Detroit's business model.

Another ad, which touted the Beetle's thirty-two miles to the gallon and ease of parking, carried a simple, two-word headline: "Think small." Volkswagen's unlikely success with its quirky car was beginning to prove that Detroit really wasn't impregnable. It was also spurring Detroit to mount a counterattack.

The first wave came from tiny American Motors Corporation, which along with Studebaker formed the "Little Two" that existed in the shadow of Detroit's Big Three. AMC chief George Romney figured that at least some people wanted practical, sensible cars with an American flavor. The recession of 1958 proved him right. That year, to the surprise of the Big Three, AMC's compact Rambler became the auto industry's third-largest nameplate—behind Chevrolet and Ford, of course, but ahead of such stalwarts as Pontiac and Plymouth. Romney's success grabbed the attention of General Motors, Ford, and Chrysler, who decided to strike back with compact cars of their own.

Two years later they did.

On October 3, 1959, just as the new 1960-model cars were appearing in showrooms, *The Saturday Evening Post* carried a lengthy article headlined: "The Big Three Join the Revolution." It described the new compact cars being launched that year by the Big Three: the Ford Falcon, the Plymouth Valiant, and the Chevrolet Corvair. "This small-car move may be a giant industrial blunder," the *Post* wrote. "Or it may be the smartest thing Detroit has done in decades." The article added that the new compacts "will be a pleasant surprise in all ways but one—price." At close to $2,000, the Falcon, Valiant, and Corvair were hundreds of dollars cheaper than Detroit's full-size cars, but still $300 to $400 above the Beetle. It was a hefty difference at the time.

The most daring and innovative of the new compacts, hands down, was the Corvair. It was the brainchild of Ed Cole, who in 1956 had been promoted from chief engineer to general manager of Chevrolet.

The Corvair's engineering architecture, like the Beetle's, featured an air-cooled engine mounted where the trunk usually was, in the rear of the car sitting above the drive wheels. Thus, like the Beetle, the Corvair had no need for antifreeze or engine coolant, and there was no driveshaft to connect a front-mounted engine with the rear-drive wheels. These and other engineering features produced considerable weight savings and made the 88-horsepower, six-cylinder engine seem more powerful than it was. But the Corvair was bigger than the Beetle—a "*six-passenger* compact car . . . designed specifically to American standards of comfort," as Chevrolet's advertising put it.

From the start the Corvair stirred controversy among some car critics, who claimed that the rear-weight load on a car of its length made the Corvair prone to spin out around curves. Worse, from GM's perspective, the Corvair was being outgunned in the market by the conventional, conservative Falcon. Ford sold more than 400,000 Falcons the first year, nearly twice the level of Corvair sales, but Cole remained undeterred. In 1961 he expanded the Corvair from a single model into an entire family of air-cooled, rear-engine vehicles. Besides the coupes and sedans, the Corvair lineup included a station wagon, three commercial light trucks, and a camper-van called the Greenbrier that could hold up to nine passengers and be outfitted for weekends in the woods—just like the Volkswagen Micro-bus. Chevrolet was the top-selling car marque in the world, and Ed Cole was determined to make the Corvair not just a single model but a brand within a brand. The decision would come to haunt him and General Motors.

Considering that the 1960s brought sexual revolution to America, fueled by the birth-control pill and unprecedented numbers of eager college kids, it's an oddity that the most blatant sexual imagery disappeared from cars. Dagmars and gonads disappeared, and the remnants of tail fins began receding in size in 1960 until they finally (and thankfully) disappeared in 1964.

The Mustang, with its youthful flair, was the defining car of the new decade. Inspired by two-seat British roadsters such as MGB and Triumph, it was championed by a new star in Detroit's executive firmament, Lee Iacocca. In November 1960, after Bob McNamara accepted John Kennedy's invitation to become secretary of defense, the thirty-six-year-old Iacocca became the youngest man to run Ford Motor's flagship Ford division (as opposed to the separate Lincoln-Mercury division). He quickly saw the need to put some pizzazz into a competent but dull product lineup and asked his underlings to develop a car that would look sporty, be suitable for a small family, and be profitable at a price under $2,500.

The price criterion was key. To reduce engineering costs, Ford's product planners decided to use the underlying architecture—engine, transmission, chassis, and so on—of the boring old Falcon.

But to create a roadster-style look, they moved the passenger compartment back to create a long hood and a short rear deck; and they chose sleek styling that made the car look like it was straining forward. It was, said one of Iacocca's underlings, "like putting falsies on grandma." The car was launched on April 17, 1964, at the New York World's Fair with a base price of $2,368.

Ford booked advertising on all three television networks and ran ads in newspapers nationwide. "Americans will have to be deaf, dumb and blind to avoid the name," wrote *Newsweek,* which put Iacocca on its cover, as did *Time* the very same week. Americans were smitten. Some dealerships had to shut their doors to control the crushing crowds inside. A New York City diner posted a sign in its window: "Our hotcakes sell like Mustangs." Ford sold 525,000 Mustangs in 1965, the car's first full year on the market, and another 550,000 the next year. One reason: by 1964 nearly 20 percent of American families had second cars, which were becoming necessities in the suburbs. Thanks to the Mustang's success and the booming economy, U.S. car sales passed 8 million vehicles in 1964 for the first time ever.

The Mustang's success caught General Motors flat-footed, but the industry leader had some tricks of its own up its white-shirt corporate sleeves. In the spring of 1963 a young executive named John Z. DeLorean was driving a Pontiac Tempest at the company's proving ground near Detroit. During a break one of his engineers remarked that it wouldn't take much effort to pop the monstrous 389-cubic-inch engine from the full-size Bonneville into the compact Tempest. The deed was quickly done, and DeLorean was wowed by the sensation of driving a small car with a big engine. He wanted to put the car into Pontiac's showrooms.

In October 1963 Pontiac introduced the Tempest with the GTO option, a 325-horsepower, 389-cubic-inch engine, that cost $295.90. The initials stood for Gran Turismo Omologato, a name DeLorean ripped off from Ferrari, which had neglected to copyright it. Pontiac's advertising, playing on the initials, called the car The Great One. American kids nicknamed it the "Goat."

The GTO landed DeLorean in the corporate doghouse because the car hadn't been officially blessed by GM headquarters. But GM's bosses were mollified when Pontiac sold more than 32,000 GTOs in the first year—six times the initial forecast. The next year sales more than doubled to 75,000 cars. Ford was selling seven times as many Mustangs, but for a car that had cost little to develop, GTO sales were awfully good, and the car bestowed a high-performance image on the entire Pontiac lineup. Part of the impetus came from a song recorded on a lark by Nashville session musicians who took the name Ronny and the Daytonas. The lyrics rhapsodized about the car's engine, transmission, and three two-barrel carburetors:

> *Little GTO, you're really lookin' fine.*
> *Three deuces and a four-speed, and a 389 . . .*

The tune soared up the charts. Together the car and the song gave birth to the late-1960s muscle car era. By 1968 the GTO had a monstrous 400-cubic-inch engine producing 350 horsepower and a host of new competitors. Ford reconfigured the Mustang, making the once-nimble chassis much heavier, to accommodate a more powerful engine. Chrysler's Plymouth division put Pontiac on the defensive with its Barracuda, which had as much power as the GTO but sold for less money. The muscle car parade also included the Dodge Coronet Super Bee, the Olds 442, and the Chevy Chevelle SS. The craze fostered impromptu drag races all around the country. It was all great fun, both for the car companies and for the kids who would blast their way to muscle car memories that would last a lifetime.

In the 1960s Detroit's car companies stood at the pinnacle of their profitability and prestige and brought new opportunities to many Americans. In September 1965, three months after Chrysler opened its new assembly plant in Belvidere, Fred Young started on the assembly line building the Plymouth Fury sedan, which sold for $3,200. The job required demanding physical work. Young would hop down into a sunken trench under the assembly line to wield a welding gun and apply welds to critical points on the underbody of the car. So many sparks flew that he was always burning holes in his coveralls, and his wife got tired of mending them.

But there were compensations: a then-princely wage of $1.85 an hour at the start, along with raises and cost-of-living increases over the years. In addition, the medical benefits were the best available anywhere, requiring Young and his co-workers to pay hardly anything out of their own pockets. And the company pension plan held out the promise of lifetime financial security. The Young family would be linked to Chrysler and the American auto industry, for better and for worse, for two generations and decades to come.

Ponies and goats supplanted dagmars and gonads in the latter half of the 1960s. From a marketing and innovation standpoint, Detroit now turned to big engines instead of tall tail fins and layers of chrome. But even at the peak of Detroit's power, not everything was idyllic. On March 16, 1966, the last Studebaker rolled off an assembly line in Canada. The company's demise would convince Detroit executives that no modern car company could survive bankruptcy.

In 1964 a young Harvard-educated attorney named Ralph Nader grew bored with practicing law and moved to Washington to work for the Labor Department—while also doing freelance research and writing on automotive safety. A year later he accepted an offer from a fledgling New York publishing house to write a book about the topic. *Unsafe at Any Speed* began with the sentence: "For over half a century the automobile has brought death, injury and the most inestimable sorrow and deprivation to millions of people." That might have been news to the farmers liberated from their isolated homesteads by Ford's Model T and its successors, but Nader was just getting started. Only the first chapter of the book was about the Corvair, but it was devastating.

Nader described the case of a California woman who had lost her left arm in a 1961 accident when the Corvair she was driving at thirty-five miles an hour spun out of control. After three days in court, Nader wrote, GM settled the case for $70,000 "rather than continue a trial which . . . threatened to expose on the public record one of the greatest acts of industrial irresponsibility in this century." He described how in early 1960, with the Corvair new on the market, several automotive "after-market" companies started selling stabilizer bars to be bolted under the car's front end to better balance the weight. GM itself had begun selling similar devices in 1961, the book continued, but hadn't advertised them. What's more, Nader wrote, GM finally overhauled the suspension on the 1964 model Corvair, but by that time more than 1.1 million Corvairs had been sold.

Unsafe at Any Speed marshaled evidence that the Corvair's concentration of weight in the rear made it prone to spin out when taking sharp curves. Nader's argument was impressive, but a book written by a no-name bureaucrat and printed by an obscure publisher wasn't about to make waves. Until, that is, GM itself handed Nader a public podium.

The company was facing more than one hundred Corvair lawsuits around the country, and the GM legal staff noted that Nader was providing expert witness testimony in many of them. The company's lawyers asked one of the company's outside law firms to find out more about Nader. The firm retained a New York private investigator, who in turn put some freelance private eyes on the case. Somewhere along this lengthy and unwieldy chain of command, the private eyes started snooping into Nader's sex life, politics, friendships, and drinking habits, in the hope of finding facts to impugn his credibility.

As the investigators got more aggressive, Nader sensed something was going on. *The New Republic,* which had published some of his freelance writing about auto safety, did a story about his suspicions. Then on March 6, 1966, *The New York Times* published a story headlined: "Critic of Auto Industry's Safety Standards Says He Was Trailed and Harassed." At that point GM had to respond. The company acknowledged that it had "initiated a routine investigation through a reputable law firm," and a sensation ensued. GM president James M. Roche, who hadn't even known about the investigation until the *Times* story broke, was subpoenaed to testify before Congress. On March 22, before a U.S. Senate subcommittee, Roche publicly apologized to Nader.

Roche's apology drew network television coverage and made Nader an instant celebrity. The debacle propelled *Unsafe at Any Speed* onto the best-seller list. The effect on Corvair sales was somewhat less salutary: sales dropped by more than half that year, to 104,000 cars. In late 1966 Nader sued General Motors for invasion of privacy. Just as bad, from the company's point of view, Congress passed the

Motor Vehicle Safety Act of 1966. The new law required, for the first time, that car companies publicly disclose any recalls of their vehicles.

The Nader hearings effectively killed the Corvair. After a couple of halfhearted attempts to revive it, GM finally pulled the plug in 1969. On December 12 of that year, Nader made the cover of *Time,* with his face depicted alongside the taillights of a Corvair, driving off into oblivion.

It's almost impossible to overstate the magnitude of the Corvair disaster for General Motors, indeed for the entire American auto industry. The scandal occurred just as the Vietnam War was fostering a new and profound mistrust of establishment institutions—the government, the military, universities, churches, and others. The Corvair added General Motors—and, by extension, all of corporate America—to the list of organizations not to be trusted. In some ways, GM's corporate reputation would never recover.

Nor would any aspirations harbored by the company's engineers to pursue innovative technology, as opposed to styling or horsepower, as the path to commercial success. The Corvair was, in many ways, ahead of its time. Its roomy interior belied a lightweight design that allowed the car to get twenty-nine miles on a gallon of gas, double the mileage of most other cars of its day. If GM had fixed the weight-distribution problem from the outset, which would have been relatively easy to do, history might have been different. But Ed Cole stubbornly believed in his design. After the Corvair, Detroit's inclination to play it safe was solidified.

Despite the Corvair, Cole went on to become president of General Motors. In the early 1970s, with government clean-air legislation looming, Cole championed a device called the catalytic converter, which required cars to run on lead-free gasoline and sharply reduced tailpipe emissions. His stand put him at odds with most other Detroit executives and thus required considerable courage on his part. Thanks to Cole, catalytic converters soon became standard on cars. But Cole, sadly, would be remembered as the "Father of the Corvair" instead of the "Father of Clean Air."

The adverse publicity from the Corvair dragged on for years, thanks to Nader's suit against GM. It wasn't until August 1970 that the two sides settled for $425,000. By then, Detroit's power was beginning to wane. Though it was little noticed at the time, the average profit margins of GM, Ford, and Chrysler had peaked in 1963 at 17 percent. By 1969 their cumulative margins had dropped below 13 percent. And during the 1970s Detroit's automotive oligopoly—now just the Big Three plus little American Motors—would be rendered asunder.

FOUR

CRUMMY CARS AND CAFE SOCIETY

On November 11, 1970, General Motors and the United Auto Workers ended a bitter sixty-seven-day strike over the union's demand for big wage increases to offset rising inflation. At a testy press conference in the GM building, reporters pressed weary executives on whether the new contract would fuel inflation, but they couldn't get a direct answer.

When the press conference ended, the frustrated journalists retreated to a nearby men's room. There *New York Times* correspondent Jerry Flint pulled a piece of chalk out of his pocket and drew two large circles on the floor. He firmly planted a foot in each circle and shouted, "Inflationary!" Then he informed his fellow scribes that they could write, with accuracy, that the contract was "described in some circles as inflationary." Which is pretty much what Flint's story would say, and not without reason.

The new GM contract granted the company's 400,000 hourly workers (triple what the Big Three's *combined* total would be forty years later) a 30 percent wage hike over the next three years. It ended the cap on cost-of-living adjustments and accelerated the payment schedule from annually to quarterly. Most notably, the new contract allowed workers to retire after thirty years on the job at age fifty-eight with a full pension of $500 per month. To the UAW's leaders, the "thirty and out" provision represented social progress. Thirty years was long enough for mind-numbing work on Detroit's assembly lines, they reasoned, and early retirements would create new job opportunities for young Americans. GM's bosses didn't like the idea, but sixty-seven days of idle factories melted their resistance.

While company officials wouldn't directly answer the "inflationary" question, they did concede that the new contract's compensation increases would outstrip productivity gains. So the contract "was thus by definition inflationary," said the next day's *Times*. Both the company and the union maintained, however, that they were victims of inflation rather than causes of it—starting a chicken-versus-egg debate that would continue for years.

The new contract was the first one the UAW had negotiated since the mid-1940s that wasn't shaped by Walter Reuther. At sixty-two, Reuther had been killed in a plane crash the previous May while traveling to the union's northern Michigan conference center. His death made front-page news around the country, because Reuther had twice graced the cover of *Time*, advised five presidents, and helped to shape American domestic policy. His biggest disappointment, in the early 1950s, had been his failure to convince the Big Three to push for national health insurance, which executives equated with socialism. Decades later Detroit's CEOs would wish that Reuther had succeeded.

Reuther had dominated the union for a quarter-century, thanks not only to his powerful social vision but also to his mastery of union politics. Both were reflected in the gains he won for UAW members in the 1950s and 1960s. Besides cost-of-living allowances and generous wage increases, autoworkers got company-paid health and hospitalization insurance, supplemental unemployment benefits during layoffs, and much more. The wages and benefits allowed UAW members to live comfortable, middle-class lives, and Reuther reasoned that similar pay and perks eventually would spread to workers in other industries. In other words, what was good for the UAW was good for America.

Another part of the Reuther vision was that the union should help its members improve not only their financial standing but also their health, education, political consciousness, and social outlook. To that end every car factory had, not just a shop committee and grievance committee to handle bargaining and worker complaints, but also an education committee, a health and safety committee, and a recreation committee. In the interest of preserving "labor peace," all these committee members and their staff appointees—a number that could be one hundred or more in large factories—got paid by the companies for doing union work instead of for toiling on the assembly line.

The committeemen and -women received the premium wages paid to skilled-trade workers such as electricians, as opposed to ordinary assembly line wages. When their plants' assembly lines worked overtime, they got extra pay too, even if they themselves weren't working. Plant committee jobs, in short, were plum posts, and the best way to get one was to ally yourself with the UAW's leadership caucus, which was the Reuther caucus. The bottom line was that in his pursuit of social justice, Walter Reuther got the car companies to fund his union patronage machine.

Thanks to Reuther, some skilled-trade workers began earning enough to join the country clubs where their managers were members, but that rarely, if ever, happened. Detroit's line of social demarcation was class as well as cash. Managers and executives (except for the few who favored the old-money enclave of Grosse Pointe, on the east side) lived west of Interstate 75, territory that included the northwest suburbs of Birmingham and Bloomfield Hills. Their kids often attended Detroit Country Day School or the Roeper School. Their social courts were elite country clubs such as Orchard Lake and the Bloomfield Hills Country Club, the latter being such a GM bastion that even a Ford was considered a foreign car.

Hourly workers, though, lived east of I-75 in Macomb County, where their powerboats, sitting on trailers, often were longer than the homes alongside them. They hung out at union halls and American Legion posts. This social-geographical dividing line continued all the way up the state to the playground communities at the top of Michigan's Lower Peninsula.

West of I-75 lay the white-collar resort towns of Petoskey and Harbor Springs on the Lake Michigan shore, and upscale inland lakes such as Torch, Walloon, and Charlevoix. The seasonal residents attended summer "up north" parties, where the women wore silk and the men wore seersucker. East of I-75 the Lake Huron shore was lined with blue-collar bungalows and blue-jean bars, where even saying *seersucker* would get you a punch in the jaw.

The 1970s would be the UAW's high-water mark; the 1970 strike was a singular victory for Leonard Woodcock, Reuther's successor. Woodcock was cut from the same ideological cloth as Reuther, but lacked his predecessor's considerable charisma. After Reuther's death the union's executive board had elected him president by a meager 13–12 margin. Thus Woodcock had to prove his mettle to his membership by winning contracts richer than Reuther's.

He would succeed, but in the process the UAW started killing the geese that had laid the golden eggs at the feet of its members. It made gains in wages and benefits, but it also single-mindedly emphasized protecting the rights of workers, often without expecting workers to fulfill their responsibilities. Rights were trumping responsibilities everywhere else in America during the 1970s, but the UAW's power in the nation's car factories had special consequences.

Many factories had to close for the first days of deer-hunting season, for example; so many workers took unexcused absences—with little fear of penalty—that it was impossible to stay open. Along with piston rings, some auto plants had gambling rings. The union's cohort of committeemen and their appointees in each factory had to be matched by a costly company counterpart to deal with the union people—which had less to do with making cars than with keeping a tenuous peace on the factory floor.

When a machine broke down and stopped the assembly line, workers would take an unscheduled break and wait for an electrician or machinist instead of rushing to fix it themselves. Only skilled tradesmen were allowed to repair machinery, even if ordinary workers were capable of doing it—rules enforced not only by the national contract but also by the separate local contracts at each factory. The electricians or machinists often took their time getting to where they were needed, so that the plant would have to go into overtime to make up for lost production, and everybody would get more money.

The culpability for accepting all this lay squarely with managers, who understood the problem but deemed giving in to the union to be the path of least resistance—especially because consumers had to pay up regardless. And when one company caved in to avoid or to settle a strike, the other two had little choice but to go along. Workers at Ford and Chrysler, for example, weren't about to settle for less than what GM workers were getting. That's what pattern bargaining, and the UAW's monopoly on automotive labor, was all about.

Labor was just one challenge that Detroit faced as the 1970s began. Ralph Nader's consumer movement and America's growing environmental consciousness were spawning new federal regulatory requirements for cars. Shoulder-harness safety belts, in addition to lap belts, became required. In the wake of the first Earth Day, on April 22, 1970, Congress passed the Clean Air Act, which phased out the use of lead as a gasoline additive—to the dismay of virtually every executive in Detroit except Ed Cole. Automotive engineers hadn't yet learned how to make high-horsepower engines run without the performance-enhancing (albeit polluting) properties of lead. So one result was that in 1976 the Chevy Corvette had to sputter along on just 165 horsepower, less than half what the car had in the late 1960s.

Detroit's engineers were already overwhelmed in trying to keep up with clean air and safety regulations, but there were more challenges to come. Because of the regulatory piling-on, in addition to the alienated workers and inept managers, Detroit's quality nose-dived just as import sales were growing. In 1960 imports had accounted for less than 5 percent of U.S. car sales, but by 1971 they accounted for about 15 percent, or 1.5 million cars out of the total 10 million sold. Most imports were from Germany, but Japanese Toyotas and Datsuns were gaining ground on the West Coast and eyeing expansion into the American heartland. Imports gained further from the trend toward small cars as rising inflation squeezed Americans' incomes and as baby boomers bought cheap wheels to take to college.

The management teams that faced these challenges were becoming increasingly inbred and sycophantic. In a telling incident in the mid-1970s, some junior GM executives had a meeting with chairman Thomas A. (for Aquinas) Murphy that happened to fall on Ash Wednesday. Murphy, a devout Catholic who attended Mass most mornings, was wearing the ritual ashes on his forehead. One of the young men dipped his finger into a nearby ashtray, dabbed a smudge on his own forehead, and—yes—walked in to meet the boss. Years later he would become an executive vice president of the company.

The new generation of "subcompact" cars that were launched in 1970 to combat the imports made Detroit's dysfunction apparent. First out of the box was AMC, which launched its new Gremlin model (appropriately) on April Fool's Day. It featured a long snout and a chopped-off back end that led, inevitably, to the joke: "What happened to the rest of your car?"

Five months later, on September 10, GM introduced the Vega, and the very next day Ford followed with the Pinto. Both were more conventionally styled than the Gremlin, and both—like the Gremlin—were conventionally engineered. That is, they were little versions of Detroit's big cars, with a heavy driveshaft to connect the front engine to the rear-drive wheels. The driveshaft created a big hump along the length of the car's floor, making a small car feel cramped and adding extra weight, thus sacrificing fuel economy.

The fledgling crop of Japanese imports weren't stylish, but they had the sort of engineering innovation that Detroit had come to neglect. Most had front-mounted engines and front-wheel drive, eliminating the need for a driveshaft and making the cars roomier and more fuel efficient. The weight of the engine directly over the drive wheels also increased traction in rain and snow.

In the spring of 1971 Ford chairman Henry Ford II saw enough troubles looming on the horizon to speak in an unusually blunt tone. On May 13, after the company's annual shareholders' meeting, he held an impromptu press conference and delivered a downbeat assessment of Detroit's future. "I frankly don't see how we're going to meet the foreign competition," he told reporters. "We've only seen the beginning. Wait till those Japanese"—instead of confining their sales mostly to the West Coast—"get a hold of the central part of the United States."

As for Washington, "holding the industry's feet to the flame might be a satisfying and politically useful kind of exercise for some people," Henry II declared, "but it's not a justifiable practice." Concerning the trend to small cars, Ford was direct. "Mini cars," he said, lead to "mini profits." It's hard to fault the man for lack of foresight.

The 1970s were the decade that undid Detroit. During the 1980s and 1990s, the Big Three would mount periodic, and sometimes spectacular, comebacks and undergo equally dramatic crises. But never again would Detroit rule the automobile industry unchallenged and unbowed. All that Henry Ford II had cited—foreign competition, government regulation, and the trend to smaller and less-profitable cars—would combine to produce the proverbial perfect storm, and the inbred industry was ill equipped to react to it.

The 1970s had been foreshadowed for General Motors on October 3, 1968, when the company opened the GM Building—a white fifty-story skyscraper—at 59th Street and Fifth Avenue in Manhattan. Chairman James M. Roche (the same man who had apologized to Ralph Nader three years earlier) chose the occasion to announce that in two years, GM would introduce an innovative small car. It would weigh less than two thousand pounds, be priced the same as the Volkswagen Beetle, and be built with the latest American manufacturing technology. Roche was throwing down the gauntlet to the nettlesome imports.

To build anticipation, in May 1970 GM started running teaser ads, saying "You'll see" but neither showing the car nor disclosing its name. That same month, by unhappy coincidence, Ohio National Guardsmen shot and killed four students during an antiwar protest at Kent State University. Kent State was located about an hour from the massive Chevrolet assembly plant in Lordstown, Ohio, where the mysterious unnamed car would be built. The Lordstown plant, which had opened in 1966, had one of the youngest workforces in the auto industry; many workers were roughly the same age—and of the same disaffected mind-set—as the kids over at Kent State. That demographic would loom large in the years to come.

The new car, christened the Vega, was launched in September 1970, with advertising that proclaimed, "Chevy's new little car is open for business." But shortly thereafter the UAW's sixty-seven-day strike against GM began. Production of the Vega, the most serious "import fighter" in GM's history, was suspended in the midst of its launch. The high stakes maximized the UAW's leverage against the company, just as the union's leaders had intended. It was brilliant timing—unless the union was concerned about the long-term threat posed by Americans defecting to Japanese cars, which it wasn't. The result: Chevy dealers, geared up to sell the Vega, wouldn't get many of them for months.

Meanwhile the Vega failed to meet Roche's weight and price targets. Four hundred pounds overweight, it was priced at $300 more than the Beetle. To be sure, the Vega had its strengths. Its sleek, distinctive styling and innovative features won it *Motor Trend* magazine's coveted Car of the Year award in 1971—even though the Pinto outsold the Vega that year, 317,000 cars to 245,000.

But that same year GM took the Lordstown plant away from Chevrolet and folded it into the new General Motors Assembly Division (with the unfortunate acronym of GMAD), which henceforth would run all GM assembly plants. The corporate restructuring move—one of many that GM would try in the decades to come— was aimed at streamlining operations, eliminating duplication, and boosting efficiency.

Though little noticed at the time, the creation of GMAD would prove a turning point. It complicated the company's quest to produce high-quality cars just when quality was becoming critical, because it constituted a new organizational layer between Chevrolet and its customers. So if Chevy's general manager wasn't satisfied with the quality of the cars coming out of Lordstown, he couldn't just crack down on the plant's management himself. He'd have to take the problem to the top man at GMAD, a move that often spawned bureaucratic infighting, with the Chevy people blaming GMAD's manufacturing methods and the GMAD guys blaming Chevy's engineering. Alas, both sides often were right. In such finger-pointing contests, finding solutions became nearly impossible.

Not long after GMAD took over Lordstown, it increased the speed of the assembly lines to make up for production lost during the strike. But instead of going from 60 cars an hour to 65 or perhaps 70, GMAD boosted the line speed at times to an incredible 100 cars an hour. GMAD also reduced the number of quality inspectors. It deemed these moves to be reasonable because the Lordstown lines had been designed to build up to 140 cars an hour. The GMAD managers also figured, incorrectly, that Lordstown's highly automated assembly process would ensure high quality without much traditional quality inspection. They didn't count on the reaction of the workers, who thought the moves were a heavy-handed speed-up that forced them to bust their butts for the bosses.

Before long the sort of angry rebellion that had blown the lid off

Kent State found its way to the factory floor, as some workers resorted to sabotage. "Autos regularly roll off the line with slit upholstery, scratched paint, dented bodies, bent gearshift levers, cut ignition wires, and loose or missing bolts," reported *Time*. "In some cars, the trunk key is broken off right in the lock, thereby jamming it." Drugs and alcohol became rampant at Lordstown, and more than a few workers carried guns or knives, either for self-defense or otherwise.

In early 1972, just fifteen months after the sixty-seven-day national strike of 1970 had ended, the Lordstown workers staged their own local strike that yet again interrupted shipments of Vegas to dealers. The repeated strife grabbed the attention of the national news media, which couldn't resist the story of oppressed young workers bucking the corporate establishment, and they dubbed Lordstown the home of the "blue-collar blues."

If Lordstown's manufacturing was a mess, the Vega's engineering was also suspect. Some of the features that had won it Car of the Year honors began to backfire. The Vega's engine had a weight-saving aluminum block and cast-iron head, but the two metals react to heat stress (which is inevitable in all engines) in different ways. In addition, the engine's "sleeveless" piston cylinders lacked the solid seals of conventional "sleeved" cylinders. These features had been intended to save weight and boost gas mileage, but they unfortunately made Vega engines prone to leak oil in copious amounts. Engineering innovation took another hit, in Detroit's eyes.

Little wonder that "the Vega seems to be recall prone," as *Consumer Reports* magazine deadpanned in September 1972. Chevy dealers replaced so many Vega engines that they joked that the engines were "disposable." As the Vega's reputation suffered, so did Vega sales. After all, Americans who wanted small cars had more and more alternatives, beyond just the Beetle.

Japanese car companies had been selling cars in the United States since the late 1950s, though they didn't sell many at first—and for good reason. They were tiny, tinny, and underpowered, qualities exemplified by the Toyota Toyopet, an awful little sedan introduced to America in 1958. The number of Japanese cars sold in the United States that year totaled all of 1,604—barely enough to fill a big-city parking deck. The Toyopet was a misfit in so many ways, beginning with its name, that Toyota soon pulled it off the American market and went back to the drawing board. But that move was a tactical retreat, not a permanent withdrawal.

In 1965 the company started shipping its compact Corona, which offered more room and more horsepower than the Toyopet, along with American-oriented options such as air-conditioning and an automatic transmission. The company sold 6,400 cars in America that year, a number that soared to 71,000 in 1968 and to 300,000 in 1971. By then Toyota's U.S.-model lineup had expanded to include the Corona Mark II, the Carina, the Corolla, and the Celica. It was a confusing plethora of soundalike names, but that didn't seem to matter.

Similar sales gains were being posted by Japan's second-largest car company, Nissan. Like Toyota, Nissan had sold its first car in the United States in 1958, but it dithered for a decade before launching its first car specifically designed for the American market—the Datsun 510. Other Japanese automakers started exporting to the United States: Subaru, Mazda, and in late 1972 Japan's newest and smallest car company, Honda. The Honda Civic subcompact, which had debuted in Japan earlier that year, was surprisingly roomy inside, was fun to drive, and got more than thirty miles per gallon, compared to the Vega's twenty-five. What's more, thanks to pure dumb luck, Honda's timing couldn't have been better.

In October 1973 the State of Israel vanquished six neighboring Arab countries in the latest Mideast war. Instead of just licking their wounds, the Arab nations slapped an embargo on oil shipments to Israel's foremost ally, the United States. Gasoline prices, which had remained remarkably stable for nearly fifteen years, surged nearly 60 percent within months. Even worse, shortages broke out. Some Americans had to line up at gas stations for hours to fill their cars. To reduce the length of the lines, some states and cities started odd-even fill-up days, limiting cars with license plates ending in an odd number, for example, to buying gas on Mondays, Wednesdays, and Fridays, and reserving Tuesdays, Thursdays, and Saturdays for cars with even-numbered plates. In 1974 Congress passed a new national speed limit, fifty-five miles an hour, to conserve fuel. In the rush to do something, to do *anything,* small cars became hot items. The emotional qualms that many Americans still harbored about buying Japanese cars gave way to practical considerations.

The experience of a young woman who graduated from a small midwestern college in 1975 was typical. While she was growing up, she had watched her grandfather religiously buy a new Chrysler every two years. But Chrysler didn't have much to offer someone on a tight budget except the Dodge Colt, which actually was made for Chrysler in Japan by Mitsubishi Motors. So she reluctantly bought a Honda Civic and adorned it with a hand-lettered bumper sticker that said: "I Would Have Rather Bought American."

The first half of the 1970s were difficult years for America. The country was reeling from defeat in Vietnam, the Watergate scandal, and "stagflation," the unholy combination of inflation and economic stagnation. Detroit's Big Three, meanwhile, were beset by an aggressively determined union, bitter strikes, unprecedented new regulations, and a fresh wave of foreign competition. All this occurred in just five years. But only in the second half of the decade did the *real* troubles begin at General Motors, Ford, and Chrysler.

In 1975 Congress passed the first Corporate Average Fuel Economy (CAFE) law, which required automakers to reach a "fleet-wide average," among all the cars they sold, of 27.5 miles a gallon by 1985 (about double the average mileage cars were getting in 1975), with interim increases along the way. The automakers protested, not only because the mileage target seemed to them too ambitious but also because of the politically convoluted way in which the law was structured.

Leonard Woodcock & Co. had foreseen that the easiest way for the Big Three to meet a single fuel-economy standard would be to import more small cars from overseas factories, which were non-UAW factories, where lower labor costs could compensate for smaller profit margins. So, at the insistence of the UAW, the CAFE law required Detroit's automakers to meet separate fuel-economy targets for cars built in the United States and cars imported from overseas, such as Chrysler's Dodge Colt.

By setting separate standards for imported and domestic cars, the new law required GM, Ford, and Chrysler to build most of their small cars in America, despite meager profits on them. It was the only way they could avoid paying fines on the higher-priced big cars that actually made money. And because of the ever-sweeter contracts that the UAW was winning, Detroit's profits on small cars were moving from meager to nonexistent. The Big Three were being squeezed in a vise between Washington's regulations and their own labor contracts, which were getting richer and richer.

Woodcock and the union had followed their gains in the 1970 strike with another bravura performance in 1973. After a two-day strike at Chrysler, the UAW won significant wage increases, a family dental plan, better benefits for retirees, seven additional paid holidays over the three-year life of the contract, and, to top it off, the right to retire at *any* age with full benefits after thirty years on the job. The new pattern deal was dutifully accepted by GM and Ford. The result was that a man or woman could start on the assembly line at age eighteen, right after high school; get full retirement benefits at age forty-eight; and then pursue a life of leisure or take a second job. If the retiree lived to be seventy-nine or older, he or she would spend more years drawing a full pension than actually working.

And more and more retired workers were living to seventy-nine or beyond, thanks to continuing advances in healthcare—which UAW members could consume without regard to cost. Their contract spared them from having to pay the co-payments and deductibles that most other Americans paid for doctor visits. As a result, UAW members and retirees had little incentive to spend the company's healthcare dollars wisely. And union members who chose early retirement got extra pension pay to compensate them until Social Security kicked in.

By 1975 GM's pension costs for UAW members had jumped to 83 cents an hour, up from just 43 cents an hour three years earlier. "Pension costs have substantially exceeded estimates," a senior UAW staffer wrote in a memo to Woodcock. In April 1977 UAW vice president Irving Bluestone conceded he was "flabbergasted" that 29 percent of GM's hourly employees who had chosen to retire the previous year were under fifty-five. "We were aware that the trend to early retirement was escalating," Bluestone declared. "But this is astounding."

Even Woodcock was frightened by the success of his union, from which he retired in 1977 to become U.S. envoy (and later ambassador) to China. On a return visit to Detroit, in a conversation with an old friend, Woodcock confided, "Our members have the best contract that people with their skills and education could ever hope to get. But we've convinced them that with every new contract, they're entitled to more." Having served up the gravy train, UAW leaders were now powerless to jump off.

Management's resistance to union gains that outstripped productivity improvements was always tempered by a salient dynamic: improvements in workers' pay or benefits would "trickle up" to managers too. The reason: the car companies were determined to keep pay spreads between managers and workers "appropriate." And they weren't about to let managers make do on benefits inferior to those enjoyed by their blue-collar masses. It wasn't quite collusion, but it sure was cozy. What was happening at the Big Three, in effect, was a sweeping transfer of wealth from shareholders to employees, blue-collar and white-collar alike. In Detroit, GM was gratefully nicknamed "Generous Motors" or "Mother Motors."

Somebody had to pay for it all, and that would be the hapless consumer. Between 1971 and 1974 the price of a typical Vega jumped nearly 20 percent, to more than $2,500. Just when Detroit needed to boost sales to pay for soaring wages and benefits for its employees, its price increases gave consumers a strong incentive to try a foreign car.

Customers had other incentives too. In early 1977 an Oldsmobile owner in Chicago was surprised to find that the engine in his new car wasn't the vaunted Olds Rocket V8 but a Chevrolet engine of similar dimensions. General Motors, it turned out, had run short of Oldsmobile engines and simply had used Chevy engines in some Oldsmobiles instead. The Olds owner complained to the Illinois attorney general's office, spawning nearly 250 state and private lawsuits against GM. The company insisted that it had done nothing wrong because both V8 engines were 350 cubic inches and produced an identical 170 horsepower.

But the whole point was that Oldsmobile had advertised its Rocket V8 engine as something better than the plain-vanilla Chevy V8 and indeed had charged a premium price for it. A year later GM agreed to pay Olds owners $40 million in compensation. It was a pittance for a company that earned billions of dollars a year, but the public-perception damage was enormous. The Rocket engine affair seemed yet another example of Detroit breaking its bond with car buyers.

So did the continued deterioration in the quality of Detroit's cars. As the 1970s unfolded, Detroit's engineers—by and large a talented and dedicated bunch—scrambled not only to adjust to new regulatory requirements but also to adopt front-wheel drive to boost fuel efficiency. In its June 1978 issue, *Consumer Reports* tested a Dodge Omni, a new front-wheel-drive subcompact billed as an import-fighter, built in the Belvidere factory where Fred Young worked. The magazine reported what Young and his co-workers knew but had little means or motivation to address because the plant's management wasn't about to listen to workers back then: the Omni was rife with problems.

Consumer Reports found thirty-seven defects. The fuel tank had been pierced by carpet tacks. The right rear tire was a different size from the other three. And a wiring short circuit caused the car's horn to blow whenever the steering wheel was turned. The findings might have been fodder for a comedy skit, except nobody was laughing. Besides, those flaws were mere nuisances compared to the problems with the Ford Pinto.

It's fair to say that some owners of the Ford Pinto—indeed, like some Vega owners—really did like their car. One, happily named Edward Pinto, graduated from the University of Illinois in Champaign, where he had been student body president, in 1971. Before he headed off to Indiana University Law School that fall, his parents bought him a new Pinto because of, well, its name. Young Ed drove it for 100,000 miles with nary a problem, before selling the car a decade later. During that time he and his girlfriend befriended another couple and often double-dated in the Pinto. Their friends had such fond memories of scrunching together in the car's tiny backseat that when they were married, they asked to be driven from the reception in Ed Pinto's Pinto.

It was the sort of charming car memory that Americans loved, evidence that their love affair with their cars wasn't limited to Corvettes or muscle machines. But the Pinto story that made national headlines was anything but charming. Instead it was tragic, even deadly.

On a humid summer night in August 1978 three young Indiana women—two sisters and a cousin—were driving to a preseason basketball game near Elkhart. Their 1973 Ford Pinto was struck from behind by a speeding van. "It was like a large napalm bomb going up," an eyewitness later would recall. Horribly, all three girls were burned to death.

A month later an Indiana grand jury invoked a year-old state law that made corporations, as well as individuals, subject to criminal prosecution. It indicted the Ford Motor Company for "reckless homicide." No individual Ford executives were named in the indictment, which carried a maximum potential penalty, oddly, of just $30,000—mere pennies to a company the size of Ford. From a purely financial standpoint, the company might have just pleaded guilty and cut its losses. But that wasn't about to happen. At stake wasn't just $30,000 but Ford's reputation.

Unfortunately, however, company officials could hardly claim ignorance of the Pinto problem. Almost a full year earlier, in September 1977, a little-known magazine named *Mother Jones* had published the results of its six-month investigation into why Pintos were prone to burn when struck from the rear. The car's gas tank was mounted behind the rear axle instead of on top of the axle, the magazine pointed out, the latter being a safer design that Ford itself had patented. Should a Pinto get rear-ended at only thirty miles an hour, it explained, "the tube leading to the gas-tank cap would be ripped away from the tank itself, and gas would immediately begin sloshing onto the road."

Ford engineers had known about this when the car was launched, the magazine wrote. But the company's cost-benefit analysis determined that the number of lives that might be saved weren't worth the additional cost of $5 a car required to strengthen the design. "Burning Pintos have become such an embarrassment to Ford," the article added, that the company "dropped a line from the end of a radio spot that read, 'Pinto leaves you with that warm feeling.' "

The *Mother Jones* piece caused a furor, and mainstream publications, including *The New York Times,* wrote articles about the article. Within weeks the Transportation Department launched an investigation. In June 1978 a California jury awarded $128 million to a boy badly burned in a Pinto accident. Soon afterward Ford said it would recall the 1.5 million Pintos built between 1971 and 1976 to fix the problem. But the letter notifying Pinto owners was delayed a few months until the repair parts were produced. The notification came too late for the three Indiana girls.

When the trial began in January 1980, the prosecutor told the jury that Ford "deliberately chose profit over human life." He tried to enter as evidence more than two hundred Ford internal documents that, he contended, showed what *Mother Jones* had concluded: that Ford had known about the Pinto problem all along and could have chosen to avoid it. The company's defense lawyers, however, convinced the judge to exclude all but a couple dozen documents by refocusing the trial from the Pinto's design to the specific circumstances of the accident.

The van that had hit the girls' car, noted Ford attorneys, had failed a state safety inspection. The van's driver had a record of repeated traffic violations and had admitted that he wasn't watching the road. Most important, the defense argued, the van was going so fast that almost any car, even one with a different gas tank design, would have burned from the collision. On March 13, after a two-month trial, the jury bought Ford's arguments and found the company not guilty.

The "not guilty" headlines were a mixed blessing for Ford. Being acquitted clearly was better than the alternative, but the trial publicity had cost the company inestimable damage in the court of public opinion. It was another affront, on top of the Vega's quality woes, the Olds Rocket engine flap, and the individual car breakdowns suffered by tens of thousands of Detroit customers. The reputations of GM, Ford, and Chrysler were undergoing a dramatic shift. After being regarded for decades as symbols of America's pride and prosperity, the companies were coming to be derided as callous corporations that had contempt for their customers. What had started with the Corvair scandal in 1965 came to full fruition with the Pinto trial.

Ironically, two months after the Indiana trial ended, Ford won a

$19.2 million federal contract to provide 4,994 Pintos to the U.S. Postal Service. The company, after all, had submitted the low bid.

In the months leading up to the Pinto trial, Detroit was moving into crisis mode on another front. In early 1979, just as Americans had begun returning to bigger cars that were more profitable for Detroit, the Iranian Revolution created the decade's second oil shock and sent gasoline prices soaring again. The economy plunged into recession, car sales tumbled, and Chrysler posted a record $207 million loss for the second quarter of the year. It was a short-lived record, however, because the third quarter's loss was a stunning (well, for its time) $460 million.

By then CEO John Riccardo had been negotiating for months to get up to $1 billion in assistance from the federal government—a request that initially was met with almost universal skepticism. "The conventional case for a bailout is to preserve jobs," editorialized *The Washington Post.* "But preserving jobs merely to preserve jobs is dangerous." President Jimmy Carter balked at Chrysler's request, as did Congress. The prestigious Business Roundtable, composed of top executives at America's blue-chip companies, declared its opposition to a bailout.

So did General Motors CEO Tom Murphy, who scarcely could have imagined that one of his successors would beg for a much bigger bailout thirty years later. But it all would be repeated: a reluctant president. A skeptical Congress. Plunging sales. An alienated press and public. Except that the price tag in 2009 would be fifty times as high.

But no one foresaw those events in November 1979, when Chrysler's desperate board ousted Riccardo and replaced him with fifty-five-year-old Lee Iacocca, who had suffered a humiliating public firing from Ford the previous year. Iacocca had been second in command and heir apparent to Henry Ford II for more than a decade, but not even a company as big as Ford was big enough for those two egos.

After being fired from Ford, Iacocca had signed on at Chrysler as Riccardo's number two—a move he later said he never would have made had he known how bad things really were. Chrysler had some eighty thousand unsold cars parked around Detroit in the "sales bank," which was a polite name for storage lots packed with orphan cars that had been built without orders from dealers. The company was a managerial disaster.

If nothing else, the crisis finally created common ground between a car company and the UAW. They launched a joint lobbying effort, and in late December 1979 Congress reluctantly passed the Chrysler Loan Guarantee Act. The government agreed to guarantee up to $1.5 billion of loans to Chrysler from private lenders, but only if Chrysler could meet strict conditions. One was selling the corporate jets. (They were uniquely visible symbols of executive excess—a lesson the Big Three would forget, to their chagrin, thirty years later.) Chrysler also had to get significant concessions from the UAW, private banks, and others.

The union agreed, though not without considerable grumbling from the rank and file. But the banks were even tougher. Getting them on board took six months of painstaking and desperate negotiations, during which Chrysler almost ran out of cash. On April 1, 1980, at a critical point in the negotiations, Chrysler's young treasurer, Steve Miller, summoned bankers to his office to announce that Chrysler had filed for bankruptcy. As his guests gulped, Miller smiled and reminded them it was April Fool's Day.

Thanks to Iacocca's sheer determination and to the chutzpah of his underlings, Chrysler got the concessions it needed, and America got its first automotive bailout. A folk music star named Tom Paxton memorialized the event with a song called "I'm Changing My Name to Chrysler," which included the verse:

I'm changing my name to Chrysler.
I'm going down to Washington D.C.
I will tell some power broker
What they did for Iacocca
Will be perfectly acceptable to me.

FIVE

HONDA COMES TO THE CORNFIELDS

*G*overnor James A. Rhodes, a towering figure in Ohio, was an old-school politician who never met a big project he didn't like. He once proposed building a bridge across Lake Erie from Cleveland to Canada to stimulate trade—one of his few ideas that never got off the ground. Throughout his political career he stuck with a single slogan: "Jobs and Progress."

On October 11, 1977, Rhodes convened a press conference at the state capitol to announce that a foreign company was going to build a new factory that would bring jobs to Ohio, albeit fewer than one hundred at the outset. Honda Motor Company of Japan, the governor said, would open a motorcycle plant near Marysville, about thirty-five miles northwest of Columbus. With smiling Honda executives alongside him, Rhodes was asked whether Honda might one day expand beyond motorcycles and start making cars in Ohio. "I wouldn't be surprised," the garrulous governor replied. "You know, these Japs are pretty smart." Everyone in the room gasped, but Rhodes immediately realized his faux pas and added, "Of course, you know that by Japs, I mean 'Jobs and Progress'!" The attendees burst into a gratefully relieved laughter.

Initially, luring Honda to Ohio was only a minor victory for Rhodes. The motorcycle factory was a small consolation prize for the state's failure to land the big fish, the new Volkswagen auto-assembly plant in New Stanton, Pennsylvania, near Pittsburgh. The factory would employ 2,500 people when it started building the Volkswagen Rabbit, the successor car to the beloved but outdated Beetle.

Honda, meanwhile, was enjoying success by exporting cars from Japan to America, where sales of its little subcompacts surged more than tenfold—from 20,000 to 220,000—between 1972 and 1977. As the company pondered the next step in its U.S. strategy, an unexpected opportunity arose: Ford expressed interest in buying four-cylinder engines from Honda to use in the next generation of Ford small cars. In 1974, after negotiations between the two companies began, Ford president Lee Iacocca even presented Honda's founder and president, Soichiro Honda, with a new Ford Mustang as a goodwill gesture.

But when the Americans asked for detailed technical specifications about the Honda engines while avoiding any commitment to buy them, Honda negotiators grew suspicious. What's more, the UAW had gotten wind of Ford's plans and opposed the idea, viewing it as a threat to union jobs in Ford's own engine plants. In the end, Iacocca was more interested in Honda engines than was the one man whose opinion mattered—Henry Ford II. After a couple of years of on-and-off negotiations, Henry II declared: "No car with my name on the hood is going to have a Jap engine inside." His decision was almost as pivotal, and as disastrous, as his rejection of Volkswagen nearly thirty years earlier.

Had Ford agreed to buy Honda engines, the little Japanese company might never have entertained the unlikely idea of building motorcycles, cars, or anything else in America. Japan's automakers would have increased their exports to the United States, but almost certainly would have sparked a political backlash strong enough to limit their U.S. sales—if not forever, then at least for many years. As it happened, however, the collapse of the Ford negotiations convinced Honda executives that they had to take the risk of making cars in America. Not only did they fear a potential U.S. backlash against rising imports, but they also viewed their growth prospects in Japan as severely limited by the dominance of Toyota and Nissan.

Honda's story, as the first Japanese company to build cars in the United States, is critical to the understanding of Detroit's downfall. The company successfully managed and motivated American workers, giving the lie to Detroit's excuses. Honda's Ohio motorcycle plant, and the car factory it opened next door five years later, blew open the dam of Big Three and UAW dominance. Even as it embarked on its risky American strategy, Honda hewed to cautious and conservative tactics. But Honda's American adventure was anything but a straight line upward. On the contrary, it was a wild ride, with periodic crises overcome by improbable and increasing success. Its yin-yang approach reflected the contrasting personalities of the two men who had built Honda Motor amid the bleak ruins of postwar Japan.

Soichiro Honda, who founded Honda Motor in 1948 when he was forty-two years old, was a self-taught engineer with enormous determination. The fledgling company's business expertise came from Takeo Fujisawa. Honda was a Japanese party animal while Fujisawa loved nights at home listening to Wagner's operas and didn't even have a driver's license. What he and Honda had in common, however, was a terrible temper. Fujisawa was nicknamed "Godzilla" by his underlings, while Honda's nickname was "Mr. Thunder." By late 1954 the company's hectic expansion caused quality to deteriorate, sales to drop, and money to run short. Only Fujisawa's intervention with Japanese banks kept the company alive. But in 1961 Honda stunned the rarified world of motorcycle racing by sweeping the top five positions in the world's most demanding and prestigious race, England's Isle of Man TT. The reputation of Honda's bikes soared. So did sales.

As for its cars, well, in 1961 there weren't any yet. Not for another two years would Honda enter the automobile business, and then only by defying its own government. In the early 1960s, Japan's powerful bureaucrats believed that their country already had enough car companies and were preparing to ban new entrants. To beat the ban, in October 1963 Honda rushed out an awful little car called the S500, which Japanese journalists promptly derided as "just a four-wheeled motorcycle." They were right, but the S500 served its purpose merely by existing. Honda had entered the game.

Meanwhile, in 1959, as it was building its car business in Japan, Honda Motor began exporting its little Super Cub 50 motorcycle to the United States. The Super Cub's open, step-through design made it easy to get on and off, even for women. The bike had a peppy, clean-burning "four-stroke" design that didn't require mixing gasoline with oil like the noisy, two-stroke engines on other motorcycles.

To offset the Hell's Angels image then associated with motorcycles, the company launched the advertising slogan "You meet the nicest people on a Honda," and sales took off. In 1964 the Super Cub got another image boost from the song "Little Honda," which was written by the Beach Boys but popularized by a group called, conveniently, the Hondells. Songs about Corvettes and muscle cars were by now predictable, but a hymn to a glorified motor scooter showed the depth of America's attachment to engines on wheels.

But motorcycles can be faddish products, and a couple years later Honda's fortunes dipped again. In 1966 the company's bikes suddenly went out of style in the United States, and sales plunged nearly 30 percent overnight. For the second time in a dozen years, Japanese banks had to see the company through the crisis.

Despite the money woes, one department that remained untouched was the company's engineering center, Honda Research and Development. Honda R&D, a subsidiary of Honda Motor, was funded by a share of the parent company's revenue and thus was safe from cost-cutting drives. Its elite group of young engineers took pride in being driven, and often browbeaten, by Soichiro, the irascible founder himself.

The denizens of Honda R&D reveled in their elite status, sometimes referring to other Honda employees as "civilians." But their snobbery was justified. After making Honda into the scourge of motorcycle racing, in 1972 they unveiled a revolutionary automotive engine that stunned rival car companies. The CVCC—for Compound Vortex Controlled Combustion—passed air through the engine in a way that burned gasoline more cleanly, making it the only engine that could meet America's new clean-air standards without a catalytic converter. Detroit, inexcusably, had been out-engineered.

The CVCC boosted sales of Honda's subcompact Civic model and solidified the status of Honda R&D as the power center at Honda Motor. Just as General Motors was led by financial people, Honda would always be led by engineers—all of them "graduates" of Honda R&D. Put another way, the bean counters ran GM, while the car guys ran Honda. It would make a critical difference between Honda's success and GM's failure.

After Honda-san and Fujisawa retired in 1973, their successors wrestled with whether, and where, to build Honda cars on American soil. To do the legwork for the project, they reached down into the ranks of the company's "civilians." One had worked for several years on Honda's American sales staff.

Shige Yoshida joined Honda Motor in 1962, when he was thirty years old. He had been working for a small company that made car components when Honda's growth in motorcycles and its ambitions in automobiles grabbed his attention. Yoshida, methodical by nature, asked people who supplied parts to Honda what the company was like, and their answers weren't encouraging. Most suppliers found the company difficult and demanding, constantly changing its engineering specifications and saddling the suppliers with the resulting extra costs. But one man told Yoshida that while Honda was difficult to please, he always found himself learning something from the company. The answer convinced Yoshida to give Honda a try.

In January 1973, after eleven years with the company, Yoshida was asked to help build Honda Motor America, the company's fledgling automotive-sales subsidiary.

One problem, he quickly spotted, was that Honda was shipping boatloads of cars across the Pacific but then bringing the boats back empty, a practice that was inefficient and expensive. So Yoshida started Honda International Trading Company to export U.S. farm products back to Japan. Once a bunch of Civics was accidentally left onboard and shipped back to Japan, flattened under tons of grain. Nonetheless the subsidiary soon became a money machine for Honda. Thanks to its success, Yoshida's career flourished. Improbably, a Japanese boy who grew up during World War II was becoming a successful businessman in America.

In 1975, with Civic sales in America hitting new heights, one issue loomed particularly large for Honda Motor. Company executives were concerned that rising American protectionist sentiment would produce trade restrictions and put Honda's U.S. business at risk. So they assigned Yoshida to a small team that would study establishing a Honda manufacturing operation in America. The task, at least to Yoshida, seemed overwhelming at first.

No other Japanese automakers, not even mighty Toyota and Nissan, were building cars in America. Honda, despite its modest American sales success, remained a fairly small company that couldn't withstand the financial fallout from a significant botched investment, such as an unsuccessful factory. And among the many things that could torpedo a Honda factory in the United States would be the wrong location.

America was a big place: in contrast to homogeneous Japan, the country was filled with myriad local customs and a diversity that baffled the Japanese. Yoshida and his colleagues needed a place reasonably close to the American auto-parts manufacturers clustered in the Midwest. Location near a major population center would help in hiring a local workforce and would mitigate the cost of shipping motorcycles and cars to dealers. Most important, they decided, would be to find an area where the local culture put a high premium on diligence and hard work.

One location eliminated early on was Las Vegas, which had made a pitch for Honda, but California was another matter. Even though it was far from the auto-components companies of the Midwest, Honda seriously considered it, both as America's most populous state and as the epicenter of Japanese car sales in America. Honda's image in the state was critically important.

So in early 1976 Yoshida and his colleagues met with Governor Jerry Brown, whose embrace of the California counterculture and public musings on existential philosophy had earned him the nickname "Governor Moonbeam."

"Please explain to us, Governor," Yoshida asked, "why we should consider putting a factory in the state of California."

There was a momentary pause before Governor Moonbeam spoke. "Hippies," he said. "Blue jeans. All the important trends start in California." A surprised Yoshida thanked the governor for his most helpful thoughts, and soon crossed California off the list.

Carefully keeping their search out of the headlines, Yoshida's team increasingly focused on four states: Tennessee, Indiana, Illinois, and Ohio, where nobody called Rotary Club Republican Jim Rhodes "Governor Moonbeam." But luring new companies to his state was the core ideology behind "Jobs and Progress."

In April 1976, Rhodes's business development director, Jim Duerk, showed him an article in a Columbus newspaper saying that an unnamed Japanese car company was looking for a manufacturing site in the United States. Rhodes suggested that he and Duerk take a trip to Japan to check it out, and Duerk said he would need two or three weeks to make the necessary appointments. "No," replied Rhodes. "We're going tomorrow."

It was nutty to go without appointments—in Japan proper protocol meant everything. But Rhodes wouldn't be deterred. The next morning he and Duerk hopped on a plane to Tokyo. They arrived late in the afternoon, only to learn that the next day was the emperor's birthday and thus a national holiday. They managed only one appointment that day, with a Toyota executive who just happened to be at work. Toyota, he assured them, wasn't planning a U.S. factory. On day two the men met with Nissan and struck out again. Only on their last day in Japan did they meet with Honda, where executives confirmed they were indeed studying a U.S. factory site—though only for a small motorcycle plant. The entire trip lasted just four and a half days, for which Duerk was particularly relieved: their return flight touched down in Columbus just two and a half hours before his daughter's wedding was to begin.

It took another fifteen months for the Honda study team to settle on Rhodes's state, and buying the land, building roads, and installing sewer lines took three more. But by October 1977 it had all been approved. Building motorcycles first enabled Honda to limit its risk; the investment was much smaller than an auto-assembly plant would require. Starting small was the essence of pursuing a bold strategy with conservative tactics. American workers were being portrayed in the media as disaffected shirkers, so many Honda executives in Tokyo were skeptical that their company could build quality products in the United States. In essence, Honda was taking a test drive. Still, some Americans wanted to go along for the ride.

One of the first to apply was thirty-seven-year-old Al Kinzer, a manager at a diesel engine factory in Canton, Ohio. A soft-spoken, easy-drawling Southerner, Kinzer made two trips to Columbus for interviews with multiple Japanese managers, after which Yoshida called to say that he and a Japanese colleague wanted to drive to Canton to have dinner with Kinzer and his wife. A husband-wife interview was weird, Kinzer thought, but both Kinzers passed muster, and he became the first American manufacturing manager to be hired by Honda. Two American secretaries were already on board. Another sixty-one employees would be hired to start the motorcycle plant; the group would become known in Honda history as the "Original 64."

Kinzer's husband-wife interview was just one example of the painstaking care that Honda took in hiring. Yoshida subjected applicants to multiple hour-long job interviews, asking them about their life goals and aspirations and giving them little tasks that were designed to test their attention to detail—which he deemed the key to success in any factory. He invariably asked applicants, for example, to write their first name on a name tag and to place the tag on their left shoulder. Some applicants would put it on their right shoulder, and others even forgot to wear it at all. They were crossed off the list. Those who did get jobs often hailed from the small towns surrounding Columbus. With farming or working-class backgrounds, they were grateful to get hired at a time when farms were consolidating and factories were closing.

Kinzer was impressed with Yoshida's methodical methods but was less impressed with his other ideas. After Kinzer was hired, Yoshida informed him that Honda's factory employees would be called "associates" instead of workers. The managers would wear the same white jumpsuit uniforms as the, um, "associates," instead of the shirt-and-tie managerial uniform of American factories. Managers wouldn't get assigned special parking places close to the factory, let alone the heated parking garages—where cars were washed and gassed up daily—that were accorded to senior managers and executives in Detroit. At Honda, parking would be strictly first-come, first-served, regardless of rank.

What's more, the managers would have no executive dining room, no separate bathrooms, and no separate locker room to change into their work clothes—all in sharp contrast to Detroit. Kinzer protested that Honda was ignoring American customs, which to Yoshida was precisely the point. Symbols were important, he explained, in getting managers and associates to view themselves as part of a common purpose. So Honda's managers would have lockers right alongside the associates. It would be the duty of bosses,

Yoshida added, to explain the reasons for managerial decisions and to get consensus where possible.

For the first few weeks Honda's "Original 64" Ohio employees did little but sweep floors and paint them with yellow lines. Then they started building motorcycles, but only three to five a day. And at the end of each day they would disassemble each bike, piece by piece, to evaluate the workmanship. The goal was to develop diligence and discipline, which most Detroit factories sadly lacked. One of the associates, a recent high school graduate, hated it and kept getting grief from his older brother for working for a Japanese company. "I thought I had made a mistake by going to work there," he recalled decades later. "It was like, 'What the heck am I doing here?'" But he stuck with it. (Thirty years later he would be managing a new Honda car factory in Indiana.)

On September 10, 1979, after months of repetitive training, the little plant at Marysville started building motorcycles. Just a few days later Yoshida received an overnight fax message from Tokyo headquarters. The Honda people in Ohio, the fax instructed, were immediately to begin planning for an automobile-assembly plant right next to the motorcycle factory.

Yoshida was shocked. Honda had barely begun making motorcycles in America; the order to start building a car plant seemed unduly hasty. But by mid-1980 one of Yoshida's colleagues, Toshi Amino, found himself negotiating with an American construction company to build the new auto-assembly plant. The contractor, the Lathrop Company of Toledo, Ohio, laid out the building plans and timetable on an elaborate cardboard-mounted chart that was nearly ten yards long.

The presentation was detailed and impressive, except for one thing: the Lathrop people said the construction project would take three years. Amino expressed appreciation for their work, then informed them that the factory would have to be finished in eighteen months. The Lathrop people protested that that timetable was impossible. Not without reason: auto-assembly plants are enormous facilities, as big as indoor shopping malls, and are filled with electronic robots, multi-ton stamping presses, and supersensitive paint shops.

But Honda couldn't afford to carry the construction costs for three years. The sooner the factory was finished, the sooner it could start building cars and producing revenue. In a bind, Amino took the posterboard factory layout home overnight, spread it out on the floor, and stared at it in hopes of finding a solution. Finally he grabbed scissors and sliced out the middle portion of the plant's proposed construction schedule. "It was all about speed, crazy speed," Amino would recall nearly thirty years later. "I really didn't know what I was doing, but we Japanese have a saying: 'A blind man is never afraid of a snake.'"

Building a factory in record time was one thing; training a workforce to build cars that met Honda's quality and productivity standards was quite another. In the spring of 1982, when the company was gearing up to begin building cars in Ohio, Honda decided to send dozens of American workers from the Marysville motorcycle plant to Japan to gain experience at the company's car factories there.

When one employee asked, "Where is the airport in Columbus?" someone asked, "And how do we get there?", Yoshida got a vivid reminder of just how green and naive Honda's young Ohio employees really were. For many, this would be not only their first trip to Japan, but also the first airplane ride of their lives.

On November 10, 1982, the first Honda Accord (a gray four-door sedan) rolled off the assembly line at Marysville. By then the Volkswagen factory in Pennsylvania, which had been organized by the UAW, was struggling with lousy quality, labor unrest, and tension between the Germans and Americans, leading many in Detroit to question whether Honda could succeed where Volkswagen seemed headed for failure. (Which it was: VW would close the Pennsylvania factory in 1988.) Even the very people who should have been enthusiastic about Honda, the company's U.S. dealers, were skeptical. Many balked at ordering U.S.-made Accords, because they suspected the quality would be inferior to the cars Honda shipped from Japan.

Some Honda customers felt the same way. Savvy shoppers learned to look at the little vehicle identification number mounted near the driver's-door latch on each car. The numbers on American-made cars began with V, but the numbers on Japanese-made cars began with J. More than a few buyers insisted on cars with a J. But the issue quickly evaporated, because it became clear that Accords from Ohio were just as good as those shipped from Japan. American workers were showing that, when they were properly managed and treated with respect, they could build cars just as well as the Japanese.

Detroit initially was unable to see the differences in strategy, and delighted with Honda's expansion into Ohio. Chrysler's Lee Iacocca declared that the move would "level the playing field" between Detroit and Japan, because Honda finally would have to deal with American labor. The UAW was pleased as well: its leaders knew they never could organize autoworkers in Japan, who had their own unions, but when Honda's hiring in Marysville hit a critical mass, those workers would surely come into the UAW fold. And in truth, Honda's senior executives back in Tokyo had assumed the same thing. From the beginning, the Honda headquarters brass figured that recognizing the UAW would be inevitable and was just part of being a "good corporate citizen" in America.

In 1983 the presidency of Honda passed to yet another graduate of Honda R&D, Tadashi Kume. It was a pivotal point in Honda's history: the United States, as opposed to Japan, was becoming its single largest market, but the company's early success in Ohio remained fragile. The man Kume installed as president of Honda American Manufacturing, Soichiro Irimajiri (pronounced *eerie-mah-jeerie*), would tell his fellow executives that Honda was like a fly buzzing around the head of a lion—meaning the giant car companies up in Detroit, especially GM. If the lion got sufficiently annoyed, it could flick his paw and kill the fly. The lion that was really focused on Honda, however, wasn't General Motors. It was the UAW.

The union viewed the nonunion plant in Marysville, correctly, as a threat that couldn't go unchallenged. Before long UAW president Douglas Fraser, who had succeeded Leonard Woodcock, was holding private discussions with President Kume. Fraser had little formal education but possessed a first-rate intellect and a personal charisma that made him respected, and even liked, by most auto executives—especially those who didn't have to deal with the day-to-day work rules on the factory floor. The talks with Kume had gone well, and Fraser believed it was only a matter of time before Honda recognized the UAW as the collective bargaining agent at Marysville.

But over in Ohio, Irimajiri and other Honda executives, especially Yoshida, had qualms. The issue wasn't money: Honda paid its factory employees wages and benefits very close to those earned by UAW workers. To have done otherwise would have been to roll out the red carpet for the union's organizers. Instead, Yoshida saw the UAW's relationship with Detroit's car companies as unduly antagonistic—a situation, he believed, for which both sides shared blame. And even when the relationship was smooth, he thought, the union's contract with the Big Three handcuffed management's ability to, well, manage. It took an outside vision to question what had been seen as inevitable. Many Detroit executives believed the same thing but felt powerless to address the issue. They didn't know how to repair relations with the union, yet ousting the UAW was unthinkable.

So Detroit executives made do with a UAW contract that, by the 1980s, had a table of contents nearly twenty pages long. Besides specifying the number of union committee members that the company had to pay in each plant, the contract limited the amount of components a car company could buy from a nonunion supplier. The result often was parts purchased at a higher cost and perhaps of lower quality. There also were detailed rules for filing grievances and for the four-step appeals process. And besides the national contract, each factory had its own local contract with still more rules and provisions governing who could do what and when.

The Japanese managers whom Honda had posted to America thought all this smacked of the excessive reliance on legalese that so puzzled them about the country. Success in the marketplace, not lawyerly language, should be the best guarantee of job security. Certainly they expected Honda's "associates" to work hard. In fact, working on the Honda assembly line was an aerobic workout that caused some associates to lose twenty pounds after a few months on the job. Factory discipline meant associates couldn't swig soda, smoke cigarettes, or munch on snacks while working, as the workers in Detroit's factories could do.

But there were benefits. Instead of being told, in effect, to check their brains at the door, Honda's workers were encouraged to contribute their ideas, as well as their manual labor, to the manufacturing process. If their suggestions produced efficiencies that eliminated someone's job, even their own, the person would be transferred to another job instead of being laid off. Workers were told they wouldn't be laid off except as a last resort, and Honda's growing U.S. sales (which rose nearly 50 percent between 1980 and 1985) meant layoffs never happened.

None of this was rocket science, but it was effective. Everybody was on the same team, rather than being divided into two factions that warily circled each other, trying to gain the upper hand. Yoshida understood the difference because he had spent more time in America than virtually any other Honda executive. He believed the bosses back in Japan didn't understand what recognizing the UAW would mean. Yoshida could duck the issue for a while but not forever.

In December 1985 the UAW presented the Marysville managers with petition cards from hundreds of Honda employees and asked for immediate recognition as their bargaining agent. Management could either recognize the union straightaway or ask for a secret-ballot election by workers. The UAW had forced the matter. Now Honda would have to react.

As Yoshida's boss and the head of Honda's U.S. manufacturing operations, Irimajiri was the man on the spot. When the UAW petition cards landed on his desk, he convened a Saturday meeting of his managers, both Japanese and Americans, at a hotel in Dublin, Ohio, an upscale suburb of Columbus. Throughout the day the group discussed the pros and cons of recognizing the UAW and decided that there weren't any pros other than avoiding a potential confrontation with the union. At the end of the day Irimajiri said simply, "I think we fight." That Monday Honda polled its associates and found that 78 percent of them wanted a secret-ballot vote.

The UAW, having been through this sort of thing before, knew what to do next. Union operatives filed three complaints against the company for unfair labor practices. Valid or not, the complaints had the potential to embarrass Honda management and to undo all the favorable publicity that Honda had reaped by building cars in America. Sure enough, President Kume soon summoned Irimajiri and Yoshida back to Tokyo, where he wanted to know why the Ohio plant hadn't recognized the UAW.

Yoshida, who bore the brunt of the questioning, wasn't foolish enough to oppose the pressure from Honda's president outright. But neither did he say yes. Instead he remained evasive and noncommittal, even though Kume was clearly getting annoyed, and Irimajiri uncomfortable, as the meeting dragged on. Finally, much to Yoshida's relief, Kume excused himself for another appointment. Later, on the flight back to the United States, Yoshida realized just how thin the ice had been. Irimajiri, seated next to him, confided that during the meeting he had been trying to kick Yoshida under the table, to signal him to agree to Kume's wishes. But Yoshida had been seated just out of reach. Years later Kume would privately thank Yoshida, telling him that he had been right.

Historians say Napoleon might have lost the Battle of Waterloo because his hemorrhoids flared up at just the wrong moment. So the UAW might have lost the Battle of Honda because Shige Yoshida was sitting just out of kicking range from his boss. The secret-ballot election at Marysville was scheduled for February 1986, but the UAW asked for a postponement. The union's organizers sensed that they didn't have the votes. A few months later, with the prospect of defeat certain, the union went further and "temporarily" withdrew its petition for a plebiscite. *Temporarily* would mean forever. The UAW never reinstated its request for recognition at Honda.

In only twenty years a little car company had come out of nowhere to challenge the Japanese government, its bigger Japanese competitors, Detroit's Big Three, and the powerful United Auto Workers. With the UAW vanquished, Irimajiri would lead Honda through a spurt of aggressive expansion. The company built more U.S. factories and pursued a "five-part strategy" that even included exporting some cars made in Ohio back to Japan.

Between 1980 and 1990 Honda's U.S. sales surged 130 percent, from 375,000 to 855,000 cars. More than half were built in America, which proved to be a marketing and public relations bonanza for the company. Iacocca's belief that Japanese car factories in America would "level the playing field" by erasing Japan's edge in quality and efficiency proved another historic miscalculation. Honda's success in Ohio prompted Japan's other car companies—Toyota, Nissan, and all the rest—to build their own assembly plants in America, which industry executives dubbed "transplants." Japan's automotive invasion of America entered a whole new phase.

The UAW's presence in the transplants would be limited to a few factories—the joint ventures between Japanese and Detroit companies, where the union was grandfathered in. But those factories got special contracts that were much more streamlined, and had far fewer work rules, than the UAW's cumbersome contracts with the Big Three. Switching to similar contracts at GM, Ford, and Chrysler would have made sense for everyone, but UAW politics made that impossible. Too many shop committeemen and grievance committee members held prized union desk jobs that depended on the existing system.

In the years to come, as Honda grew exponentially, it inevitably lost some of the entrepeneurial, "crazy speed" spirit that had caused it to buck the status quo. But after Honda came to Ohio, nothing ever would be the same for the UAW or the Big Three. Just as Japanese imports had broken Detroit's market oligopoly in the 1970s, so Honda broke the UAW's labor monopoly in the 1980s.

SIX

REPENTANCE, REBIRTH, AND RELAPSE

American business history is filled with spectacular corporate crack-ups and a smaller number of remarkable recoveries. But not much resembles the round-trip roller-coaster ride that Detroit took between 1980 and 1992. The twelve-year period began with Chrysler nearing collapse and begging for a government bailout, and Ford reeling from red ink and not far behind. It ended with the Big Kahuna, General Motors, struggling to remain solvent and with a frightened GM board sacking its CEO for the first time since Billy Durant was ousted some seventy years before.

In between, the Big Three, especially Ford and Chrysler, staged incredible comebacks and earned record profits that shocked even the executives. Chrysler's Lee Iacocca became America's first celebrity CEO, starring in television commercials and writing a best-selling autobiography in which he exacted sweet revenge on Henry Ford II for firing him. The book described Henry Ford II as "a real bastard" and an "evil man." One passage described Henry II boasting that his favorite food in the Ford executive dining room was hamburger. No one dared reveal, Iacocca wrote, that for the boss's burgers the corporate chef was grinding up prime strip steak.

Iacocca was even touted, briefly, as a candidate for president, before both he and the politicians thought better of it. GM's CEO Roger Smith, in turn, became corporate America's anticelebrity, starring unwittingly and unwillingly in Michael Moore's 1989 film *Roger and Me.* The wicked satire lampooned GM and its chairman for the factory closings and worker layoffs that produced the demise and decay of Flint, Michigan—the birthplace, as it happened, of both GM and Michael Moore.

Perhaps the one thing General Motors did right during the decade was to lead Detroit in establishing U.S. joint ventures with Japanese car companies. General Motors and Toyota partnered to build small cars at a shuttered GM plant in Fremont, California, near Oakland. The venture, called New United Motor Manufacturing Inc., or Nummi (pronounced *new-me*), was announced in February 1983, just three months after Honda started building cars in Marysville.

Nummi was followed by Diamond Star Motors, a joint venture between Chrysler and Mitsubishi Motors in Illinois, and American Automotive Alliance, a Ford-Mazda factory in the Michigan town of Flat Rock (which the men from Mazda invariably pronounced as "Frat Lock"). All three manufacturing partnerships were intended to give Detroit an up-close, firsthand look at how the Japanese competition really worked.

So the Big Three discovered, for example, that the Japanese didn't store weeks' worth of parts in their assembly plants, at great cost, just to keep from running short, as the Detroit companies did. Instead the Japanese kept inventories lean, a few hours' worth at most, and expected suppliers to deliver parts just in time, without fail. They expected and rewarded workers for suggesting improvements in the production process, such as ergonomic assembly lines. Instead of expecting workers to bend down to attach components underneath a car, the Japanese elevated the assembly line and angled it so the workers could perform the task standing up. Thousands of such things gave the Japanese their edge in quality and efficiency.

The disastrous 1970s, followed by record losses in the early 1980s, provided enough motivation for Detroit to begin to change. Big organizations, and the people in them, often resist fundamental changes unless prompted by pain. And in the early 1980s, pain was prevalent in Detroit.

In late 1979 a scornful new word entered the lexicon of the United Auto Workers. On November 27, the UAW agreed to $403 million in "givebacks"—reversals of wage-and-benefit gains previously won at the bargaining table—as part of a new three-year contract with Chrysler. The cuts in pay and benefits were required by law so that ailing Chrysler could qualify for government assistance, but the union's rank and file were reluctant to accept them. President Doug Fraser, knowing full well that Chrysler could collapse, campaigned hard for the deal. Iacocca, meanwhile, cajoled the workers and Congress by agreeing to work for one dollar a year. Instead he got Chrysler stock options, which later would be worth millions.

The United States was entering a three-year recession that hit the Big Three especially hard, because they were facing the economic downturn and growing Japanese competition simultaneously. Betwen 1979 and 1982 Chrysler and Ford would post cumulative losses exceeding $5 billion—a breathtaking number at the time.

In 1981 even mighty GM lost money, $763 million, which the company had managed to avoid even during the Great Depression. Early the next year both GM and Ford got their own givebacks from the union: a wage freeze to last two and a half years, the postponement of cost-of-living allowances, and the elimination of some paid holidays. But GM's Smith immediately made a historic blunder.

On the same day that union members voted to approve the givebacks, GM disclosed a new pay plan—buried in the fine print of its proxy statement but noticed nonetheless—that made it easier for executives to earn larger bonuses. A sense of entitlement clearly wasn't limited to UAW members. Fraser and the union cried foul, but the damage was done. In decades to come, General Motors would pay for this blunder many times over in combative labor relations.

In February 1982 the number of autoworkers on indefinite layoff at all three companies topped 250,000 (nearly double the total number of hourly workers whom Detroit still would employ in 2009). White-collar workers got whacked as well. Chrysler slashed its managerial ranks to 22,000 people in 1983, compared to 40,000 five years earlier.

Detroit's pain served its purpose, however, especially at Chrysler, which made the harshest cuts. In 1983 the company staged a recovery that allowed it to repay its government-guaranteed loans a full seven years early. The repayment ceremony featured Iacocca standing in front of an $863 million check the size of a billboard—"like Patton in front of the flag," boasted Chrysler's PR men, referring to the opening scene of the movie Patton, where the general fronts an American flag that fills the entire screen.

Between 1979 and 1983, the draconian cost cuts chopped Chrysler's break-even point—the number of vehicles it had to sell each year to make money—in half, from 2.4 million cars and trucks to just 1.2 million. "We intend to hold it there," Iacocca wrote in the company's annual report for 1984. (Once the government loans were repaid, however, the company quickly bought a fleet of corporate jets.)

As Chrysler's CEO, Iacocca was proving a surprisingly effective pitchman and was becoming famous in the company's television commercials. "If you can find a better car, buy it," he intoned on TV. And the United States, finally, was beginning to enjoy the fruits of the Reagan economic recovery. After dropping to 10.6 million vehicles in 1982, total U.S. car and truck sales soared to a record 16.3 million in 1986, an increase of more than 50 percent. The effect was like rain after a long drought, because in the car business, volume—as in sales volume—cures all ills.

To develop a new car and bring it to market, companies incur enormous fixed costs. They pay salaries for engineers, designers, and safety experts; add nine-figure outlays for factories, production machinery, and components; and spend millions more on marketing, as well as on wages and benefits for the workers who actually build the car. Only after sales hit a certain volume level (which varies by car and by company) does the automaker recoup the costs and start making money. But once that happens, it's all cream thereafter, and the higher the sales volume, the richer the cream. Chrysler's cream was especially rich in 1984, thanks both to the economic recovery and to the work of its combative but brilliant product development chief, Hal Sperlich.

Sperlich had been a key figure in developing the Ford Mustang in the early 1960s. But he ran afoul of Henry Ford II, who in 1977 fired him, and he landed at Chrysler a year before Iacocca arrived. When he left Ford, Sperlich carried with him plans for a vehicle that Henry Ford II had stoutly refused to develop despite Sperlich's repeated urgings. It was a small passenger van that would be built on a light, front-wheel-drive car chassis instead of on the heavy, rear-drive platform used on existing vans and pickup trucks. Ford didn't have such a platform, but lo and behold, it existed at Chrysler when Sperlich arrived. It was as if Michelangelo had happened upon the perfect piece of marble.

It wasn't stone that he found but metal: a 2.2-liter four-cylinder engine and a front-wheel-drive transaxle from Chrysler's small European subsidiary, Simca. It formed the underpinnings of the Dodge Omni and Plymouth Horizon, whose early quality shortcomings were remedied after a shaky start, and the "K cars," the Plymouth Reliant and Dodge Aries, that spurred Chrysler's recovery. The same underlying architecture proved ideal for the underpinnings of Sperlich's proposed small van. And Iacocca, unlike Henry Ford II, was willing to listen.

Chrysler introduced minivans in the fall of 1983, the onset of the industry's 1984 model year. It was basically a K-car chassis topped by a big box, with optional third-row seating occupying what would have been the trunk on an ordinary sedan. The minivans were woefully underpowered, especially when carrying a family and full kid gear; Chrysler didn't make any six-cylinder engines due to its recent cost-cutting efforts and had to make do with four-cylinder motors only. Also, the quality could be suspect. When Chrysler staged a press event for Iacocca to drive the first minivan off the assembly line, the van's sliding rear door got stuck, locking in the dignitaries seated in the backseat. When reporters snickered, the company's PR chief announced that the childproof lock had been accidentally engaged. The minivan didn't even have a childproof lock—but the journalists didn't know that.

The minivan's shortcomings, though, were outweighed by it obvious advantages. It was small enough to fit in a garage—and thus was named Caravan, for "car and van"—but big enough to seat up to seven people. Women drivers were seated high enough to see the road, and children had space to spread out, not fight, and not drive their parents nuts. "The Caravan is a true multipurpose vehicle, ideal for a multitude of family and individual lifestyles," said Chrysler's sales brochures.

The minivan factory was in Canada, but Chrysler nonetheless asked Bruce Springsteen to license his hit "Born in the USA" for commercials. The singer said no, so Chrysler commissioned a knock-off called "Born in America."

In 1984, with Sperlich's minivan leading the way, Chrysler sold more than 1.7 million cars and trucks, half a million vehicles above its

break-even point. That year the company ran every one of its factories on full, flat-out overtime. Profits boomed to $2.4 billion, more
than Chrysler's profits of the preceding fifteen years combined. The
company didn't have to pay income taxes, thanks to the tax credits
that stemmed from the prior years' losses, but that benefit was just
icing on the cake. After years of crisis Chrysler had everything going
its way.

At the Belvidere factory Fred Young was working nine hours a day
and a full shift every other Saturday. He had been with the company
nearly twenty years and had seen it go from the brink of oblivion to
incredible prosperity. The Japanese challenge had forced Chrysler to
improve its quality, which still wasn't fully competitive with Honda
and Toyota but was far better than before.

Just a few years earlier Young and other Chrysler workers had
worried that the company might fail. Now the good times were
rolling at Belvidere and at other Chrysler plants. The "givebacks" of
a few years earlier got restored (as they did at Ford and GM). Fred
Young and his co-workers reveled in their overtime pay and took to
calling Iacocca "Uncle Lee."

Iacocca's growing celebrity earned him a guest cameo appearance
on television's *Miami Vice*. When *Parade* magazine reported, in error,
that Iacocca was available for free appearances at "birthday parties,
benefits and bar mitzvahs," so many requests poured in that Chrysler
had to hire three extra staffers just to handle his mail. *Time* magazine,
which had dubbed Iacocca the "Comeback Kid" in 1983, honored
him again in April 1985 with a cover story titled "America Loves to
Listen to Lee."

The man indeed was quick with quips, though not all of them
were suitable for the pages of *Time*. Once after *The Wall Street Journal*
ran a negative article right next to a Chrysler ad, Iacocca angrily be-
rated Chrysler's top PR guy. When the hapless publicist explained
that the *Journal*'s news and advertising departments were strictly separate, Iacocca waved his ever-present long cigar and snapped, "Are
you saying we've been fucked by juxtaposition?"

The f-word was used about as often as, say, *minivan* in Chrysler's
sharp-elbowed, towel-snapping executive suite. Its senior occupants,
like Iacocca and Sperlich, had all fled the buttoned-down halls of Ford

and thus called themselves the "Gang of Ford," a parody on the "Gang of Four" clique of hard-core Maoists in China. Most had risked their careers by coming to Chrysler, lured by Iacocca's persuasiveness coupled with generous grants of stock options. When Chrysler's stock soared from under $1 a share in 1981 to more than $22 six years later (adjusted for stock splits), the Gang of Ford made very capitalist fortunes.

During this time another man tied his fate and fortune to Chrysler. At thirty-six, after nearly fifteen years as a high school teacher and coach in Maine, Gene Benner wanted a new challenge. A friend of his, an older man who had a Chrysler dealership in the little town of South Paris, suggested that Benner buy a small stake in the business and come aboard.

His timing was couldn't have been better. Americans were in their postrecession car-buying spree, and Benner's many contacts from his years as an educator provided a ready-made pool of potential customers. Just as in teaching and coaching, he quickly concluded, in selling cars "people skills" meant a lot, because if people trusted you they would buy from you. Soon he was selling enough cars to make a better living than he had as a teacher and to improve the overall fortunes of the dealership.

While Chrysler was raising itself back from the near-dead with the minivan, Ford was betting its recovery on a new midsize sedan with edgy styling called the Taurus. Its development was championed by Ford's president and number-two man, Donald E. Petersen, a temperamental but talented veteran of Ford's product-planning ranks. In the early days of the Taurus "program" (Detroit's term for developing a new vehicle), Petersen drove over to the Ford Design Dome and asked the stylists if they liked the car they were creating. When he got blank stares, he suggested that they draw a car that they'd actually want to drive.

That might have seemed a simple, commonsense suggestion, but in fact the designers were surprised and dumbfounded. Ford had a decades-long habit of following the lead of GM, which was wedded to upright, boxy, bland styling because it was judged to be safely nonoffensive—like Velveeta cheese on wheels, though nobody would admit that. But Petersen pressed his point, and Ford's designers went back to the drawing board. By the time they were finished, the Taurus and its near-twin, the Mercury Sable, sported sleek, rounded, European-type styling, more like an Audi sedan than anything made in America.

Ford's engineers, meanwhile, "identified over 400 of the best features available on competitors' automobiles around the world," as the company put it, and tried to beat those benchmarks in everything from the seats to the suspension system. Some $3 billion and five years later, the Taurus and Sable were nearing completion. In December 1985, after Petersen ascended to CEO, the cars went on sale at a base price of $9,645.

Ford's Detroit competitors sniped at their styling right away. Iacocca said the Taurus resembled a "flying potato," and a fast-rising GM vice president named Bob Stempel called the Taurus and Sable "the bulls and furry animals." Some early cars, like the first minivans, were plagued by quality glitches, including faulty emission-control systems that emitted a sulfur-dioxide odor and smelled like a giant fart. Ford executives held their breath—figuratively, of course—because they were betting the ranch on the new cars.

It turned out to be a great bet. Within months Ford was selling every Taurus and Sable it could make, and the company's older models showed surprising sales strength too. For several years Ford executives had fretted that they were spending so much money to develop the Taurus that they couldn't afford to downsize the Ford Crown Victoria, Lincoln Town Car, and other aging land barges in their lineup. But that proved to be a blessing in disguise. In the mid-1980s, contrary to all forecasts, gas prices were dropping and Americans started buying big cars again. The "Crown Vic" and Town Car didn't get the praise accorded to the Taurus and Sable, but they actually were far more profitable because their development costs already had been depreciated.

The company sold six million cars worldwide in 1986, about the same number as in 1979, but the profits were three times higher because Ford had cut $5 billion in costs in the interim. In 1985 and 1986 the company boosted its stock dividend five times and threw in a three-for-two stock split.

Petersen also launched a concerted effort to change Ford's factional, combative culture, albeit with mixed results. Employees attended training sessions where they were asked to hug the person next to them. Executive vice president Bob Lutz heaped scorn on such sessions. He wrote a satirical guide to the "new Ford-speak," lacing it with such terms as "team-oriented transformational buy-in" and "interactive post-adversarial consensus." His irreverence didn't wear well, and not long afterward Lutz departed for Chrysler, becoming the latest addition to the Gang of Ford.

At the same time Ford developed a cooperative new labor-management relationship that was unique in Detroit—and a sharp contrast to the surly worker sabotage that had plagued the Vega in Lordstown. At Petersen's behest Ford began using "statistical process control," which empowered workers to monitor the manufacturing process and ensure quality. Ironically, the method had been developed in America, but it was spurned by the Big Three and initially adopted in Japan instead—a classic consequence of Detroit's inbred arrogance. Ford seemed to be breaking out of that mind-set, however, and was boosting quality close to Japanese levels.

In the process, the company was becoming a profit machine. In 1986, for the first time in 62 years, Ford's income of $3.3 billion topped that of General Motors, even though GM was 40 percent bigger than Ford. In 1988 profits rose to $5.3 billion, a record for any car company in history. Betwen 1980 and 1989 Ford's stock price surged 1,500 percent. The only blip on the company's windshield was the death of the patriarch, Henry Ford II, on September 29, 1987, at the age of seventy. His passing deprived the company's controlling family—which had just 4 percent of the stock but 40 percent of the votes, thanks to their supervoting shares—of its longtime leader.

But Petersen's public profile was on the rise, thanks to Ford's incredible success. Because of Ford's quality ratings and amazing financial performance, Detroit's once-unknown CEO began to supplant Iacocca as the Motor City's latest media hero. Roger Smith professed that he wasn't worried about GM's performance vis-à-vis Ford. He explained that Ford was playing a short-term game, while GM was investing for the twenty-first century.

.   .   .

In Smith's view, Ford was developing only new cars, while he himself was developing something far bolder: a brand-new corporation. In 1984 Smith abolished the General Motors Assembly Division, the ill-fated outfit that ran the assembly plants, and Fisher Body, which ran the stamping plants, and replaced them with two enormous car groups, Chevrolet-Pontiac-Canada (CPC) and Buick-Oldsmobile-Cadillac (BOC), with integrated responsibility for manufacturing and marketing. The sweeping corporate reorganization was intended to eradicate GM's powerful, balkanized fiefdoms. At the outset, however, it created organizational disarray.

GMers grimly joked about the apocryphal manager who walked out of his office and told his secretary, "If my boss calls, please get his name." Smith, undeterred, moved next to modernize GM's electronic infrastructure—not by hiring a computer services company but by buying one: Electronic Data Systems of Dallas. With the financial acumen he had acquired during his ascent through GM's financial ranks, Smith paid for EDS not with cash but with an innovative new class of GM stock—Class E shares—that would pay dividends tied to EDS's results.

EDS's founder and CEO, billionaire H. Ross Perot, joined the GM board and stayed at the helm of EDS, overseeing the effort to over-haul GM's technology infrastructure, everything from record keeping to factory automation. In the September 1984 union contract negotiations, to ease the UAW's fears about automation, GM offered a pioneering program called the Jobs Bank, which would pay workers displaced by factory automation 95 percent of their wages until the company found them a new job.

GM initially proposed Jobs Bank eligibility for workers with at least ten years seniority and wanted to cap the program's spending at $500 million over three years. But the UAW—still smarting from Smith's bonus sleight-of-hand a couple years earlier—demanded more. By the time the contract was finished, the company agreed to a spending cap of $1 billion, and soon afterward it lowered the eligibility threshold to just one year's seniority.

Ford and Chrysler were forced to accept the Jobs Bank too, to avoid a potentially crippling strike. UAW members' jobs were "more secure than ever in history," the union told its members. Perhaps, but

years later it would become clear that Smith and the union had created a monster.

But Smith was busy teasing the press, in early 1985, about another
acquisition that would be, in his coy midwestern expression, "a lulu."
It was the multibillion-dollar purchase of Hughes Aircraft, the aerospace arm of the Howard Hughes empire, which made night-vision
devices, satellite systems, and other technology that Smith deemed
the key to the car of the future. He wasn't alone: Ford was eager to
buy Hughes as well, for the same reason. Ford was so confident of
winning that it hired a painting crew to paint its blue-oval logo on the
roof of Hughes's Los Angeles headquarters. But Smith built his bid
around another new class of shares, GM Class H, which would pay
dividends tied to Hughes's results, like the Class E shares at EDS.
After learning that Smith's financial wizardry had won the day, Ford
sent its painters packing—and a jubilant Smith told reporters, "Lulu
is home!"

There were still more blockbuster moves in Smith's headlong
charge to transform General Motors into a twenty-first-century corporation. Besides partnering with Toyota in California, Smith also announced that General Motors would launch its first new brand in half
a century, Saturn, to build small cars with innovative labor relations
and high-tech manufacturing. Smith further embraced advanced
technology—with help from EDS—to make GM's existing cars by
building new factories or refurbishing old ones. Headquarters kept a
"robot count" for each factory, and rewarded managers who had the
most.

The only thing that didn't seem exciting about General Motors between 1983 and 1985 was, well, its cars. In August 1983 the cover of
Fortune magazine pictured four maroon sedans that were GM's new
entries in the critical midsize segment, which the company had dominated for decades. The magazine was making the point, in visually
striking fashion, that the Chevrolet Celebrity, the Pontiac 6000, the
Oldsmobile Cutlass Ciera, and the Buick Century all looked alike.
They were products of a system GM called "badge engineering," in
which the company saved billions in development costs by taking the
same basic car and then tweaking it for the different divisions—some
plastic body cladding on the Pontiac, a special front grille for the

Buick, square taillights for the Olds, and so on. Far from being chastened by the Olds Rocket engine scandal of a decade earlier, GM was
further blurring the identity of its decades-old brands. Increasingly,
the only meaningful difference among its cars, alas, was their price.

The *Fortune* cover caused a stir, but not for long. General Motors
seemed to be reorganizing and revitalizing with a veritable industrial
blitzkrieg. For a brief time, after the press had tired of Iacocca and before it discovered Don Petersen, Roger Smith actually became a
media darling. In April 1985 *Financial World* magazine named him
CEO of the Year. Two months later *BusinessWeek* called him the
"cherubic chairman of General Motors," a reference to his pudgy
physique and ruddy complexion, and quoted Smith's prediction:
"You're going to see the greatest corporation in the world."

That was precisely the fear at both Ford and Chrysler. By the mid-
1980s both companies were enjoying unaccustomed success in competing against "the General," but they had spent too many years
following in GM's footsteps to kick the habit completely. If General
Motors deemed diversification to be a prudent hedge against the
threat from the Japanese, well, they would diversify too.

So the cover of Chrysler's 1985 annual report carried the company's newest model—not a car, but a Gulfstream executive jet.
"Chrysler is diversifying into industries and businesses that can sup-
plement our core automotive operations," Iacocca wrote to shareholders. "Gulfstream gives us a strong entry into the growing aerospace
and defense industries"—where, he didn't have to add, the Japanese
weren't a factor.

Iacocca also bought consumer-finance and commercial-finance
companies and restructured Chrysler itself as a holding company.
The car business, Chrysler Motors, became just one of four divisions,
along with Chrysler Financial, Gulfstream, and a new entity called
Chrysler Technologies that was created to seek high-tech acquisitions. Chrysler's only automotive deal during this buying spree was
the 1987 purchase of American Motors from its controlling shareholder, the French automaker Renault. The crown jewel of AMC was
Jeep, a specialty brand for which Iacocca saw significant potential.

Ford likewise began a $6 billion diversification drive, buying a big
savings and loan in California and a consumer finance company in

Dallas called the Associates, where the name of the CEO was (no joke) Reese Overcash—which added some public relations luster to the deal. Petersen also made some small acquisitions in the aerospace and defense industries and kept hunting for his own "lulu" to make up for the last-minute loss of Hughes. In late 1989 he got a measure of revenge by outbidding GM to buy Britain's Jaguar, a prestigious luxury car marque that had fallen on hard times. It would prove an empty victory, bringing Ford billions of losses for nearly twenty years.

For companies that had been at death's door at the beginning of the decade, the buying binges were surreal. Author David Halberstam had spent the early 1980s researching and writing *The Reckoning,* using the respective stories of Ford and Nissan to describe the demise of Detroit and the rise of the Japanese. But by the time the book was published in 1986, the tables were turning: Ford was resurgent, and Nissan was sliding into one of its periodic funks. An inspirational industrial comeback, with the potential to restore American pride and Detroit's prosperity, seemed to be taking shape.

Between 1984 and 1989 General Motors, Ford, and Chrysler spent some $20 billion on acquisitions, most of them outside the car business. The acquisitions came on top of dividend increases, stock splits, and share-buyback programs, all generated by that ultimate enabler of corporate spending—copious amounts of free cash flow. The diversification moves were intended to outflank the Japanese, who were busy with the boring business of building more automobile factories in America. The real question was, who was outflanking whom?

While Detroit was diversifying, the Honda Accord became the best-selling car in America. Unlike the Big Three, Honda and the other Japanese automakers were investing heavily in new automotive technology—engines with direct fuel injection, overhead camshafts and multiple valves per cylinder, and four-speed automatic transmissions. The Japanese were using all these advances to improve the driving performance of their cars without sacrificing fuel economy. But such basic engineering investments didn't produce headlines. And anyway, the Big Three were producing impressive financial results, at least for the short term.

But no sooner had it peaked than Detroit's diversification started to backfire, with GM and EDS leading the way.

Even after General Motors bought EDS, the automaker remained EDS's biggest customer, by far. And because EDS had its own class of stock, GM Class E, General Motors let EDS set its own prices to avoid any hint that it was shortchanging holders of the Class E shares. · What followed was price gouging, pure and simple.

Knowing they had a captive customer, EDS executives demanded premium prices for every GM contract they got, big and small. Any GM manager who tried to bargain down EDS's price was risking his career. Even worse, GM wasn't getting much for its money. At a new high-tech assembly plant in Detroit, the automated guided vehicles that were supposed to replace old-fashioned forklifts stayed frozen in their tracks for nine months, because the EDS software didn't work.

Other automation-software malfunctions were downright comical. Spray-painting robots at the same factory went haywire, taking aim at each other instead of the cars. At another factory robots equipped with suction-cup arms to install windshields broke as many as they installed, because they pressed down on the glass too hard. Roger Smith's factories of the future were becoming industrial houses of horror—and expensive ones at that.

Adding insult to injury, Ross Perot was becoming disenchanted with General Motors and with Smith himself, whom he derided none too discreetly as a buffoonish bureaucrat. "Roger Smith works on everything in the world but GM business," Perot told two *Wall Street Journal* reporters in a six-hour off-the-record monologue in May 1986. "He is the basic problem here; you're looking at the cancer."

A month later Perot went on the record with *BusinessWeek*. "The first EDSer who sees a snake kills it," he said. "At GM, the first thing you do is organize a committee on snakes. Then you bring in a consultant about snakes. Third thing you do is talk about it for a year." Perot hoped his sniping would convince Smith to sell EDS, but Smith proved tougher than that. Instead, he proposed buying out Perot's GM shares for $753 million, in return for Perot's resignation from EDS and from GM's board. Basically, Smith wanted Ross Perot out of his hair, and on December 1, 1986, Perot agreed to take the money and go.

The Perot buyout was a watershed for General Motors and for Smith. The Dallas billionaire was mercurial, but many Americans sensed—correctly—that his folksy criticisms of GM and Smith were spot-on. Perot's departure produced a barrage of bad press for GM; the company's market share dropped overnight from 45 percent to 41 percent, a low it hadn't seen in decades.

In early 1987, shortly after the buyout, GM hired New York PR guru Gershon Kekst to assess the public relations fallout. When Kekst's research team finished its work, he flew to Detroit for a private breakfast with Smith, whose ruddy face by then had developed a blotchy red rash that his doctors attributed to stress. Kekst suggested a variety of steps that GM could take to adjust its marketing message. Then, with all the gentleness he could muster, he suggested the only real way to fix GM's image. After an honorable period of time, say a few months, he said, Smith should announce he was retiring early from General Motors to make way for a new generation of leadership.

Kekst held his breath waiting for Smith's reaction, which was surprisingly calm. Without missing a beat, Smith looked up between bites and said, "What's Plan B?" It was a classic rebuff from a man who knew that his corporate fortress was impregnable because he was, after all, the chairman of General Motors. His successors would never be so secure, but Smith couldn't fathom that. With more than three years to go before hitting GM's mandatory retirement age, Smith wasn't about to turn tail and run. He would stay the course— unfortunately for the company and its shareholders.

GM's messy divorce with Perot showed the real danger of Detroit's diversification drive: management took its eye off the ball. While Smith was busy building the twenty-first-century corporation, GM was building lousy twentieth-century cars. The Pontiac Fiero, a sporty two-seat roadster, suffered an alarming incidence of engine fires that prompted massive recalls. The Cadillac Allante, a $60,000 two-seat coupe, featured a sleek body that was built in Italy and then shipped to Detroit on jumbo jets for assembly. Not only was the process expensive, but the long-distance assembly line resulted in leaky roofs.

As these and other missteps took their toll on GM's earnings, Roger Smith sought salvation in his comfort zone: accounting. General Motors stretched out its factory-depreciation charges over forty-five years instead of thirty-five, increased the projected investment returns from its pension fund, and changed its accounting assumptions for inventories and auto leases. Each of these moves increased earnings under accepted accounting standards, enabling GM in 1998 to report a record income of $4.9 billion.

But one-third of that amount came from the accounting changes—meaning that the entire increase came out of the accounting department, not the car department. It was all perfectly legal, analysts noted, but it amounted to earnings trickery nonetheless. Smith was undeterred. "GM is well positioned to achieve . . . industry leadership into the twenty-first century," he wrote in the company's 1988 annual report.

By this time, over at Chrysler, the distractions of fame and diversification were pushing Iacocca into making his own blunders. Chrysler had invested $400 million in the Italian luxury car maker Maserati, but the $30,000 car that resulted was a resounding flop. Iacocca moved production of the Omni and Horizon subcompacts twice, to factories in two different states, costing another $400 million—after which Chrysler decided to kill the cars anyway.

Those fiascos were just part of the nearly $5 billion that Chrysler squandered between 1985 and 1989 on production snafus, diversification, and stock buybacks—money that could have been spent to develop new cars, which Chrysler amazingly had neglected. Worse yet, spending discipline collapsed, Chrysler's break-even point soared, and the company's 1989 earnings plunged more than 60 percent.

It was a wake-up call that prompted Iacocca to shift his diversification drive into reverse, selling Gulfstream and Chrysler Technologies. The moves "reflect the company's renewed commitment to the automotive industry," Iacocca declared. It was a strange statement for a car company, like the Yankees announcing a newfound affection for baseball.

Chrysler also launched a stringent cost-cutting campaign from which little was exempt—except $2 million for gold-plated faucets and other amenities at the company's suite in New York's Waldorf Towers, which was reserved almost exclusively for Iacocca. Tone-deaf executive excess would be a constant in Detroit, right up until the Big Three CEOs boarded their corporate jets in 2008 to beg for a government bailout.

In 1990, with Chrysler's red ink mounting, Las Vegas investor Kirk Kerkorian snapped up 10 percent of the company's stock for an average of $12.37 a share, about one-fourth of the stock's price just three years earlier. Before the decade was out, Kerkorian would change Chrysler's future.

But for now Kerkorian's arrival played right into Iacocca's hands. The directors, lacking an obvious successor to Iacocca and worried about Kerkorian's intentions, lavished more pay and stock awards to keep their CEO from retiring—even though the last thing Iacocca wanted to do was retire. So obsessed was he with the CEO lifestyle that his exasperated executives took to describing it as "the Four P's: Power, Podium, Perks, and Pay."

Being CEO or a top executive at any Detroit car company offered plenty of those. Courtiers always hovered to arrange transportation, place phone calls, fetch drinks, and pave the way for everything. Executives could drive any car they wanted, always fully gassed, freshly washed, and perfectly primped. Iacocca's travel entourage included two cars of security guards—one in front of his limousine and the other in back—whenever he was chauffeured from place to place. His chariot of choice, like that of Detroit's other CEOs, was a Gulfstream G5 jet or something similar, always outfitted to the chairman's personal specifications.

At Ford some executives even complained when the corporate jets served broken cashews instead of whole nuts. (Whole nuts, indeed.) In 1988 a lavish Persian carpet ordered for the Ford executive suite was so big that it couldn't be hauled up the elevators at headquarters. Windows had to be temporarily removed so a helicopter could lower the rug into the building. The operation occurred on the day after Thanksgiving, so ordinary employees wouldn't notice. Predictably, the corporate grapevine spread the news anyway.

Amazingly, after swinging from repentance to recovery during the

1980s, the Big Three were going astray again, unable to learn from their failures or to be satisfied with their success. Leading characters in the morality play, their executives had started their Detroit careers right after World War II, climbed the corporate ladder during the industry's glory years, and then struggled to cope with the invasion of the Japanese—the same enemy that some of them, or their fathers, had fought during the war. But as the 1990s neared, these men were preparing to leave the stage.

On November 10, 1989, Ford's Don Petersen announced that he would retire early, at age sixty-three. It shocked the business world because Petersen was the most lauded CEO in the country, not just in Detroit. But he had fought with the young Fords—Edsel Ford II and William Clay Ford, Jr., the son and nephew, respectively, of Henry II—about their roles on the board of directors. He had alienated key board members, who feared Petersen's press clippings were going to his head. Petersen explained simply that he was resigning to "repot myself" in the new soil of retirement.

Next to go was Roger Smith, who despite his many and manifest missteps did make it to GM's mandatory retirement age. In July 1990, just before he turned sixty-five, Smith was feted at the traditional "pickle dish" party for GM's retiring executives—so named because the retiree got a silver-plated tray engraved with the signatures of every other active officer of the company. The attendees watched a film showing highlights from Smith's career: the acquisitions of EDS and Hughes, the Saturn announcement, and the launch of the Nummi joint venture with Toyota. But much else was omitted, including the Perot buyout and GM falling behind Ford in earnings. Most of Smith's fellow officers were relieved to see him go, but each dutifully raised his glass in a simple toast: "To Roger Smith."

The last 1980s CEO to depart Detroit was Iacocca, though it would take him a couple of years and plenty of melodrama to do so. Iacocca hated the thought of someone stealing his spotlight, especially his ablest underling, Bob Lutz. The last member of the Gang of Ford remaining at Chrysler, Lutz was a talented "car guy" and Iacocca's obvious successor. But Iacocca vetoed Lutz, and it was a stalemate until Chrysler's desperate directors made a surprise choice: Bob Eaton, an affable GM executive whose biggest qualification was his lack of any enemies at Chrysler. By the time Eaton came to Chrysler in 1992, another CEO succession drama, indeed a full-fledged crisis, was unfolding elsewhere in Detroit.

In many ways the man who succeeded Roger Smith at General Motors, Robert C. Stempel, was Smith's polar opposite. Instead of a career-long finance man, Stempel was an engineer, the first man who actually had developed cars to run GM in nearly forty years. In contrast to the short, squeaky-voiced Smith, Bob Stempel was big and burly, with a deeply resonant baritone. Stempel didn't mind occasional verbal jousting—he once greeted three journalists who came to interview him by saying, "I see it's three against one this morning. That ought to make the odds about even."

Stempel had hardly settled into the chairman's chair when, on August 2, 1990, Saddam Hussein invaded Kuwait, and the United States plunged into a recession. Six weeks later, in the midst of contract negotiations with the UAW, Stempel agreed to expand the six-year-old Jobs Bank. No longer would the program be reserved only for workers idled because of factory automation. Now workers idled for virtually any reason—including a slowdown in sales during a recession—could collect 95 percent of their regular wages even though they weren't working. And they could remain in the Jobs Bank for years, without any time limit, and without looking for another job.

Despite Stempel's high-minded intentions, his timing couldn't have been worse: GM's earnings were evaporating in the recession. Money that might have been used to develop efficient, high-tech engines or to upgrade the tacky plastic on GM's dashboards was used to fund elaborate "job security" provisions that were actually becoming instruments of job destruction. Instead of protecting UAW members, the Jobs Bank and the rest of the "safety net" threatened the very existence of the companies that employed them.

Nobody wanted to connect the dots, at least not publicly. But after the United States went to war in the Persian Gulf, the recession deepened, and car sales plunged. Ford's cash drain in 1990 alone exceeded its negative cash flow in 1980 through 1982. GM lost $2 billion in 1990, and in 1991—Stempel's first full year as chairman—the company lost a stunning $4.5 billion, partly because of expanded outlays for the Jobs Bank. By 1992 the situation was critical, and GM directors were stirred to action.

Chastened by their complicity in Smith's missteps, GM's directors vowed to be more rigorous in evaluating GM's management, starting with Stempel himself. The board wanted radical change at the company, but Stempel was hardly a change agent. He kept every member of Smith's executive team, merely shuffling each man's assignment—like the proverbial shuffling of the deck chairs on the *Titanic*. His plan to address GM's crisis called for plant closings and layoffs that would be phased in only gradually, over a period of years, through the mid-1990s. By that time, the board feared, General Motors might not be around. GM's crisis wasn't all Stempel's fault, but he was the wrong man to handle a crisis.

In November 1992, with the company perilously close to bankruptcy, GM's directors ousted Stempel as CEO and installed one of their own—John Smale, the retired CEO of Procter & Gamble—as nonexecutive chairman. It was the first time the GM board had dumped a CEO since the days of Billy Durant. As the new CEO, the directors turned to a quiet GM executive named Jack Smith. No relation to Roger, the fifty-four-year-old Smith was a finance man who had transformed GM's international operations from a money-losing mess into the company's only source of profits. The directors also bypassed several layers of management to install a new executive team of Young Turk reformers, including Rick Wagoner, who became chief financial officer at the tender age of thirty-nine. In the nick of time, GM's board had asserted itself (in striking and ironic contrast to the unstinting support that the directors during GM's next crisis would give the CEO, Wagoner).

So the ride was coming full circle. Between 1980 and 1992 GM, Ford, and Chrysler had tried robots, reorganization, diversification, Japanese joint ventures, and more. They had gone from record losses to record profits and back to record losses. Detroit's quality had improved, but it still trailed the Japanese, who weren't standing still. Toyota, Honda, and Nissan were expanding their U.S. factories and launching new luxury brands—Lexus, Acura, and Infiniti, respectively—that posed a direct threat to Detroit's high-profit sweet spot.

There was no mistaking the challenge confronting the Big Three. "We realize the urgency of change," Jack Smith wrote in his first letter to GM's shareholders in early 1993, "and will not let this opportunity slip by." Fortunately for Smith, Detroit was about to get a timely boost from a shift in the car market that the Japanese could neither foresee nor comprehend.

SEVEN

"CAR JESUS" AND THE RISE OF THE SUV

National cultures can be opaque to outsiders. Most Americans probably never figured that their national sport, baseball, would be embraced enthusiastically by the Japanese, complete with professional teams called the Kintetsu Buffalo, the Yakult Swallows, and the Hiroshima Carp. Then again, the Japanese didn't foresee that the inscrutable Americans would start paying premium prices for off-road sport-utility vehicles with little intention of taking them off-road. Or that towns named Naperville, Irvine, and Ho-Ho-Kus would spawn "suburban cowboys" behind the wheels of big, brawny pickup trucks—whose following previously was limited to farmers, contractors, and other guys who hauled plywood to make a living, as opposed to, like, show off.

The trend was so illogical, it was little wonder that the Japanese missed it. So did, initially, *The Wall Street Journal,* which refused to include SUVs and pickup trucks in its regular reports of U.S. car sales until the late 1980s. The newspaper viewed car sales as an indicator of consumer spending, and heck, everyone knew that most SUVs and pickups were really commercial vehicles. Which was absolutely true . . . until it wasn't.

The change started, as did so many automotive trends of the time, with Lee Iacocca. The surprising success of Chrysler's minivans suggested to him that many Americans aspired to "active" lifestyles that required vehicles more versatile than ordinary sedans or station wagons. That insight had prompted him to buy American Motors and thereby acquire its Jeep brand. Jeeps were perfect for hauling the kids to school Monday through Friday, then for trekking off into the woods for a weekend of mountain biking, trail hiking, and campfire building. Of course, such weekends in the woods, minus hot showers and indoor toilets, meant stinky kids, creeping spiders, and mosquito bites, which weren't what the well-heeled suburbanites who used invisible-glide deodorant envisioned as their lifestyle.

So they bought Jeeps and other sport-utility vehicles but then rarely, if ever, ventured off a paved highway, where they might encounter something icky or gooey. A rugged-looking Jeep SUV or a brawny Chevy Silverado pickup became the perfect complement to a Patagonia windbreaker: a fashion statement, the sports car substitute for soccer moms.

At first Toyota, Honda, and Nissan missed the trend, and after that they refused to believe it would last. Honda executives told each other that SUVs were just a fad that they would be foolish to chase. Anyway, Toyota, Honda, and Nissan were preoccupied with launching their luxury divisions. Their new marques were aimed at Mercedes-Benz and BMW instead of Cadillac or Lincoln, which sold mainly on the north side of the generation gap. Subaru did make all-wheel-drive vehicles, but they weren't tough-looking trucks, and Subaru had little presence outside New England and the Rocky Mountain states.

The bottom line was that the truck boom made the car business resemble the 1960s: hardly any Japanese vehicles in an exploding new segment of the market that the Big Three thus had virtually to themselves. So SUVs and pickup trucks commanded premium prices, helped along by the EPA, which classified SUVs, pickups, and minivans as "light trucks," giving them a lower fuel-economy standard than cars. The heavy four-wheel-drive apparatus that underpinned most pickups and SUVs made them proverbial gas hogs, but who really cared? Gas was cheap in the 1990s, and seemed destined to stay that way. In the mid-1990s SUVs and pickups were like a powerful shot of adrenaline delivered straight into the hardening arteries of Chrysler, Ford, and General Motors.

By 1990, pickup trucks had been around for decades. Dust-bowl Okies had used them to trek westward to California on Route 66. Farm families stuck with either Ford or Chevy pickups from generation to generation, demonstrating fierce brand loyalty, in contrast to the fickle habits of ordinary car buyers. Jeeps, for their part, had been the staple of GI transport during World War II, when they were made by Willys-Overland, one of the companies that had merged to form American Motors. From the end of the war until the mid-1980s, Jeeps had limped along as niche vehicles for the Coleman stove set. AMC, meanwhile, came under the control of Renault in 1980. The French automaker tried to use the AMC dealer network to sell its cars in America, mostly in vain.

When Chrysler bought AMC in 1987, the most powerful engine in the Jeep Cherokee was an anemic 135-horsepower V6 that made merging onto a freeway an act of courage. Chrysler quickly installed a new 177-horsepower in-line six-cylinder engine that improved the Cherokee's acceleration from nonexistent to acceptable. Chrysler also created a gussied-up version called the Cherokee Limited with leather seats, gold-paint body stripes, and gold-tinted aluminum wheels. It looked like a tarted-up tin can, but the combination of more horsepower and a bit of bling proved to be a winner. Dealers around the country begged for increased allocations, especially of the four-door version, as opposed to the two-door models that had been Jeep's staple for decades. Four years after hitting a home run with the minivan, Chrysler was doing it again, amazingly, with a reconfigured relic of World War II.

Cherokee sales jumped 33 percent in 1988 and rose another 5 percent in 1989, to more than 156,000 vehicles. It was a rare bright spot for Chrysler, which dipped into the red that year as it paid the price for Iacocca's diversification detour. Having been caught flat-footed by the minivan's success, Ford was quicker to respond this time. In the spring of 1990 it replaced its aging and uncomfortable Bronco II with a new four-door SUV called the Explorer, outfitted with power leather seats and other creature comforts more attuned to the lure of the shopping mall than to the call of the wild. The Explorer "has given Jeep's renowned Cherokee a good whacking," wrote *USA Today.* Indeed, in its first year the new Explorer actually outsold the Cherokee.

Even as Ford mounted a bumper-to-bumper challenge to Chrysler with the Explorer, it accelerated its running war against GM with pickup trucks. For years it had consisted mostly of rural battles, fought beyond the notice of the news media in little towns such as Paxton and Piper City, Illinois—both of which happened to be located in rural Ford County, about 120 miles south of Chicago.

Ford County was a place where, some clever researchers at a GM ad agency discovered, Chevy pickups outsold Ford's. So the agency dispatched a crew to Ford County to film real-life residents—at least those who owned Silverados—talking about their trucks. "I love the horses," as in horsepower, declared a ninety-one-year-old woman named Agnes, a Silverado driver who was filmed stitching quilts with her friends. (More pickup drivers were hunters than quilters, but shooting a deer wouldn't have looked good on TV.) Agnes added: "That Chevy really hauls." As the camera panned to a Silverado standing strong on a rural, windswept landscape, the commercial's narrator delivered the punch line: "People from Ford prefer Chevy trucks."

Ford quickly cried foul, claiming its numbers showed that the F-series (a lineup that extended from the basic F-150 to the enormous F-350) really outsold the Silverado in Ford County, as it did all over America. Chevy retorted that Ford was counting certain types of medium- and heavy-duty trucks that Chevrolet didn't even make. Both companies probably were right, but that didn't matter. Sales of pickup trucks, like those of SUVs, were going mainstream. With sales surging and the stakes getting higher, new rules of combat were emerging. It was a crosstown contest that Detroit loved because it didn't involve the Japanese, who hadn't suited up for the game.

The bottom line was that in the mid-1990s GM, Ford, and Chrysler were handed a golden opportunity to rebuild their balance sheets, regain market share, and return to something approaching dominance in their home market. The truck boom wasn't the only reason. During these years, much to Detroit's delight, Japan's car companies hit some unaccustomed speed bumps of their own.

Greed and hubris in the auto industry weren't limited to people who worked for General Motors, Ford, and Chrysler. One prospective Honda dealer learned that firsthand in the late 1970s, when he was trying to get a dealership in Georgia. The would-be dealer was waiting to finalize the paperwork when he got a visit from John "Jack"

Billmyer, Honda's district manager and a rising star in the company's sales hierarchy. Billmyer explained that Honda sales managers really didn't make much money, then added, "Nobody really loves you but your momma, and everybody else got to pay a little cash up front."

A Honda dealership was valuable, he then explained, worth at least $20,000 and the title to a new car. The prospective dealer knew a shakedown when he saw one. He threw Billmyer out and a few weeks later learned that his application for a dealership had been denied. One of the largest commercial bribery scandals in the history of the United States was beginning to unfold, right in the heart of Honda. It would be given impetus, ironically, by government actions designed to help Detroit.

In 1980 the American and Japanese governments had agreed to "voluntary" restraints on Japan's automotive exports to the United States, with the stated purpose of giving Detroit time to "adjust" to a new competitive landscape. Because the auto industry loomed large in America's psyche as well as its economy, even the free-market Reagan administration didn't want to watch it get run over by the Japanese. The "voluntary" limits started with about 1.7 million cars a year and would rise to more than 2 million annually by the mid-1980s; each Japanese car company would get a share of that quota. The fears that had prompted Honda to start building cars in America proved fully justified: while the deal mollified Detroit and satisfied both governments, it also imposed a de facto tax on Americans who wanted to buy Hondas. As demand outstripped supply, even after Honda's U.S. production began, dealers found they could often add $2,000 to the sticker price of each car.

Honda dealers used various techniques, sometimes requiring customers to buy expensive floor mats, or sometimes brazenly adding a charge they labeled ADM, as in "additional dealer markup." Many Americans paid the price, though grudgingly, because Honda's cars were reliable, fuel efficient, and fun to drive. The profit potential sent car dealers around the country scrambling to add Honda franchises to their portfolios. Existing Honda dealers, meanwhile, were desperate to increase their allocations of cars from the factories, knowing that each extra car meant extra profit.

So began the process that some Honda dealers called "kissing the ring," a term that conjured up images of Mafia-style payoffs, which wasn't far from the truth. The operation was centered at the Los Angeles headquarters of American Honda, the company's U.S. sales division, a separate entity from the manufacturing operations in Ohio. Billmyer had joined American Honda in 1970 as a district sales rep in the mid-Atlantic states and rose to become national sales manager in L.A. in 1980.

As his bribery-and-kickback scheme blossomed, Billmyer got a $10,000 Rolex from a dealer near Washington, D.C., in return for favorable allocations of cars. So many other Honda sales officials followed suit that company sales meetings became known as "Rolex conventions." Other distinctive gratuities that Billmyer got from dealers included a helicopter tour of Hawaii, an all-expenses-paid shopping spree in Hong Kong, and regular Federal Express envelopes containing cash for "consulting fees." He also got new cars, including several BMWs, as he ironically outgrew his taste for Hondas.

Throughout the 1970s and 1980s Honda cars were selling above their sticker prices even as dealers were being forced to discount the prices of Chevys, Fords, and Dodges. The American government's effort to protect Detroit was backfiring, though nobody wanted to admit that publicly. And as events unfolded, Billmyer wouldn't be just a single rogue executive.

The others at Honda who joined his hidden enterprise included Jim Cardiges, whose name (pronounced *car-dee-jus*) prompted Honda dealers to nickname him "Car Jesus." It was an appropriate moniker, because Jim Cardiges could work all sorts of miracles. When an old friend wanted to land a couple of Honda franchises in Pennsylvania, Cardiges made it happen—collecting nearly $200,000 in cash in return. Another dealer who contributed to the Car Jesus collection plate financed a California home for Cardiges, then sent him monthly cash payments to cover the mortgage.

Most dealers weren't in on the action, and some of them were afflicted with business problems that seemed hard to explain. One New England dealer collected $300,000 in new-car deposits from customers, who then became irate while they waited for months to get Hondas that never arrived. Finally the frustrated dealer sold out to a nearby rival, who seemed to have no trouble getting regular deliveries of *his* brand-new cars. But the lucrative kickback scheme was too widespread to remain unnoticed. In 1991 an uninvolved district sales manager blew the whistle to Honda's higher-ups, and a few months later Cardiges resigned from the company by "mutual agreement." Honda hoped its housecleaning would resolve the mess discreetly, but that wasn't about to happen.

A New Hampshire Honda dealer who hadn't been part of the scheme sued the company, claiming that Honda's sleazy sales practices had cost him money. That brought in the FBI, which found that the scheme of bribery and kickbacks had spanned at least fifteen years and involved at least $15 million. In 1994 a federal grand jury handed up racketeering, conspiracy, and fraud indictments against Billmyer, Cardiges, and others. In the ensuing months nearly twenty Honda dealers and former executives pleaded guilty to various charges. And on the eve of his trial Cardiges himself agreed to provide state's evidence.

Fortunately for Honda, when the trial began in out-of-the-way Concord, New Hampshire, on February 7, 1995, media coverage was sporadic. Less fortunate for the company was that, from the very start, nobody really denied what had happened. Billmyer's attorney argued rather that all the booty had just been favors among friends and that key Honda executives, including some Japanese, had just winked at the scheme. It was a variation of the "Everybody does it" argument that most people stop using at age twelve or so. And it worked just about as well as it did for most kids.

In May 1995, after a trial of some three months, the jury found Billmyer and another former Honda official guilty. The judge said that Honda itself "could well be accused of being negligent" for ignoring the warning signs so long. The remark provided ammunition to dealers who claimed they had been harmed by the company's negligence. In July 1998 Honda agreed to pay those dealers nearly $330 million. Billmyer and others would continue their appeals even longer, without success.

The scandal, in a perverse way, provided evidence of Honda's surging popularity in America. A similarly large-scale shakedown never could have happened at the Detroit companies because their cars weren't nearly as popular as Honda's, at least not in relation to the available supply. More important, the scandal proved a huge distraction to Honda executives just as their momentum in the U.S. market had seemed unstoppable. At the same time, the Japanese car companies suddenly found themselves facing a seismic shift in the global foreign-exchange market. The land of the rising sun had become the land of the rising yen.

In 1991, the same year Honda started coming to grips with its payola scandal, the company quietly cut 25,000 cars out of its first-quarter production plans. Within a month it rented a former army depot in Ohio to store two thousand cars that had been built but that dealers didn't want to order. And shortly after that Honda gave its U.S. dealers an allowance of $900 a car to spur sagging sales.

The allowance was small potatoes by Detroit standards, where rebates were $2,000 or more. But it was a sea change for a company whose dealers, just a couple years earlier, had clamored for extra cars and in some cases paid bribes to get them. The problem, simply put, was that Honda had sharply raised its prices along with other Japanese car companies. In 1993 the price of a Toyota Corolla, once the quintessential inexpensive Japanese subcompact, soared to more than $17,000, about the same as a midsize Ford Taurus.

Toyota, Honda, and the others were raising prices to cope with the value of the Japanese yen, which had begun to soar in 1985. By 1993 the yen had more than doubled in value against the U.S. dollar, despite the onset of recession in Japan. The country's bubble economy had burst in 1990 after the collapse of hyperinflated real estate prices that had been supported by a glut of bad loans. (Wouldn't that sound familiar to Americans twenty years later?) Maybe it didn't make sense for the yen to rise while Japan's domestic economy tanked, but foreign-exchange markets can swing in directions that defy explanation.

For Japanese car companies, the effect of the strong yen was to pay twice as much for everything that they made in Japan and exported to America. And despite the growing number of transplants, exports still accounted for most of their U.S. sales.

As the yen caught the Japanese by surprise, so did something else:

Detroit started making major quality and productivity gains. After years of delay and denial, the Big Three started adopting some of the manufacturing techniques and worker-involvement ideas developed by the Japanese. Detroit's strategy had become "If you can't beat 'em, join 'em," and some of the results were palpable.

A newly retired Japanese executive who had become an automotive consultant visited a Chrysler plant in Canada that built the company's new line of midsize cars. He was amazed to see an exhaust system that was designed to be attached to the car easily and seamlessly in a single piece, thus boosting both both quality and productivity. It was a page straight out of Japan's playbook, along with just-in-time inventory, worker participation in quality circles, and a host of other innovations.

After fifteen years of explosive growth, the rising yen, recession in Japan, Detroit's self-help program, and the payola scandal at Honda seemed to be bringing the Japanese automotive juggernaut to a halt. At a Japanese assembly plant in Indiana, some seven thousand vehicles sat in storage because buyers couldn't be found. Mazda abruptly canceled plans to launch its own luxury division.

To everyone's shock, in 1992 Honda announced it was pulling out of Formula One racing to save costs. Honda had just won its sixth straight world F1 championship. What's more, ever since the days of Soichiro Honda, the company had used racing to test the capability of its cars and to test the mettle of the hotshot engineers at Honda R&D.

At the end of 1992 the Ford Taurus dethroned the Honda Accord as the top-selling car in America. The next shoe to drop, in February 1993, was Nissan's decision to close one of its assembly plants in Japan. By then factory closings were old news in the United States, but Nissan's move was the first such closing in the history of Japan's auto industry.

In 1993 the combined U.S. market share of Japanese automakers dropped to 23 percent, down from nearly 26 percent in 1991. It seemed sort of like the Battle of Midway in World War II: after sustaining humiliating defeats, the Americans had stemmed the Japanese advance. At least that's what many experts believed. "I don't think they'll regain the share of the U.S. market they once had," Jonathan Dobson, an automotive analyst at Jardine Fleming Securities, told the Associated Press. "It's a case of damage limitation."

Meanwhile the Japanese still didn't have much to compete with Detroit's newest weapon: the SUV. When Bob Lutz drove a new Chrysler Grand Cherokee into the Detroit auto show in January 1992, he was launching not just a new vehicle but a whole new era. Lutz, then the president of Chrysler, didn't drive through the door. Instead, he steered the company's newest SUV straight up the steps of the Cobo Hall exhibition center and right through an enormous plate glass window. The stunt was basically bogus, because a special window had been installed beforehand and rigged with tiny explosive charges to shatter at just the right moment. But it grabbed headlines around the country and provided millions of dollars of free publicity for Chrysler's newest Jeep. The Grand Cherokee retained most of the original Cherokee's rugged persona but was far more refined, with everything from sleeker styling to a more comfortable interior.

Lutz's drive was the first of numerous, ever-more-elaborate publicity stunts to launch big pickup trucks and SUVs—the vehicles that symbolized America's economic boom of the 1990s, just as tail fins had defined the postwar prosperity of the 1950s. Chrysler's next stunt, at the 1993 auto show, was to drop a new Dodge Ram pickup truck from the ceiling of Cobo Hall—a feat that required painstaking preparation and considerable expense.

The company had removed the truck's seats and other interior parts to reduce its weight. Then the vehicle was hoisted on a giant forklift that had been hidden behind a black curtain—with only the black-painted (and therefore invisible) twin forks sticking through. After weeks of trial and error, Chrysler engineers figured out how to siphon out the forklift's hydraulic fluid fast enough to make the pickup truck seem to be in free fall, but not so fast that the fall would kill nearby onlookers. There was a last-minute crisis when Lutz, who relished the notoriety he had received for crashing the Cherokee through the window, insisted on being in the truck when it was dropped. The PR guys talked him out of it, but barely.

The new Ram pickup dropped from the fake suspended ceiling

with a loud and convincing thud. Its sales, however, went right through the roof. The truck had been completely reengineered and redesigned, with a"drop-fendered" front end that looked like muscular shoulders and that added a vaguely menacing Mack truck sort of look. The design was developed in consultation with Clotaire Rapaille, a French-born medical anthropologist who viewed burly trucks and SUVs as natural expressions of man's repressed reptilian instincts.

Adopting the aggressive styling was risky because 80 percent of the attendees in Chrysler's customer focus groups said they hated it. But Lutz had decided on a new design strategy that was the polar opposite of GM's. Instead of settling for styling that was inoffensive but also uninspiring, Chrysler would adopt styling that aroused passion in some buyers, even at the risk of offending others. It worked wonderfully.

Chrysler rebounded from an $800 million loss in 1991 to record earnings of $3.7 billion in 1994, partly because Ram sales surged. Chrysler's share of the pickup truck market, historically stuck at less than 15 percent, soared to nearly 19 percent in 1995, an astounding increase in an industry where companies fought over tenths of a percentage point. Chrysler was becoming a truck company instead of a car company. In 1986 its sales mix had been roughly two-thirds cars and one-third trucks. But by 1995 that ratio was reversed, with 64 percent of overall sales consisting of minivans, pickup trucks, and SUVs. It seemed a brilliant strategic shift. (Nobody knew it would backfire a decade later.)

The truck boom of the 1990s produced a windfall for Chrysler dealers, including one of the newest ones, Gene Benner. In 1994, when the principal owner of Bessey Motors was ready to retire, he offered to sell his 90 percent interest to Benner, and the former football coach jumped at the chance. He depleted his personal savings and borrowed every penny he could lay his hands on—from his retirement account, from local banks, and from Chrysler Financial. When he was still a little short, he made up the difference with a small loan from his mother. Benner was going deeply into debt to bet his future on Chrysler.

And just as in 1984, when he had become a car salesman right when minivan sales hit high gear, Benner's timing was perfect. Sales of SUVs, pickup trucks, and minivans boomed at his little dealership in Maine, as they were doing in the rest of the country. Benner was able to pay off all his loans within five years, far faster than he had expected. He was riding the wave of Detroit's truck boom.

The prosperity was also spreading to Fred Young in Belvidere, where Chrysler was putting renewed emphasis on quality. Young was chosen to become a "process team member," helping design work stations on the assembly line. The really dirty work that Young had done two decades earlier—hopping into a pit to weld car underbodies—had been assigned to robots. His task as a PTM member was to go further and help improve the layout of the assembly line to make it easier for workers to do their jobs.

Chrysler had discovered what the Japanese knew: that better ergonomics would boost quality and productivity and avoid on-the-job injuries that increased workers' medical bills. The company adopted all sorts of innovations, such as redesigned wrenches that could be used repeatedly without causing stress injuries to workers' wrists. Young and other team members joked that PTM really meant "part-time management," because they felt like they were acting as quasi-managers as opposed to workers. But that was a good thing. PTM, whatever it stood for, was just the sort of worker involvement that the Japanese had used successfully for years.

PTM wasn't perfect. Young believed some members were shirkers who had been named to the team because of their friendship with local union officials and were quick to pad their hours with extra overtime. But he liked the assignment and took it seriously, often traveling to Auburn Hills to work with the manufacturing engineers at company headquarters.

Ford, like Chrysler, was trucking down the road to success. In 1995, for the first time, the company sold more trucks than cars. Two years later trucks totaled nearly 58 percent of its U.S. sales, helped by a new full-size SUV, bigger than the Explorer, called the Expedition. It could seat eight people and, with the optional 5.4-liter V8 engine, could tow boats, horses, snowmobiles, Jet Skis, or anything else that weighed up to eight thousand pounds—much more than any other SUV at the time. A less flattering number was the Expedition's fuel-economy rating of just fourteen miles a gallon in combined city-highway driving, which drew criticism from the environmental lobby. But who really cared, when gasoline was cheaper than bottled water in most of the country?

Nor did it seem to matter that in 1997, the same year the Expedition debuted, the Ford Taurus fell from first to third place on the list of America's top-selling cars, to be supplanted by the Toyota Camry and Honda Accord. The Taurus wasn't important anymore, in Ford's view. Americans wanted big SUVs, and Ford wanted big profits. The Expedition happily met both needs. There seemed little reason for Ford to invest more money in the Taurus.

Detroit's come-lately to the truck party was General Motors, traditionally the most cautious of the Big Three. Throughout the 1990s GM remained the only Detroit company that was selling more cars than trucks. It acquired Saab, the Swedish maker of upscale cars, to add to its lineup. GM's competitor for the Grand Cherokee and Explorer was the outdated Chevy Blazer, whose narrow chassis made it feel more "tippy" and less secure than its crosstown competitors—a big drawback, especially with women drivers. But GM had an SUV ace in the hole: the enormous Chevrolet Suburban.

Bigger than any other SUV, this ancient warrior had first appeared in the mid-1930s but didn't get four doors until 1973. After that GM left the Suburban's utilitarian body style basically unchanged for a couple decades. In 1996, however, the Suburban got sleeker styling and a 290-horsepower engine, and GM started catching the truck wave too. It became common to see Suburbans sitting in the prosperous driveways of Darien and Lake Forest, right alongside Mercedes and BMW sedans.

The Japanese remained dumbstruck by it all. Honda not only lacked an SUV, it didn't have anything in the pipeline, much to the dismay of its dealers. Already restive over the bribery scandal, Honda dealers demanded an SUV, forcing the company to toss aside its oft-professed policy to "carry our own torch," as company executives put it. The result was the pathetic Honda Passport, launched in 1993 as the company's first SUV. It actually was built by Isuzu and then tweaked a little so it could be badged with an *H* and sold as a Honda. Inside the company the Passport was an acute embarrassment, because Isuzu's quality was so uneven that the vehicle depressed Honda's overall quality ratings in the widely watched J.D. Power surveys.

As for Toyota, until the mid-1990s its 4Runner SUV basically was an underpowered pickup truck with an enclosed back end. The 4Runner got high quality ratings, but the absence of defects couldn't make up for the lack of interior space or for an awkward seating position that made drivers feel like they were sitting in a living room recliner. The company's Previa minivan, introduced in 1990, had an anemic four-cylinder engine that was crammed under the front seat. Nissan had a more conventional minivan, the Quest, but it was actually built by Ford in Ohio.

The Japanese were missing the truck boom, while Detroit's Big Three were selling ever more powerful, sophisticated, and comfortable trucks right in the market's sweet spot. Profits on the Chevy Suburban topped $10,000 per vehicle, and those on the Expedition, Grand Cherokee, other SUVs and pickups weren't far behind. One Chrysler executive told his colleagues, "We wish we could just shrink-wrap the way it is right now." But things were about to get even better for Detroit, or so it seemed.

On the afternoon of Wednesday, May 6, 1998, a group of weary Chrysler road warriors piled into a van after attending a daylong preview of their new cars near Atlanta. Suddenly everyone's cell phone began ringing, with each person getting the same message from his or her boss: There'd be an important special meeting at five P.M. back at the hotel. When the meeting convened, the bosses confirmed a report from *The Wall Street Journal* that morning. Chrysler would be joining Germany's Daimler-Benz AG, parent company of Mercedes, in a transatlantic merger that would redraw the map of the global auto industry and perhaps create a template for a postnational corporation. "We started jumping for joy," recalled a Chrysler PR man some years later. "Mercedes-Benz was a great brand name with enormous prestige. It had what we at Chrysler aspired to—sort of like penis envy."

Chrysler executives had more concrete reasons to rejoice. Even though Daimler was the acquiring company, the deal was billed as a "merger of equals." For the next three years Daimler's Jürgen Schrempp and Chrysler's Bob Eaton would serve as co-CEOs of the new DaimlerChrysler. The terms called for Daimler-Benz to exchange more than $38 billion of its stock for Chrysler, a 30 percent premium for each Chrysler share. Chrysler's top thirty or so executives would reap a windfall of nearly $1 billion on their stock options. Chairman Eaton alone would get an immediate $70 million, plus new stock options in the combined company that could be worth tens of millions more.

The biggest winner was Kirk Kerkorian, Chrysler's largest shareholder. In 1995, five years after first buying his stake in Chrysler, Kerkorian had tried to acquire the entire company and take it private—only to be rebuffed by Eaton. It was the luckiest miss ever for Kerkorian. After dropping his bid, he had maneuvered behind the scenes for Chrysler to be acquired and had assured Schrempp he would support the deal. In 1998 Kerkorian owned nearly 14 percent of the company and stood to reap profits of nearly $5 billion on his original investment.

After toasting their deal with champagne in London's Dorchester Hotel on the night of May 6, the next morning Eaton and Schrempp strode into a press conference in the city's Docklands to be greeted like rock stars, almost blinded by flashing cameras and bright television lights. Analysts projected that "synergy savings" of $3 billion a year would flow from the deal, about half of that in the first year. Schrempp immediately began talking about yet another megamerger, maybe buying one of the weaker Japanese car companies, such as Mitsubishi or Nissan. "We'll have the size, the profitability, and the reach to take on everyone," the Daimler chief said as he beamed at the press conference.

After a full day of media interviews, Eaton hopped on a helicopter with Chrysler's PR chief, Steve Harris, to head for the airport. As the sun set over the ancient city of London, shedding the day's final rays on some of the best-known buildings in the world, the existential moment moved Eaton to eloquence. Not about synergies, or about developing great new cars, or about making further acquisitions: instead, Chrysler's CEO rhapsodized about the the riches that he and Chrysler's other executives would reap from the deal.

Back in America, Chrysler dealers were rejoicing as well. Chrysler's marriage to one of the most prestigious car companies in the world, they figured, surely would give them more and better vehicles to sell. When the deal was announced, Gene Benner was at a used-car auction for dealers. He returned later that day to find a surprise gift from his employees—the three-pointed Mercedes-Benz logo—sitting on his desk.

General Motors and Ford executives in Detroit also figured that the new DaimlerChrysler would become a competitive powerhouse. But for the moment GM and Ford were themselves enjoying unprecedented prosperity. GM earned $6 billion in 1999 and Ford earned $7.2 billion, a new record for any car company in history, surpassing the previous record Ford had set a decade earlier. It was all because of America's love affair with the SUV.

And even better results promised to come. In early 1999 Ford's senior sales executives, in giddy anticipation, privately unveiled a new vehicle to a handful of company officials. It was a bitterly cold day, typical of Detroit in winter, and the attendees huddled in their topcoats in the company's drafty design studio. When the cover was pulled off the new vehicle, however, not everyone in the room shared the sales staff's excitement. Some attendees gasped, "Oh my God!" and "Jesus Christ!" Others shuffled away and averted their eyes.

The vehicle was the new Ford Excursion, the biggest SUV the world had yet seen. Nearly as big as a small hotel room in Tokyo, the Excursion had a V10 engine, weighed more than three and a half tons, and was fully seven inches longer than the Chevy Suburban. Its fuel-economy rating would be barely ten miles a gallon—even less when it was loaded with people, luggage, and maybe a ten-thousand-pound boat on the towing hitch. Ford's PR people knew the Excursion would send the Sierra Club and other environmental groups into a frenzy of anti-SUV outrage. But company executives had been feeling their own penis envy over the Suburban, and they didn't intend to let GM's fat profits on its behemoth continue unchallenged.

At the close of the millennium, times were good in Detroit: The cycle of crisis and recovery during the preceding two decades appeared to be gone forever. For the first time the Japanese car companies were on the defensive, beset by scandal, by currency swings, and by their gross underestimation of America's appetite for trucks. Nissan was suffering with lackluster cars and inept management, hovering on the brink of bankruptcy. In 1999 Japan's second-largest car company took a once-unthinkable step. The company sold a controlling block of its stock to the leading French automaker, Renault, which dispatched one of its own executives—a non-Japanese—to take Nissan's helm.

On January 8, 1999, *The Wall Street Journal* carried a front-page article declaring the end of the twentieth century to be the dawn of a new golden age for General Motors, Ford, and Chrysler. It would be different from the Big Three's oligopolic dominance of the 1950s and 1960s, to be sure, but a plethora of exciting new products to meet every consumer taste would make it in many ways better.

The year 2000 would bring the debut not only of the Excursion but also of Chrysler's hot PT Cruiser, which sported 1930s retro styling that made it a cross between a small station wagon and an Al Capone squad car. "It's wonderful to be in this industry now," a product development executive at Chrysler told the *Journal*. "We've come from where all those dummies said we were going to die in 1980 to now, where it's more products than ever."

EIGHT

POTHOLES AND MISSED OPPORTUNITIES

*W*ith Detroit on a roll, General Motors announced it would build "the largest auto show exhibit ever in North America" for the January 2000 Detroit auto show. The company's publicists reached for superlatives. If the exhibit's 230 tons of steel were melted down and laid end to end, GM announced, the beams would stretch seven miles—equivalent to rounding the bases at the Tigers' ballpark ninety-nine times, crossing the Ambassador Bridge between Detroit and Canada four times each way, or running the length of a soccer field 105 times. As a final flourish, GM said the steel would rise three times higher than Mount Fuji. Take that, Japan.

Detroit might have been entitled to some hyperbole. General Motors, Ford, and Chrysler had mounted odds-defying comebacks from their near-death experiences in the early 1980s and early 1990s. Profits stood at record levels, and the stock prices of both GM and Ford were close to their all-time highs. (Chrysler, as part of Daimler-Chrysler, didn't have its own stock anymore.) The Big Three were the market leaders in light trucks, the fastest-growing—indeed, the only growing—segment of the American car market. In 2001 Americans would buy 8.7 million minivans, pickups, and SUVs compared to just 8.4 million sedans, coupes, and station wagons. For the first time trucks actually outsold cars 51 percent to 49 percent—which was amazing, considering that the ratio had been 80 percent cars to 20 percent trucks just twenty years earlier. All this was good news for the Big Three.

Or so they thought. Their survival struggle during the previous two decades had sparked an urgency to boost quality, increase productivity, and meet the threat of foreign competition, which was becoming a little less foreign as the Japanese, German, and even Korean car companies built more factories on U.S. soil. But at the turn of the century Detroit's success with trucks caused the impetus for ambitious efforts at self-reform to fade. On the labor front, the debate over cooperation versus confrontation continued between the UAW and the car companies, especially General Motors. The union saw its GM workforce drop from 500,000 people in 1980 to just 220,000 in 1998. GM, for its part, had almost gone bankrupt in 1992 and seemed determined not to continue business as usual.

The debates meant that GM and the union tried lots of things to change their relationship, often with initial success, but then followed through on virtually nothing. As a result, their prosperity wasn't as sound at it seemed. Major problems lurked like rocks below the water's surface and sometimes jutted up into public view. The issues and uncertainties were amply evident at GM's most ambitious effort to reinvent itself, the Saturn Corporation. There the company and the UAW tried a new model for enlightened labor relations and then abandoned it, retreating into their old pattern of discord and eventual disaster.

Saturn had started modestly in 1983 at the sprawling General Motors Technical Center in suburban Detroit as a project—one of dozens—aimed at improving the company's manufacturing efficiency and performance. But in December 1984 in Fremont, California, Roger Smith hinted that he had bigger ideas. Smith was there to help reopen a factory that had been shuttered because it was one of the very worst in the GM system, with terrible quality and nonstop warfare between management and union. For Fremont's new incarnation as Nummi, the joint venture between General Motors and Toyota, the companies had enlisted the help of two hard-bitten union leaders (named, believe it or not, George Nanno and Gus Billy) to give the factory another chance under Toyota management methods. Before long, Nummi would be building higher-quality cars than any other GM factory.

At the "line-off" ceremony to celebrate production of the first car, Smith said GM would take the labor-management techniques from Nummi and combine them with high-tech manufacturing to leapfrog the rest of the industry—including, by implication, Toyota itself. Some listeners thought Smith's remarks were insulting to the Toyota executives, including members of the founding Toyoda family, who were attending the ceremony. The bigger problem, however, was that Smith had a grand idea but had given little thought to "details," such as how to make money and how to spread any innovations to the rest of GM.

The grand idea was unveiled when Smith made a "historic announcement," as he himself put it, in Detroit on January 8, 1985. General Motors would upgrade Saturn, he said, from an anonymous project to GM's first new brand in seventy years, to take its place alongside Chevrolet, Pontiac, Oldsmobile, Buick, and Cadillac. Unlike the others, Saturn would be established as a separate subsidiary with its own factory chock-full of the latest technology, as well as a separate workforce with its own unique labor agreement. Saturn would be empowered, Smith explained, "to develop and produce an American-made small car that will be fully competitive with the best of the imports," meaning the Honda Civic and Toyota Corolla.

"Saturn is the key to GM's long-term competitiveness, survival and success," declared Smith, adding that Saturn would "affirm that American ingenuity, American technology and American productivity can once again be the model and the inspiration for the rest of the world." It was a national crusade, and Americans rushed to join, besieging GM with thousands of unsolicited job applications. Seven governors went on television's *Phil Donahue Show* to plead publicly for the Saturn plant—with its thousands of jobs and high-tech infrastructure—to be located in their state. More than a dozen others trekked to Detroit to state their case in person. After a media circus that ran for months, the winner was Tennessee, where GM put the plant in the bucolic hamlet of Spring Hill, some forty-five miles south of Nashville. More important, it was five hundred miles from the hidebound union-versus-management mores of Detroit.

In July 1985, while the site search was still under way, negotiators for Saturn and the UAW reached a "memorandum of understanding" stating that Saturn wouldn't be bound by the union's master contract with General Motors. Saturn would have just five or six job classifications compared with dozens and dozens at some other GM factories, where the classifications and myriad work rules basically were featherbedding provisions. With Saturn, the union tacitly admitted that the traditional job classification structure was inefficient—though it wasn't willing to scrap it at other GM factories, because one man's inefficiency was another man's job.

The memorandum further established "the principle of risk and reward" in setting workers' pay, meaning that wages would be tied to Saturn's success or failure. And it stated: "We believe that all people want to be involved in decisions that affect them, care about their jobs and each other . . . and want to share in the success of their efforts."

It was a revolutionary, even inspiring document. The memorandum reflected the views of a blue-collar philosopher who was one of the UAW's more remarkable leaders, Donald Ephlin, who had stood at Roger Smith's side when Saturn was announced. Ephlin, a disheveled and overweight man, spoke with an accent that betrayed his roots in Massachusetts, where he had started building cars in the late 1940s at GM's assembly plant in Framingham. He had risen through the UAW's ranks to become Leonard Woodcock's administrative assistant when Woodcock led the union in the 1970s.

As head of the UAW's Ford department in the early 1980s, Ephlin had traveled with Ford executives to Japan to observe Japanese management methods firsthand. And with his help Ford had forged the most cooperative and productive union relationship among the Big Three. By the time Ephlin moved up to head the UAW's GM department, he was the union's leading intellectual, sometimes to the irritation of his colleagues.

"Don read books—and let the other guys know that he read books," one former union official would explain. If Roger Smith wanted a laboratory for technology, Don Ephlin wanted a proving ground for a new era of labor-management relations in which GM and the union would bury their bitter, combative past.

The new Saturn contract, built on the memorandum of understanding, pledged both the company and the union to go well beyond the Japanese in joint decision-making. Each Saturn executive and many managers—about four hundred in all—would have a union counterpart. The two would share responsibility for their assigned operation, reaching consensus decisions on matters big and small. Workers would receive only 80 percent of the UAW master contract wage, with the other 20 percent tied to quality and productivity.

Instead of a traditional fixed-benefit pension, Saturn workers would get a profit-sharing plan akin to a 401(k). Seniority rights, traditionally sacred to the union, would be limited. In return, GM pledged to devote at least 5 percent of each worker's annual working hours to skills training, and not to lay off more than 20 percent of the workforce under virtually any circumstances. Admirably, though perhaps naïvely, the contract was a template for democracy in the workplace.

To make it work in the trenches, Ephlin would need a like-minded person to lead the new UAW Local 1853 in Spring Hill, which would represent Saturn's workers. He found his man in a most unlikely place: the union's militant heartland of Flint, Michigan, the UAW's equivalent of Bunker Hill, where the violent 1936 Sit-down Strike is still celebrated every year with local parades and festivities.

Mike Bennett, a mild-mannered Flint native with a flat midwestern accent, knew the playbook of labor-management confrontation very well. As president of UAW Local 326, he'd used it to considerable advantage in the past. "Our job was to prevent management from managing," he would say in recalling his early years as a union leader, when his most potent weapon had been the grievance pad. Local union officials would write grievances—formal complaints that a manager had violated a worker's rights—at a moment's notice. While some were legitimate, many amounted to reverse harassment to bend managers to the union's will. This system had worked remarkably well over the years, but in the long run cowering managers and inefficient factories weren't in either side's interest.

By the mid-1980s Bennett was coming to view company-union relations in a different light. Detroit's crisis early in that decade had convinced him that "the greatest threat to our livelihoods is an unprofitable company," as he would explain to union colleagues, adding that the UAW had to "keep the goose healthy" instead of killing the bird that laid the golden eggs of high-paying jobs. Bennett's readiness to look for common ground with the company was just what Ephlin needed. In April 1986 Ephlin appointed him head of UAW Local 1853 at Saturn, a job that would become an elective position once the new operation got up and running.

At the outset Bennett was disappointed that Saturn gave hiring preference to workers from other GM factories, whom he believed might bring old attitudes with them. But he quickly forged a close relationship with R. G. "Skip" LeFauve, the personable executive whom GM had installed as Saturn's president, and together the two men forged a brand-new environment, with joint union-management meetings on everything from parts procurement to work schedules.

While the factory was being built in Spring Hill, LeFauve and Bennett led their growing band of cohorts through team-building exercises at a nearby company obstacle course. Workers and managers had to scale a forty-foot wall while roped together and lie in each other's arms while being passed through a giant net. And they took "trust falls," flinging themselves backward off an elevated platform and into the arms of their (hopefully) supportive colleagues. Recalcitrant workers were told to take a day off to, like, come to grips with their negativity. The Age of Aquarius was meeting the automotive assembly line.

Hokey as it sometimes seemed, the new culture invigorated many workers—or "technicians," as they were called at Saturn, evoking but not copying the term *associates* at Honda. One young woman had transferred in from a GM components factory in Alabama, where her job had been to shove a bootlike contraption onto a steering mechanism; she endured shoulder pain from the minute she started until her shift ended eight hours later. Years later she would recall that Saturn was "like heaven; a nice, clean new plant," where physical work was made easier by robots and other machinery. "You felt more loyal," she would explain, "because you were really part of it all."

But the majority of General Motors employees *weren't* part of Saturn. They were reminded of that constantly by Chairman Smith, who publicly praised Saturn as the role model for the rest of the company before it had built a single car. The result was a passive-aggressive backlash against Saturn, which many GM managers came to view as the proverbial Goody Two-shoes. One GM engineer who

had joined Saturn encountered the resentment when he tried to recruit other engineers from General Motors. "People would shoot
back: 'You Saturn guys are supposed to be the experts,' " he would recall of those early years. " 'Why do *you* need *our* people?' "

And all along Chevrolet dealers resented Saturn for siphoning off
product development dollars that could have been earmarked to develop new Chevrolets. Saturn was portrayed as "a special vehicle built
in a special place by special people," a Detroit Chevy dealer griped to
BusinessWeek. "Where does that put the rest of what GM builds?"

In 1987 doubts about Saturn even surfaced within the executive
suite. GM already was saddled with unused plant capacity, Smith's
colleagues argued, so it didn't make sense to build two new Saturn assembly plants that could produce another half-million cars a year.
They convinced the chairman to scale Saturn back to a single assembly plant at the start, with the option of adding a second plant later.

One senior executive wanted to go further and pull the plug on
Saturn entirely, believing it was an expensive boondoggle. In December he even raised the issue with GM's directors, but Smith wasn't
about to lose a battle in his own boardroom. The executive was rebuffed, and soon afterward resigned.

Meanwhile the labor-management cooperation that Saturn symbolized was spawning a backlash within the UAW as well. A rump
group called New Directions began arguing that the union's leadership had gone overboard in cooperating with management and demanded a return to the traditional confrontational approach.
(Ironically, New Directions wanted the union's old direction.) The
dissidents gained public backing from the aging Victor Reuther, a
younger brother of Walter, and launched personal attacks on Don
Ephlin, coining the term *Ephlinism* as a derisive description of collab-
oration with management.

As the attacks continued, Ephlin became a prophet without honor
in his own union. In July 1989, after forty-two years with the UAW, he
would limp into retirement—a sad symbol of a new vision for the
UAW that might have avoided the disaster of twenty years later.
When Ephlin retired, the union praised him with more formality
than conviction. "The UAW thanks Brother Ephlin," it stated, "for

giving so many years to the betterment of UAW members and re-tirees." It was a bittersweet parting indeed.

A year after Ephlin's departure Roger Smith also retired, at age sixty-five, but not before fulfilling his vow to drive the first Saturn car off the assembly line. Normally, such "line-off" ceremonies are public celebrations: journalists are not only invited but encouraged to attend. But by then Smith's public image was so battered that Saturn's publicists held the drive-off ceremony in private, to avoid tainting their promising new brand with the bumbling image of their boss.

Ironically, at least in concept, much was right about Saturn: the promise of a fresh start for GM, an innovative approach to labor relations, a new brand unencumbered by the blemishes of GM's past. The trouble was, Saturn couldn't avoid being a part of GM.

To go beyond a noble experiment, and to bring change to the entire company, Saturn needed broad support from GM's management, the UAW's leadership, and GM's overall dealer body. But in each of those groups suspicion of Saturn ran high, for some reasons that were legitimate and others that weren't. Some people felt threatened, others were just jealous, and still others believed—understandably—that GM had too many factories and brands already.

In October 1990, when its first cars went on sale, Saturn landed on the cover of *Time*. "Can America Still Compete?" asked the headline, a question that the article answered with a resounding yes. Saturn "scares the liver out of" the Japanese, one automotive consultant told the magazine, while another added that "General Motors is about to kick butt." Body-part analogies were flying like welding sparks.

The Japanese indeed had been concerned about Saturn. Toyota executives believed Saturn had the opportunity to heal the wounds of GM's labor-management strife, and Honda fretted that Saturn might surprise them with some revolutionary automotive technology. But when Honda engineers bought a Saturn and disassembled it, they found that the car was surprisingly ordinary. The SL1 and its big brother, the larger and more powerful SL2, had high-revving multi-valve engines with overhead camshafts, functional interior design, and a notable absence of chrome. The dashboards, however, had overlapping plastic panels that made them look cheap, and the engines emitted a harsh noise that stemmed from inferior motor mounts.

The cars' one unique feature was their plastic-polymer doors, which were intended to protect the car from getting dinged in parking lots. But the gaps between the doors and the steel fenders were twice as wide as those on the Civic. As they pored over the Saturn's parts piece by piece, the surprised engineers kept shaking their heads and exclaiming *"Shinjirarenai"* ("Unbelievable") over and over again. And it wasn't a compliment.

There was one thing, however, that the Honda engineers couldn't see. Cars are more than just hardware. They evoke emotions, images, and feelings, and by tapping into America's long-running love for the automobile in a brand-new way, Saturn hit a home run. The advertising showed Saturn workers, their dogs, their kids, and the long white fence surrounding the factory. The themes were quite the opposite of 1950s tail fins and 1960s muscle cars: teamwork, down-home values, and the noble effort to prove that America could still compete.

"I never felt this way about any job, any car, or anything I ever built," a factory technician—that is, a worker—declared in one ad. In another ad, a technician was shown kneeling beside his Irish setter and saying: "What's happened here is something I'd like my grandchildren to know about." And one advertising line, "It's spring in Spring Hill," echoed the "Morning in America" slogan that had helped Ronald Reagan win the White House a decade earlier. That was no accident: both were produced by the same San Francisco ad agency. Saturn's tag line was "A Different Kind of Company. A Different Kind of Car."

Maybe the car wasn't all that different, but the company really was—and the message often was driven home by real employees. Saturn's management asked one man, whose burly frame and huge hands made him the central casting version of an autoworker, to speak to a dealer group in California. Though nervous and awkward, he talked about teamwork, innovation, and the Saturn cause—and the dealers rose in a standing ovation. Saturn began sending him to make promotional appearances at Disney World and professional baseball games.

Dealers were equally enthusiastic. One from Wisconsin was dismayed the first week that his store opened, when the first sixteen cars he received had a bad batch of engine coolant. But Saturn, amazingly, replaced not only the coolant but the entire car—an expensive solution, but one that endeared Saturn to the dealer and his customers alike. Saturn stores rang a bell every time a car was sold, and every time a customer drove away in a brand-new Saturn, the dealership's employees would gather around the driveway to wave and applaud. Saturn's image got a further boost on June 7, 1993, when Vice President Al Gore visited the Spring Hill factory and declared that he wanted to "Saturnize" the federal government.

Saturn was flourishing because it felt so honest, so genuine, so *different* from Detroit's bloated bureaucracies, and from the public's images of white-shoed car salesmen trying to sneak in hidden charges for, say, insurance against sun damage on odd-numbered Thursdays in Alaska. Many Saturn buyers were the very upscale types, in terms of demographics and income, who had abandoned Detroit for foreign cars but yearned to "buy American" again. In June 1994 more than forty thousand Saturn owners and their families trekked to Spring Hill for the first Saturn Homecoming. It was the sort of "cult car" gathering usually attended only by owners of 385-horsepower Corvettes and other high-octane sports cars, not by ordinary folks driving around in 85-horsepower econoboxes.

But Saturn owners loved being treated to factory tours, country-music concerts, and barbecues with the workers who actually built their cars. It was a genuine public relations coup, something General Motors hadn't had for decades. Saturn sold fewer than 75,000 cars in 1991, but by 1995 sales soared to more than 286,000. That year Saturn topped the respected J.D. Power Customer Satisfaction Survey—a distinction normally won only by high-priced luxury brands—because in the minds of most buyers, getting red-carpet treatment overcame the occasional quality glitches. Saturn's workers were awarded thousands of dollars apiece in performance bonuses.

Despite its many birthing pains, including the baggage of Roger Smith's image and the counterattacks from UAW right-wingers, Saturn was fulfilling its promise of showing the rest of GM that there was a different way, a better way, to do things. As far as the world could see, the issue was how quickly General Motors could spread

Saturn's innovations throughout the company. But there was a lot that the world couldn't see about Saturn. The qualms of key people in the company and the union had abated for a while but had never entirely gone away.

The early 1990s might have been glory years for Saturn, but they weren't for General Motors. Jack Smith, whom the GM board had installed as CEO after Bob Stempel, found that his first task was to repair the company's battered balance sheet. Smith was a decent, self-effacing man who had started his General Motors career at the Framingham factory, the same place as Don Ephlin, though Smith was keeping the books instead of building cars. Smith wasn't particularly passionate for or against Saturn, but he had neither the time nor the money for grand experiments.

GM was always cagey about whether Saturn actually made money. The answer depended on which accounting system was used: on a stand-alone basis, Saturn was profitable, but when Saturn was assessed for corporate-wide product development on top of the cost of its own engineering organization, the picture changed. When it came to developing new models or even making major enhancements of existing cars, GM, Smith decided, had other spending priorities.

So while Honda and Toyota were developing new versions of the Civic and Corolla with more powerful engines and other improvements, Saturn couldn't do the same. And when Saturn asked for funding to develop an SUV, the response was that customers could buy SUVs from Chevy instead. Maybe GM's stance made sense for a company battered by losses, but Saturn was being starved for product. It was becoming Exhibit A for GM's inability to follow through on its initiatives.

Meanwhile the costs and limitations of workplace democracy were becoming evident. Saturn had hundreds of "sourcing teams" for machinery and components, and each one had a UAW member. Suppliers were chosen by a "point system" that awarded extra points to unionized companies. So Saturn paid a higher price for its engine pistons, among other components, than it would have paid without getting the union involved.

In these decisions Mike Bennett tried to play the good-faith middleman. But like all local UAW leaders, he had to run for reelection regularly and thus couldn't afford to antagonize his constituents. When UAW team members insisted that Saturn build its own manual transmissions and polymer parts—with union labor—even though the components could have been purchased for less money from an outside supplier, Bennett agreed.

On top of that, as the procurement process was wrapping up, some UAW team members didn't want to return to the assembly line to build cars again. Such dilemmas didn't exist at the Japanese car factories in America. The Japanese worked hard to engage their hourly workers, encourage their suggestions, and foster consensus decision-making, but they made no pretense of workplace democracy. Management retained the right to run the place, period.

Saturn might well have managed its way through such awkward issues. But just as GM's commitment to Saturn was cooling, the UAW's suspicions were hardening into antagonism. In the early 1990s a new and forceful figure was gaining power in Solidarity House, the union's international headquarters on the east side of Detroit. He was Stephen P. Yokich, the child of two UAW activists who had hauled their son to his first picket line in 1937 when he was just twenty-two months old.

The anti-Ephlin in virtually every respect, Yokich was muscular and fit, thanks to regular workouts at a public gym near his home in Detroit's blue-collar suburbs. Unlike the cerebral and soft-spoken Ephlin, Yokich had a violent temper that could erupt without warning. He once shocked two visiting journalists by launching into a tirade against Detroit's Catholic cardinal, who had disciplined a priest who was friendly with Yokich. "The cardinal's a fucking prick!" Yokich screamed, his face turning bright red and veins popping out of his neck. "Just a fucking prick!"

Yokich was a proverbial union firebrand who had made his mark by leading a long, bitter 1979 strike against International Harvester, and then moved further up the UAW hierarchy. It wasn't hard to understand why a man of his nature would be suspicious of Saturn. To Yokich, the union had given up far too much in the Saturn contract for what it received in return. UAW orthodoxy put a premium on seniority rights, which the Saturn contract threatened. Tying workers' pay to corporate results would leave union members too vulnerable to bad decisions by management, in Yokich's view, and GM obviously had made plenty of those. Likewise, he believed that substituting a 401(k) profit-sharing plan for a fixed pension was a blow against the security of UAW retirees.

The major problem with the Saturn contract, in Yokich's eyes, was that it might eventually apply to the rest of General Motors—which, of course, was Saturn's original goal. "Saturnizing" might have been okay for the federal government, if that's what Al Gore wanted, but it was the last thing Steve Yokich wanted for GM. So step by step, with a canny knack for UAW politics that Don Ephlin always had lacked, Yokich began his campaign to undo Saturn.

In 1993 he dispatched one of his relatives, a staffer at union head-quarters, as a representative to UAW Local 1853 at Saturn. Bennett rightly regarded the man as a spy. Saturn's management had the fac-tory on flexible schedules that might leave union members working the day shift one week but the night shift the next. It was an efficient system that allowed three-shift days when necessary, but it was anath-ema to Saturn workers who had transferred with high seniority from other GM plants. They wanted traditional fixed-shift scheduling, in which seniority determined the choice of shifts.

Mike Bennett supported management on the flexible-shift sched-ules, but in 1994 Yokich forced a vote on the issue. Saturn workers backed Bennett in two plant elections, one in November and the other in early December 1994. But Yokich insisted on a third election later that month, and this time his political power within the union prevailed, and flexible shifts were defeated. It was a sign of Steve Yo-kich's ascendancy, and there was more to come. In mid-1995 Yokich would be elected president of the United Auto Workers. It was great for union traditionalists, but bad for Saturn—and for the new labor model that Saturn hoped to create.

The following year, after lobbying from Yokich, General Motors announced that a new Saturn midsize sedan would be built at a GM factory in Delaware instead of at Spring Hill. It was a sea change for Saturn, which had built its image on being distinct from General

Motors—"a different kind of company," where labor and management worked in harmony amid the down-home values of Spring Hill. The Delaware factory, in contrast, had the regular UAW contract, with all its work rules and job classifications. But in a hardnosed way, the Delaware decision suited both the company and the union. GM was able to utilize spare manufacturing capacity and avoid closing the Delaware plant, while Yokich and his UAW allies were able to rein in the heresies at Saturn.

Despite Detroit's overall prosperity as the new millennium neared, the hope that Saturn would spawn an era of company-union cooperation at General Motors was fading. Any illusion otherwise would meet with harsh reality in 1998, some 550 miles north of Spring Hill, in the UAW citadel of Flint.

On the night of June 4, 1998, General Motors moved some dies— giant cookie cutters used to stamp car body parts out of steel sheets—out of a metal-processing factory in Flint. Equipment moves were common, but this one was ordered because the company's manufacturing executives were fed up. Workers at the Flint facility were filling their daily production quotas (which had been negotiated between management and the union local) after working just four or five hours, then taking the rest of the day off. But they were getting paid for a full eight hours. If GM needed to schedule extra work, it had to pay them overtime.

It was the sort of utter craziness that had come to seem normal because it had gone on for years. And it was among the reasons GM's labor costs for each car were $700 higher than those of Japanese manufacturers. Determined to take a stand, GM warned the union leaders in Flint that the system had to change. When it didn't, they decided to move some of the work to other factories.

The move was a direct public challenge to the UAW and Yokich, and workers at the plant walked out the next day. Six days later, on June 11, workers at another Flint factory walked out in sympathy. Only 9,200 workers were on strike, but their impact was enormous. The two factories produced components that were critical to most of the GM assembly plants in the United States and Canada. Within a week or so those plants were shut down, idling their 175,000 workers as well as tens of thousands more workers at plants owned by other companies that produced parts for GM.

The strike's impact caused the entire industrial production of the United States to drop nearly 1 percent for the month, the sharpest monthly decrease in five years. It was like Sarajevo 1914: neither side had believed things might escalate so quickly, nor that the result would be so destructive. In Spring Hill, even Saturn workers voted to authorize a possible strike—something that would have been unthinkable just a few years before.

In late June, with the strike three weeks old, the UAW's leadership adjourned to Las Vegas for the union's triennial convention. A GM executive taunted them, in voice-mail messages to employees, for cavorting in Vegas instead of engaging in negotiations. "I mean it's nuts," Yokich told reporters in Las Vegas. "It's like a madman's in control of the company." The irony of Steve Yokich calling a GM executive a madman was rich. The union's real concern, though, was that the company seemed to have some legal leverage.

The GM-UAW contract forbade strikes during the life of the agreement, except on issues involving production standards, subcontracting, and safety. The number of grievances on those issues in the Flint factories had surged magically from just six to 259 shortly before the strike. Most of them were blatantly bogus. What followed showed how dysfunctional the GM-UAW relationship had become.

GM's lawyers suggested suing the union. But the company's timorous labor relations staff retorted that the move would be unduly antagonistic. It was as if GM's labor staffers were suffering from an industrial version of Stockholm syndrome, the strange tendency of hostages to sympathize with their captors. In mid-July, with its losses topping $1 billion, GM finally mustered the gumption to sue the UAW, citing the sudden increase in grievances as evidence that the strike violated the contract.

It was the first time GM had sued the union since the Sit-down Strike, in the same city, sixty-two years earlier. Yokich phoned GM executives and screamed, "You can't do this!" He was antagonized all right, just as GM's labor staff had predicted, but what more could he do? GM was already almost entirely shut down.

By late July fear was mounting inside Solidarity House that the union might actually lose the case—with potentially devastating consequences. If the court deemed the strike illegal and ordered the UAW to reimburse GM for its losses, the union would be bankrupted.

Then suddenly, just a day before the judge was ready to rule, GM's senior executives lost their nerve. They convinced themselves that even winning the lawsuit would be a no-win proposition, because they would have to live with embittered workers who might, conceivably, resort to sabotage after returning to their jobs. The reality was that the UAW was the devil GM knew. On July 28, after fifty-four days and $2.2 billion losses, the company and the union settled, and GM's costliest strike in twenty-eight years came to an end.

The ramifications, however, were just beginning. While the company got some concessions on work rules, the dies that had launched the war were returned to the Flint metal-stamping plant in broad daylight—cheered by UAW members in a public victory parade. GM replaced its veteran chief of labor relations with another executive who had marching orders to get along with the UAW, no matter what. The company began requiring managers to fill out an internal "score sheet," assessing the potential for planned productivity improvements in any factory to trigger another strike.

Newsweek, BusinessWeek, and *Barron's* assessed the developments and concluded, correctly, that General Motors had caved. Instead of either standing up to the union or spreading the Saturn model, wrote *Barron's,* General Motors had taken the ineffectual middle ground of "building 'lean and agile' plants too quickly to keep the union quiet and too slowly to make big annual gains in productivity." In the Flint strike, yet again, GM lacked the will to finish what it had begun.

A week after the settlement General Motors announced it would spin off its components operations, including the Flint facilities that had been ground zero in the strike, to its shareholders. They would become a new, independent company called Delphi Corporation. GM's board of directors finally had become fed up with paying inflated prices for parts from "captive" components plants whose workers had the ability, and the will, to shut the whole company down. Spinning off Delphi would give GM flexibility to buy components from other, independent suppliers. The company's show of resolve went only so far, however. GM agreed to the union's demand to guarantee the pensions of Delphi workers, in case Delphi couldn't pay them. It was a critical concession, because subsequent events would prove that GM hadn't really washed its hands of Delphi after all.

In early December Jack Smith and Rick Wagoner (who by now was the president of GM and Smith's heir apparent) held a peace parley with Yokich over dinner at the Whitney, a restaurant housed in the elegantly restored mansion of a Michigan lumber baron just north of downtown Detroit. It was part of the company's new charm offensive. Steve Yokich, however, was still on the warpath.

In the fall of 1998 a young GM executive named Mark Hogan took four senior staffers from the UAW's headquarters on a fact-finding mission to Brazil. The personable Hogan had served as president of GM Brazil before being recalled to headquarters by Wagoner to lead U.S. small-car operations. His marching orders from Wagoner were clear: Do whatever it takes to make the company's small cars profitable.

So Hogan traveled back to Brazil with the UAW staffers to look at Project Blue Macaw, which Hogan himself had launched shortly before returning to the United States. Blue Macaw achieved significant efficiencies by shifting much of the responsibility for building a car to components companies, which usually had more flexibility and lower labor costs than the automakers themselves.

The suppliers would deliver preassembled modules, as opposed to individual components, to the assembly plant, where the final work would be done at a fraction of the previous cost. Hogan wanted to adapt Blue Macaw to the United States under a new code name, Project Yellowstone, but with essentially the same concepts. The potential savings were huge: some $2,000 off the cost of building each car.

Yellowstone would be GM's third bite at the apple of small-car profitability and a new labor-management relationship. The first had been the Nummi joint venture with Toyota, which remained an isolated outpost of the GM empire, regarded in Detroit as too Toyota and not enough GM. The second was Saturn, which neither GM nor the UAW seemed willing or able to embrace. Hogan, however, figured that Yellowstone would succeed if he lined up backing from key people in the company and the union. He was energized to try a concept that was working—despite some initial glitches—in Brazil.

The trip with the union staffers went well, so when Hogan returned to the United States he paid a visit to the chairman of UAW Local 652 in Lansing, Michigan, Art Baker. Baker had run Local 652 for nearly twenty years, a rare achievement, and was an avid hunter whose trophy room had enough antlers to outfit an entire herd of deer.

Baker's top priority, possibly excluding hunting, was to secure future jobs for his local union, so when Hogan talked about building a new assembly plant near Lansing, he listened eagerly. Hogan acknowledged that the plant would need fewer workers—far fewer—than existing GM factories. But he also said GM would guarantee the jobs of all existing employees in Lansing and would manage the reductions over time through attrition and retirements instead of layoffs.

For Baker, who had proved his negotiating savvy with management over two decades, that was the clincher. "I'm optimistic," he told *Automotive News,* the industry's leading trade publication, in mid-January 1999. "I think we'll make it work."

Yellowstone, it seemed, was falling into place. The idea had passed muster with key staffers at Solidarity House and with Baker. The only disconcerting note came when reporters asked Steve Yokich about the concept. "I haven't been involved in the discussions," he replied. "If you don't know what's going on, you're concerned about a lot of things."

The comment was puzzling to Hogan, because he had kept senior union staffers informed all along. But Yokich's public statements were often calculated to enhance his negotiating position at the bargaining table, and this seemed no different. So in late April Hogan outlined the Yellowstone concept in a speech to the Society of Automotive Engineers. He also agreed to make a similar presentation for early August, at a high-profile automotive conference in Traverse City, Michigan. And then all hell broke lose.

In early May 1999 Yokich flew into a public rage, angrily telling reporters that General Motors should "put a muzzle" on Mark Hogan, or better yet just fire him outright. It wasn't entirely clear what had

provoked Yokich. But as a traditional unionist, he was inherently suspicious of any "innovations" in labor relations, and as the UAW's
president, he didn't like being upstaged by local leaders like Baker.

Hogan, for his part, was caught completely off guard. He didn't
even hear about Yokich's remarks until he got home that night and
his wife said, "So, I hear you've just been fired by the head of the
UAW."

The next day at work, Hogan was told to stop talking publicly
about Yellowstone, so he canceled the August speech. "I've got to go
dark," he told the conference's organizers. "I've got to disappear."
Just as Yokich had demanded, General Motors put a muzzle on Mark
Hogan.

The company's executives, it was clear, were afraid of Steve Yokich, the man who was eviscerating Saturn and had gone to the mat-
tresses in Flint. Less than a year after the Flint strike, they dreaded
doing anything that might offend the UAW chief. Before long Yellowstone was pronounced dead by GM, even before it got going. And in
August Wagoner summoned Hogan to his office and told him he was
being transferred to a new job.

Hogan would take charge of e-GM, a new initiative to harness the
growing power of the Internet to help the company's business. The
idea was to get him out of Yokich's crosshairs, Wagoner explained,
for his own good and that of the company. Hogan, then forty-eight,
would retain his rank of group vice president, but his career was
clearly derailed. He wasn't being formally fired, as Yokich had demanded, but was being consigned to GM's version of the witness
protection program.

By the time Hogan was exiled, more than a few unionists were hoping that somebody—*anybody*—at General Motors would stand up to
Steve Yokich. One of them was Art Baker in Lansing, who regarded
Yokich as a bully whose affinity for confrontation was hurting not
just GM but also the UAW itself.

Another was Mike Bennett at Saturn. In June 1999, at the same
time Yellowstone was coming unraveled, Bennett stepped down from
the chairmanship of the local union at Spring Hill after a bruising defeat for reelection. His opponents had strong backing from Yokich,

who added yet another scalp to his belt. Standing up to Yokich, it seemed, was career suicide, for both union leaders and company executives.

Lansing eventually did get a new GM assembly plant, but it provided only half the efficiencies that Yellowstone would have offered. As for Saturn, in 2003 the local union members would vote to scrap their special contract and return to the UAW's national agreement with GM—with its plethora of job classifications, work rules, and seniority clauses. Before long the Saturn name was taken off the Spring Hill factory, which was assigned to build Chevrolets instead of Saturns. America might have been ready for Saturn, but GM and the UAW weren't. Sadly, both sides had found Saturn too different and too alien—which was Saturn's great strength but also its unfortunate weakness.

Over a twenty-year period General Motors had launched ambitious efforts to redefine its relationship with the UAW—Nummi, Saturn, and Yellowstone—only to turn its back on all of them. The missed opportunities didn't appear to mean much at a time when SUV profits were rolling in, but would that really last forever? After the trauma of the Flint strike, GM's labor relations strategy—unstated but nonetheless clear—was the appeasement of Steve Yokich. From retirement, Mike Bennett watched it all in sadness. "I wake up at night sick," he would say, "thinking about all the things that might have been."

NINE

FROM RICHES TO RAGS

Though their internal dynamics were different, all three Detroit companies had one thing in common as the new millennium began: virtually the only vehicles on which they were making money were trucks, not cars. Gas-guzzling pickups, SUVs, and (to a lesser extent) minivans were their sole sources of profits. The reason was that their cost structures were bloated by soaring healthcare costs, gold-plated pensions, union work rules, and lavish white-collar perks. At Chrysler, for example, every retired executive got free use of two new cars, every year, for life.

It was an inherently unstable business model, though it would take a few years for the Big Three to understand that. They had ended the twentieth century on a roll, still providing nearly seven out of ten vehicles sold in America, partly because the Japanese weren't major players in trucks and SUVs. But each of the Big Three would spend the next five years struggling with fundamental issues—and at Chrysler and Ford, fierce internal politics—that threatened to snatch disaster from their unprecedented prosperity.

While the destructive warfare between GM and the UAW was grabbing headlines, the people at DaimlerChrysler were busy fighting each other, equally insanely, in the biggest German-American clash since the Battle of the Bulge. It hadn't seemed that way at first; the entire year after the transatlantic "merger of equals" was announced in May 1998 was party time, at least on the surface.

A month after the announcement ten top executives of Daimler-Benz flew to Chrysler's headquarters in Auburn Hills, Michigan, to test-drive Chrysler cars. As they drove minivans around the test track, they kept muttering about the "fipers." Their hosts thought it meant windshield wipers until they realized that the boys from Benz actually were asking about the Dodge *Viper,* Chrysler's 450-horsepower V10 sports car.

The Germans did get to drive Vipers, and each guest was given a Matchbox-toy Viper. CEO Jürgen Schrempp's special gift was a new olive-green Jeep Wrangler, not a Matchbox toy but the real thing. In return, Chrysler's Bob Eaton got a new $47,000 Mercedes CLK convertible sports car. Eaton got the better deal, but who was keeping score? They were all family now.

When the deal closed on November 17, each of the 428,000 employees of the merged company, DaimlerChrysler, got a Swatch embossed with the new corporate logo. Marching bands with cheerleaders trooped through the factories in Europe and America. Company quartermasters in Germany served American Thanksgiving fare in their cafeterias, while Chrysler returned the compliment by serving spaetzle and strudel in the United States.

In early December the first joint management meeting in Seville, Spain, was highlighted by a raucous bash. Schrempp led the executive revelers in singing "Bye, bye, Miss American Pie . . ." Well after midnight he tossed his assistant (and future wife), Lydia, over his shoulder, grabbed a bottle of champagne, and shouted "See you later, boys" before heading upstairs. At the Detroit auto show in January 1999, Chrysler set up a cabaret in a rented warehouse, where the cochairmen, Eaton and Schrempp, hosted journalists while a swing band named Squirrel Nut Zippers revved up the party.

But by then fights were breaking out behind the scenes. Not fights about product development strategy, parts-purchasing policies, factory automation, or anything like that. Instead, the first contretemps was about something really important—the size of the business cards. Standard European business cards were slightly larger than American business cards, and neither side wanted to compromise. The debates dragged on for hours in the conference rooms of Stuttgart before the Germans and Americans agreed on a compromise— DaimlerChrysler would have American-size business cards but with a European "style."

Then both sides moved on . . . to another squabble, compounded by the fact that the culture clash wasn't just krauts versus cowboys but also patricians versus plebeians. The Germans were scandalized that the Americans would desecrate their corporate logo by putting it on paper napkins and plastic cups—items that people would dirty with their mouths and then toss in the trash. After hours of arguing back and forth on that one, the two sides agreed to disagree.

It was a solution that wouldn't be used much in the months and years to come. The early fights about business cards, paper napkins, and other silly things were just a prelude to events that would destroy high-powered careers and billions of dollars of wealth and eventually send Chrysler to the brink of oblivion.

Compared to the high-level infighting at Chrysler as the turn of the century neared, General Motors was a model of management stability. Sure, the company had pushed aside executives who offended Steve Yokich, but collateral damage was part of life in the corporate big leagues. That aside, consensus and stability reigned. The unanimous choice to succeed Jack Smith as CEO was the all-American boy. G. (for George) Richard Wagoner hailed from Richmond, Virginia, where he had captained the high school basketball team and graduated third in his class before moving on to Duke University, where he also played basketball in the early 1970s.

But Wagoner—president of Delta Tau Delta, where his frat-boy nickname was "Wags"—would graduate summa cum laude and Phi Beta Kappa and head for an MBA instead of the NBA. After getting his advanced degree from the Harvard Business School in 1977, Wagoner quickly was identified within General Motors as a "high pot," GM-speak for a high-potential individual. He moved through the "T.O.," GM's New York treasurer's office, which served as the company's executive boot camp and where one of his compatriots was E. Stanley O'Neal. Both were future CEOs—Wagoner of GM, O'Neal of Merrill Lynch. Years later their paths later would cross again on the GM board.

When he became chief financial officer after GM's boardroom revolt of 1992, Wagoner, three months shy of his fortieth birthday, jumped over a slew of senior executives. His progression after that to president and chief operating officer en route to becoming CEO made Wagoner the perfect person to lead General Motors into the twenty-first century—at least on paper.

.   .   .

Some of the disputes between the Daimler-ites and the Chrysler-ites at DaimlerChrysler were more substantive, of course, than the size of the business cards or the designs on paper napkins. Daimler-Chrysler was like any blended family, where the two sets of kids had grown up with different standards on dating, curfews, and allowances. One key difference was executive pay, which was considerably richer in American corporations than it was in most German ones.

In 1997, the last year before the merger, Eaton had received $16 million in total compensation, while Schrempp got a mere $2 million. And when the two companies merged, the Americans were the biggest winners financially. Bob Eaton, who had jumped to Chrysler from GM at just the right time, was paid $70 million for his personal Chrysler holdings, while Schrempp got nothing because his company was buying instead of selling.

Much of the pay imbalance was due to Chrysler's lavish stock options and bonuses, which were typical for American companies but not significant in the pay packages of German executives. It was unrealistic to expect the imbalances in compensation to be resolved immediately. It was equally unrealistic, however, to expect that resentment wouldn't fester in the meantime.

The operating styles were different too. The key to Chrysler's success had been a philosophy that "fast is better than big," but Jürgen Schrempp believed firmly in "bigger is better." In early 1999, just a couple months after closing the deal with Chrysler, he launched negotiations to take control of ailing Nissan and thus create a tripartite automotive colossus that would span the globe. It was classic Schrempp overreach: trying to grab another prize even before he had made the Chrysler deal work. The Chrysler team, joined by some allies from the Daimler side, managed to dissuade him.

The Chrysler people were already getting annoyed by the new company's many formalities, committees, and innumerable conference calls between Germany and America. The heads of staff departments such as marketing, finance, and public relations had dual reporting lines—to an operating executive at Chrysler and to the group staff chief in Stuttgart—that slowed every decision. As 1999 unfolded, some Chrysler executives resented making one-day trips to headquarters in Stuttgart to attend meetings. They would grab an overnight flight from Detroit, shower and shave when they landed, and attend a full day of meetings, then get the late-afternoon flight home.

The Germans, for their part, were confounded by Chrysler's preoccupation with quarterly earnings reports, which weren't required in Germany. But the Americans knew that Wall Street analysts watched the quarterly reports closely and expected to be signaled in advance if their profit forecasts were out of whack. That's exactly what happened in July 1999, when DaimlerChrysler reported that its earnings for the second quarter had been flat, after most analysts had forecast a handsome increase. Chrysler's finance men had advised issuing a profit warning before the disappointing report, but the Germans had rejected the idea. DaimlerChrysler's shares dropped 9 percent that day to $77—down from a high of $107 right after the merger.

One reason for the earnings shortfall was that DaimlerChrysler wasn't getting anywhere near the $1.5 billion in first-year cost savings that Eaton and Schrempp had promised. When the Chrysler executive charged with delivering these "synergies" had the temerity to tell Eaton and Schrempp that he needed more direct authority to deliver them, he was soon dismissed.

Then Chrysler's sales chief, Jim Holden, was promoted to president, because Eaton believed his polished style would wear well with the Germans. In November 1999 Holden convened the Chrysler executive team and told them to "get back to doing what we're really good at" while putting postmerger angst behind them. Fat chance. The next shoe dropped on January 26, 2000, when Eaton announced that he himself would retire eighteen months ahead of schedule, leaving Schrempp solely in charge.

The Chrysler people weren't terribly surprised. They knew Schrempp was running the show anyway, and many were angry at Eaton, whom they viewed as either a traitor or a dupe for selling their company. Publicly, Eaton explained that he was leaving because the merger was well on the way to fruition. Privately, however, he told friends that "the biggest business mistake of my life was misjudging the character of one man," meaning Jürgen Schrempp, whom he be-latedly concluded was a power-hungry egomaniac. Bob Eaton was no traitor, but he sure had been duped.

Eaton got out just in time. In early 2000 Holden flew to Stuttgart to tell Schrempp that Chrysler's earnings for that year would be less than half the $5 billion that the premerger plan had predicted. The Germans went ballistic, and not just because they had paid nearly a 40 percent premium for Chrysler's stock compared to its premerger price. (Maybe they, instead of Eaton, had been duped.) Mercedes was a German national icon, and Schrempp had promised not only Daimler-Benz shareholders but also the entire nation that its stature would be enhanced by Chrysler. Schrempp and his team shouted that Holden should do whatever it took to make the $5 billion target.

The young executive walked out of the meeting shaken. "If this business plan was a movie it would be *Old Yeller,*" he told his Chrysler colleagues when he returned to Auburn Hills. "And I would be the dog that gets shot at the end."

A movie that debuted that very year, *The Perfect Storm,* was also ap-propriate because that's what was hitting Holden and Chrysler. The fallout soon would reach Belvidere, where by now two generations of Youngs, Fred and Gene, were working at the factory. In 1999, at age thirty-two, Gene had taken a job on the Belvidere assembly line, where having a family connection didn't hurt.

Gene's wages were more than double those in his previous job—which was more important to him, understandably, than the high-level infighting between the Germans and the Americans. When he went to buy a new SUV (a Dodge Durango) and said he worked at the Chrysler plant, his loan was instantly approved.

Nonetheless both Youngs, father and son, took notice when, shortly after the merger, Belvidere's assembly line speed was cranked up to 85 or 90 cars an hour from the previous 70. The idea was to im-prove profits, but the unfortunate side effect was to reduce quality as managers and workers scrambled to meet their new production quo-tas. Before long the PTM program that allowed workers to help de-sign their workstations was scaled back in another effort to save costs.

The PTM program would be eliminated entirely in a couple years, right around the time Fred Young retired. He decided to depart in

2001, at sixty-three. During his thirty-six years on the job, his wages had grown from $1.85 an hour to about $35 hourly. He had saved money, had a comfortable pension and generous medical benefits—and was confident that both were guaranteed by Chrysler's contract with the UAW. Times were getting tough again for Chrysler, he knew, but over the years he had seen the company swing repeatedly between crisis and prosperity. This time, Fred figured, wouldn't be any different.

The DaimlerChrysler merger's "synergies," meanwhile, continued to fall short of projections; forecasting them was one thing, but actually producing them quite another. It wasn't like the fussy engineers at Mercedes were going to start using Dodge door handles on their cars. And the Mercedes door handles were too expensive to put on Dodges.

Instead of reaping synergies, in fact, Chrysler was experiencing an alarming increase in costs. One reason: since winning Company of the Year honors from *Forbes* magazine in 1996, Chrysler's top engineering and manufacturing executives—including Bob Lutz, the guru behind Chrysler's string of product hits—had departed. Without the A-team, Chrysler had lost much of its cost-control expertise, and the new executives were preoccupied with jockeying for position in the newly merged company. In addition, customer rebates were rising to levels that the Germans couldn't comprehend.

Rebates weren't how Mercedes cars were sold. But rebates were critical in the lower end of the market where Chrysler competed, especially because the company was encountering tough new competition in both the minivan and SUV markets, which it once had dominated. Having missed the truck boom entirely during the prior decade, the Japanese were getting into the game. The new Honda Odyssey minivan had a convenient third-row seat that could be folded flat into the floor—a feature that the new Chrysler minivans to debut in the fall of 2000 conspicuously lacked.

The Germans might have been more sympathetic to Holden if the entire U.S. auto industry were hitting a slump, but in 2000 U.S. car and truck sales would hit a record 17.3 million vehicles. Honda's sales jumped 34 percent in the third quarter while GM and Ford were doing well too; only Chrysler was the outlier, with a 14 percent sales drop in the same period. On October 26 DaimlerChrysler reported its third-quarter earnings had plunged 92 percent because Chrysler had managed to lose an astounding $532 million during one of the biggest U.S. car sales booms in history.

The pressure on Jim Holden was immense, and it would multiply four days later when Schrempp acknowledged in an interview with London's *Financial Times* what everyone already knew: that the whole "merger of equals" business had been a ruse. "It had to be done for psychological reasons," Schrempp said. "If I had said Chrysler would be a division, everybody on their side would have said, 'There is no way we'll do a deal.' But it's precisely what I wanted to do."

Now Holden went ballistic, but his feelings about Schrempp's impolitic remarks, or anything else, didn't matter anymore. On Sunday, November 12, he flew from Detroit to Stuttgart for a private meeting with Schrempp, who confided that he had to take decisive action. That action, of course, would be to fire Jim Holden, which came as no surprise to the young Detroiter. In the two years since the merger—um, acquisition—Chrysler had gone through two presidents, not to mention Bob Eaton and a slew of other senior executives. By then Schrempp wasn't about to trust yet another American to run Chrysler.

He sent in a German, a Daimler veteran with a slim build and a walrus mustache named Dieter Zetsche, with orders to clean up the mess in Auburn Hills. Zetsche's number two would be a German as well. Any pretense of German-American partnership was being wiped away. This was a conquest, pure and simple, even though the vanquished had been made rich and the victors were struggling with their new prize. Journalists started calling the company "Occupied Chrysler."

Zetsche quickly closed plants and slashed production—moves that would save costs in the long run but meanwhile produced a jarring $1.3 billion loss at Chrysler for the fourth quarter of 2000. He further cleaned house in the executive suite, disposing of Chrysler veterans and luring outsiders. His new marketing chief promised to reduce Chrysler's reliance on rebates by enticing shoppers to take test drives, a strategy he termed "getting butts into seats." Well, that was appropriate. As the year came to a close, there were a lot of butts sitting in hot seats at DaimlerChrysler.

In contrast to the German-American clash within DaimlerChrysler, the infighting occurring at Ford around the same time was an old-fashioned sort of power struggle. Ever since Henry Ford II retired in 1980, ·the Ford family had wanted to restore one of its own to the helm of Ford Motor. The family's favorite was the young and well-liked William Clay Ford, Jr., a board member and nephew of Henry II who had been educated at Princeton and MIT. But in the mid-1990s Ford Motor was being led, and successfully so, by British-born Alex Trotman, a self-made man who had started in the purchasing department at a Ford factory in England before climbing the corporate ladder.

The blunt-spoken Trotman regarded the Fords as rich dilettantes ill equipped to meddle with one of the world's largest companies, even if their name was on the building. Trotman had managed Ford operations in every part of the world, while young Bill had held only midlevel management positions (e.g., managing director of Ford of Switzerland) with lofty titles but far less real responsibility. He did help run the Detroit Lions, which his father had bought in 1957—the year Bill was born—but they were pro football's perennial doormats.

Nonetheless, the Fords controlled the company with their super-voting shares that gave the family 40 percent of the votes. What's more, Bill Jr. found a formidable ally in Trotman's ambitious second in command, Jacques Nasser. Nasser, who went by "Jac" and pronounced it "Jack," was a Lebanese-born Australian whose cost-cutting prowess had earned him the nickname "Jack the Knife" within Ford.

While Bill Jr. lacked the experience to be CEO and Nasser lacked the genes to be a Ford, together they had all the right stuff. In mid-1998 the two men concluded months of private discussions by reaching an entente cordiale to share power. Once the impolitic Trotman was shown the door, they would split his titles and duties, with young Bill becoming chairman of the board and Nasser becoming president and chief executive officer.

Ford's board approved the succession plan in September 1998, even though Trotman's scheduled retirement was still fifteen months away. The quiet coup continued a tradition of executive suite ousters that had begun with the whims of Henry I and continued through the firing of Lee Iacocca by Henry II, but it caught Trotman by surprise anyway. The deposed CEO turned to the forty-one-year-old Bill Jr. and snapped in his crisp Scottish brogue: "So now you have your monarchy back, Prince William." The latest palace intrigue at Ford, however, was just getting started.

When Nasser took the helm at Ford on January 1, 1999, he took the company by storm. He immediately announced plans to shake up the hidebound culture and remake Ford as a "consumer company" instead of just a car company. He replaced executives, shuffled managers, and imported from General Electric the Six Sigma program, a sort of samurai business regimen that taught managers to attack problems with rigorous analysis.

He hired an "executive coach" for himself and brought in business professors to teach Ford's managers to think like entrepeneurs. Once, when Nasser was preparing to address a gathering of the top four hundred people at Ford, his coach fired him up beforehand with films showing speeches by Jack Welch, the legendary CEO of General Electric. Jac wanted to be like Jack, his business hero.

And he wanted Ford to be like GE or even—of all companies— Enron, whose shenanigans hadn't yet been uncovered. Enron seemingly had transformed its mundane business model by shedding fixed assets—natural gas pipelines, in its case—and becoming a trading firm. So Nasser commissioned an internal Ford study to explore selling Ford's fixed assets, the car factories, and leasing them back. Nasser wanted to reengineer Ford's structure as opposed to Ford's cars, but fortunately he was dissuaded from the factory sale maneuver.

Ford also considered dropping cars entirely and switching solely to trucks and SUVs, which was where the money was, after all. An internal bar chart of the company's profits from each region of the country showed Texas and the Southwest—America's pickup-truck capital—protruding up like a phallic symbol, because Ford's profits there were enormous compared to the other regions. Ford did keep making cars, as it turned out, but its heavy focus on trucks caused the

Taurus and other models to slip further and further behind the Japanese.

Nasser also overhauled employee performance reviews to grade managers on a curve and began one speech by saying: "I see too many white male faces out there." Predictably, a couple of class action lawsuits from passed-over white males soon followed. The silver lining was that Ford's relationship with the UAW remained relatively calm, partly because Nasser was too busy fighting his own managers to upset the union.

Amid the cultural revolution Nasser tapped Ford's $23 billion cash kitty for a corporate shopping spree. Within a month of becoming CEO he spent $6.5 billion to buy Sweden's Volvo, where amenities for workers included tanning beds and a hot tub for soaking away the aches of the assembly line. But Volvo at least was a car company. In April Nasser spent another $1.6 billion to buy Kwik-Fit, a chain of car repair shops based in England. Then he acquired a big junkyard company in Florida, which he envisioned as a base for entering the automotive-recycling business.

A year later, in May 2000, Ford spent $2.9 billion to buy Land Rover, the English maker of landed-gentry SUVs. The pace of Nasser's purchases was frenetic, just like his management style. He also removed the giant blue-oval Ford logo from the top of company headquarters and replaced it with script lettering that said *Ford Motor Company*, which he deemed more appropriate. The logo remained on virtually every Ford car worldwide, but Nasser even tinkered with that. He ordered that a little more blue tint be added to produce a darker shade, which some Ford staffers dubbed "Australian blue" in honor of the boss.

In Nasser's headlong rush to reshape Ford, the fundamentals of car quality and factory productivity were taking a backseat, though that wasn't yet apparent. His hyperactivity reflected an activist, even combative bent that Nasser had displayed since boyhood. Growing up as an ethnic outsider in 1950s Melbourne, young Jac and his brother would "be in a fight almost every day. And if we weren't, we'd . . . start to look for one," he recalled years later.

Nasser and Bill Ford were the proverbial odd couple. Jac reveled in the trappings of success and power, from his collection of expensive watches to the entourage that accompanied his travels. He was such a workaholic that on U.S. holidays he often would take a company jet to Europe to work for the day, then hop back to Dearborn for the next American workday.

Blue-blooded Bill, in contrast, tried to be one of the boys and dispensed with stuffed-shirt formality, sometimes dramatically so. A month after he and Nasser took their new posts, an incident occurred that brought out the best in his character. An explosion blasted through Ford's Rouge manufacturing complex a couple miles from Ford headquarters, killing six workers. The young scion tossed on a windbreaker and rushed to the scene to console families, then spent the night visiting hospitals to call on the wounded. It was a genuine and powerful gesture—all the more so because his ever-protective underlings had tried to dissuade him from going.

The differences between the two men became readily apparent at the company's annual shareholders' meeting in May 2000. Bill quoted the Sierra Club's description of the Excursion SUV as "a gas-guzzling monument to environmental destruction." A few minutes later Nasser took the podium to declare that Ford would keep building the vehicles anyway because "our customers love them." The two men's power-sharing marriage of convenience was soon to be tested.

Three months after that yin-yang performance, disaster struck. On August 9, Ford announced the recall of 6.5 million Firestone tires on its Explorer SUVs. The recall was big by any standard, but there were added complexities.

Ford and Firestone had a hundred-year-old relationship that was built on family as well as business ties. While Bill Jr.'s paternal great-grandfather was Henry Ford, his great-grandfather on his mother's side was Harvey Firestone—and one of Henry's closest friends. The Firestone company had passed from family hands when it was acquired by Japan's Bridgestone in 1988, but the dynastic ties to Bill's branch of the Ford family still ran deep.

Even worse, Ford's recall was prompted by government reports of forty-two deaths linked to Explorer rollovers. The treads of the tires had suddenly ripped off while the SUV was traveling at highway speeds. To reassure the public, Ford decided to run television commercials in which Nasser would address the issue head-on. In the first one, which aired during a preseason NFL football game, Nasser offered his "personal guarantee that no one at Ford will rest" until the problem was solved.

The CEO's stiff manner and thick Australian accent made him seem "a cross between Al Gore and Crocodile Dundee," *Fortune* declared, referring to the Democratic candidate for president that year and the Australian hero of the popular film. There was no doubt, though, that Nasser was sincere. He ordered three Ford factories shut down, at huge cost, so their tire stockpiles could be used for the recall. Nor did Nasser flinch at testifying at congressional hearings on the recall. A high-powered Washington consultant prepped him, counseling that the congressmen would be convivial over coffee before the hearings began but would snarl like attack dogs when the cameras started rolling.

That's exactly what happened, and Nasser fought back—not just at the congressmen but especially at Firestone, which he painted as desperate to save its corporate hide instead of protecting the public. "We virtually pried the claims data from Firestone's hands and analyzed it," Nasser testified during a grueling seven and a half hours of hearings on September 6.

Firestone fired back that Ford had recommended a low tire-inflation pressure that, while providing a comfortable ride, caused undue heat buildup that shredded the tires in hot weather. Indeed, most of the Explorer accidents had occurred in southern states or in hot-climate countries such as Venezuela and Saudi Arabia.

The mutual finger-pointing confused the car-buying public and annoyed the congressmen. "It's like tying two cats by the tails and throwing them over the clothesline and letting them claw each other," snapped Senator Fritz Hollings. By mid-September reports of deaths linked to the accidents had more than doubled, to 101. Surveys showed that both Ford and Firestone were suffering big black eyes in public opinion.

Nonetheless, Bill Ford publicly stood by his CEO. At an employee meeting in September, Bill said that "nobody could have done a better job than Jac Nasser" in addressing the crisis, and led four hundred employees in a standing ovation for their boss. In fact, Nasser had

The man and the car that changed the world: Henry Ford and his Model T, in 1919. The Model T's modest price and durability made it the first "people's car." Ford used the car to pioneer the moving assembly line, mass production, and the five-dollar day, all of which revolutionized American society. (FORD MOTOR ARCHIVES)

The twentieth century's premier corporate manager, GM chairman and CEO Alfred P. Sloan, Jr. (left), shown with his predecessor and chief sponsor, GM board member Pierre S. DuPont, in 1933. Sloan devised a brand hierarchy that allowed GM to surpass Ford as America's largest car company. (ASSOCIATED PRESS)

Ford Thunderbird, 1955. The original Thunderbird was a two-seater that seemed destined for head-to-head battle with the Chevrolet Corvette, but Ford added a rear seat to the 1958 model to broaden the car's appeal. It worked, but at the expense of abandoning the American sports-car market to Chevy. (FORD MOTOR ARCHIVES)

Edsel Citation, 1958. There were four Edsel models in all, including the top-of-the-line Citation. All four shared an ungainly design with a large, oval-shaped front grille that helped make the Edsel the most celebrated new-car flop ever. (FORD MOTOR ARCHIVES)

GM's 1959 Cadillac Eldorado, which sported the largest tail fins ever. Note the red tail light, two of which were mounted on each fin, and were nicknamed "gonads." After 1959 tail fins were gradually downsized, disappearing for good in 1964. (GENERAL MOTORS ARCHIVES)

1960 Chevrolet Corvair. This GM publicity photo shows five different views of the car, including two with an elegantly dressed model. The Corvair's rear-mounted engine put extra weight in the back of the car—a design harshly criticized by Ralph Nader in his 1965 book *Unsafe at Any Speed*. (GENERAL MOTORS ARCHIVES)

GM's 1964 Pontiac GTO, which launched the "muscle car" era of oversized engines in relatively small cars. Muscle cars began to fade in 1970, thanks to environmental regulations, rising gas prices, and changing social mores. (GENERAL MOTORS ARCHIVES)

Ford Mustang convertible, 1965. The car captured the youth culture of the 1960s and caught GM off guard, but Ford remained well behind GM in overall sales. (FORD MOTOR ARCHIVES)

UAW president Walter Reuther testifying before Congress in 1966. Reuther won the union's presidency in 1946 and provided the social vision combined with hard-nosed political leadership that led the UAW to win increasingly generous contracts from Detroit's Big Three. He died in a plane crash in 1970, just before the Japanese invasion of the U.S. car market accelerated. (ASSOCIATED PRESS)

Henry Ford II. The grandson of Ford Motor's founder took control of the ailing family empire in 1945, brought in a new professional management team, and called the shots at Ford Motor for the next forty years. This photo was taken in late 1969 or early 1970. (FORD MOTOR ARCHIVES)

The first Jeep Cherokee sport-utility vehicle, made in 1974, looks clunky and ungainly, which it was. But a decade later a streamlined version with four doors began to increase the Cherokee's popularity. By 1990, America was developing a love affair with the SUV. (CHRYSLER ARCHIVES)

UAW president Leonard Woodcock at a press conference in 1976. Woodcock succeeded Reuther in 1970 and four months later led a landmark sixty-seven-day strike against GM that won unionists the right to retire with full benefits after thirty years on the job, which would come to haunt the Big Three and the UAW. (ASSOCIATED PRESS)

The car that proved Honda's engineering prowess, the 1975 Civic CVCC. The letters stood for "Controlled Vortex Compound Combustion," an engine design that allowed the car to meet strict U.S. air-quality standards without a catalytic converter device. (HONDA MOTOR ARCHIVES)

Honda founder Soichiro Honda and colleagues inspect plans for the company's first U.S. factory, a motorcycle plant in Ohio, in 1977. (HONDA MOTOR ARCHIVES)

Shige Yoshida, the executive who decided to put Honda's first U.S. factories in Ohio, and hired the company's early employees there. His careful screening of applicants for diligence and a strong work ethic was critical to Honda's success in the United States. (HONDA MOTOR ARCHIVES)

FIRST U.S.A. PRODUCTION!
OUR PRODUCT WITH PRIDE
WE SHIP QUALITY
TO CUSTOMERS WORLD WIDE
SEPT 10, 1979
HONDA of AMERICA MFG., INC.

RESTRICTED AREA
AUTHORIZED PERSONNEL ONLY

A Honda executive rides the company's first U.S.-built motorcycle off the assembly line in Marysville, Ohio, 1979. (HONDA MOTOR ARCHIVES)

Ohio governor James Rhodes and Honda president Kiyoshi Kawashima break ground for the company's automobile assembly plant in Marysville, in 1980. Rhodes avidly pursued Honda, a decision that since has brought tens of thousands of jobs to Ohio. (HONDA MOTOR ARCHIVES)

Consumer activist Ralph Nader and UAW president Douglas Fraser at a press conference in 1981. Nader's 1965 book *Unsafe at Any Speed* exposed safety flaws in the Chevrolet Corvair, giving GM an enormous black eye. Fraser led the UAW during the deep recession of the early 1980s, and agreed to painful contract concessions that helped Detroit's Big Three survive that crisis. (ASSOCIATED PRESS)

Lee Iacocca introduces Chrysler's first minivan in late 1983. Iacocca led Chrysler from near oblivion to record prosperity—appearing in television commercials and writing an autobiography that made him an international celebrity. The minivan was a new type of family vehicle that took America by storm. (CHRYSLER ARCHIVES)

GM chairman and CEO Roger Smith poses in front of one of the company's cars shortly before his retirement in July 1990. Smith led GM for a decade, during which its market share began a thirty-year descent that eventually helped put the company into bankruptcy. (ASSOCIATED PRESS)

The first Saturn sedan, the 1991 SLI. Roger Smith viewed Saturn as the key to modernizing GM. Despite the initial popularity of the brand, opposition from within GM and the UAW eventually doomed Saturn and its cooperative labor-relations model. (GENERAL MOTORS ARCHIVES)

Chrysler's Bob Lutz drove a new Jeep Grand Cherokee through a window, rigged with tiny explosives set to go off at the right moment, at the 1992 Detroit Auto Show. Lutz's drive generated wide publicity and launched an era of ever-more-elaborate publicity stunts that captured the over-the-top spirit of America's fifteen-year SUV boom.
(CHRYSLER ARCHIVES)

Ford Excursion SUV, 2000. This was the largest SUV ever, and symbolized the Detroit companies' reliance on SUVs and trucks as their sole source of profits. The strategy backfired badly when gas prices began to soar in late 2005—the Excursion's last year of production. (FORD MOTOR ARCHIVES)

Ford CEO Jacques Nasser in June 2001, being sworn in for his congressional testimony on the recall of Firestone tires on Ford Explorers. Dozens of deaths were attributed to the defect, and Nasser publicly squabbled with Firestone executives over who was to blame. During Nasser's three years as CEO, the company's performance plunged in almost every respect. (ASSOCIATED PRESS)

Opposite: UAW president Steve Yokich at an informal press conference in 1998. The firebrand Yokich had just led a bitter strike against GM in Flint, Michigan, that cost the company more than $2 billion. An unstinting opponent of cooperation with management, Yokich also led opposition to the innovative labor-relations methods at Saturn. (ASSOCIATED PRESS)

Gene Benner in front of Bessey Motors, his Chrysler-Jeep-Dodge dealership in South Paris, Maine. The quintessential small-town car dealer and all-American success story, Benner took tough action to restore his business to profitability during 2008, enabling him to survive Chrysler's culling of its dealer ranks in 2009. (BESSEY MOTORS)

Fred Young, retired auto worker in Belvidere, Illinois. Young started at Chrysler's Belvidere factory in 1965, shortly after it opened, and worked there until 2001. During Chrysler's crisis of 2008 and 2009, Young worried that he might lose his pension. The pension remained intact, but his medical benefits were reduced. (GENE YOUNG)

Gene Young, Fred's son, shown aligning headlight beams in the Belvidere plant in 2007. Gene started at the factory in 1999 and worked there ten years—bouncing back and forth between the assembly line and the Jobs Banks, thanks in part to periodic "inverse layoffs." (GENE YOUNG)

The hefty 2006 Chrysler 300C sedan, which helped revive Chrysler's fortunes under Daimler, but only briefly. When gas prices soared after Hurricane Katrina, sales of the 300C—along with those of Chrysler's SUVs—plunged. Chrysler returned to red ink and Daimler sold the company in 2007. (CHRYSLER ARCHIVES)

Ford CEO Alan Mulally and chairman Bill Ford, Jr. In late 2006, with Ford in crisis, Bill Jr. stepped aside as CEO, and Ford brought in Mulally. It was the first of several critical steps that enabled Ford to emerge as the only American car company to avoid bankruptcy. (FORD MOTOR ARCHIVES)

Left to right: GM's Rick Wagoner, Chrysler's Bob Nardelli, Ford's Alan Mulally, and the UAW's Ron Gettelfinger appear before the House Financial Services Committee on November 19, 2008, to request emergency financial aid. When ABC News reported that the three CEOs had flown into Washington on their corporate jets to beg for a bailout, the result was a PR fiasco for Detroit. (ASSOCIATED PRESS)

SUVs parked around the altar during a prayer service for government assistance for Detroit's car companies on December 7, 2008, at the city's Greater Grace Temple. The SUVs were all gas-electric hybrids—a Ford Escape, a Chevrolet Tahoe, and a Dodge Aspen.
(CHARLES V. TINES, *THE DETROIT NEWS*)

Steven Rattner, chief of President Obama's Automotive Task Force. Rattner delivered the bad news to GM's Rick Wagoner that the Obama administration wanted him to resign. Rattner and his colleagues also developed the bailout plan that required GM and Chrysler to declare bankruptcy. (STEVE RATTNER)

UAW president Ron Gettelfinger at a press conference in May 2009. He abandoned UAW orthodoxy to make healthcare concessions to the Detroit car companies in 2007—but the move was too little and too late to allow GM and Chrysler to avoid bankruptcy. (ASSOCIATED PRESS)

Ron Bloom, who along with Rattner led Obama's Automotive Task Force, and crafted the deal that gave Italy's Fiat operational control of Chrysler. His work with the United Steelworkers union gave Bloom credibility with the UAW, but he pushed the union hard to make concessions in the bailout. (ASSOCIATED PRESS)

Harry Wilson, a senior member of the Automotive Task Force who took the lead in developing GM's post-bankruptcy restructuring plan. (HARRY WILSON)

Sergio Marchionne, CEO of Fiat—and now of Chrysler, too. Because Fiat was Chrysler's only suitor, Marchionne drove a hard bargain that allowed Fiat to take control of the company without putting in any cash. (CHRYSLER ARCHIVES)

GM's new CEO, Frederick "Fritz" Henderson, speaks to reporters after departing federal bankruptcy court in lower Manhattan on June 1, 2009, the day GM's became the second largest bankruptcy filing in U.S. history. (ASSOCIATED PRESS)

President Obama, in a pensive pose, as he passes a portrait of George H. W. Bush on June 1, 2009, just prior to addressing the nation about the bankruptcy of GM. Bush's son, George W. Bush, stood at the opposite end of the ideological spectrum from Obama, but both men committed billions of taxpayer dollars to keep GM and Chrysler afloat. (ASSOCIATED PRESS)

President Obama, flanked by members of his cabinet, addresses the nation on June 1, 2009, just hours after General Motors filed for bankruptcy. The federal government ultimately committed more than $100 billion to bail out the American auto industry. (ASSOCIATED PRESS)

been unduly combative against Firestone, but that was his style on almost everything.

In November, however, the daily Ford-Firestone headlines were eclipsed by a far bigger story: the constitutional crisis of a razor-thin presidential election that would be decided by the Supreme Court. The controversy was receding, the tire recall was progressing, and in early 2001 Ford would introduce a brand-new version of the Explorer that would be lower-to-the-ground and less prone to roll over. Ford Motor and Jac Nasser seemed to have weathered the storm.

But they hadn't. While the Ford-Firestone dispute faded from public view in the early months of 2001, the fight over who was at fault continued behind the scenes. On May 21 and 22 both companies went nuclear.

The first to strike was Firestone, which announced that, after a century of supplying Ford, it would no longer sell tires to the company. The next day Ford announced it was recalling another 13 million Firestone tires because it could no longer vouch for their safety, a claim that Firestone labeled outrageous. The move, the biggest recall in automotive history, would cost Ford $3 billion.

Both companies launched new salvos of public accusations at each other. Bill Ford appeared with Nasser at a company press conference and declared, "This decision is a painful one for me personally," alluding to his dual family heritage. Ford versus Firestone was becoming Detroit's version of the Iran-Iraq War. But bad as it was, the crisis was just one of many problems festering inside Ford Motor.

Running a car company, like running a restaurant, requires constant attention to detail and at least reasonable management stability. But Ford had neither. While Nasser was shaking up everyone and everything at Ford, executive turnover was soaring. The company began losing its grip on the basics of its business.

Two days after Ford announced the new tire recall, the respected J.D. Power Initial Quality Survey reported that Ford had dropped to dead last among major automakers. The quality woes were widespread. Ford Focus, the company's new subcompact car, was recalled six times during its first year on the market. The Escape, a downsized SUV, had five recalls in its first nine months. Even the new Explorer had suffered an embarrassing recall to repair tires (not Firestones) that had been accidentally slashed on the assembly line at Ford's factory in Louisville.

What's more, Ford's productivity, like its quality ratings, was heading south in a hurry. The annual *Harbour Report,* the auto industry's bible for measuring factory efficiency, found Ford's productivity had dropped 7 percent in 2000, while GM's had increased 8 percent. Employee morale at Ford was so bad that insiders joked, "Jack Welch has 10 guys around him who would take a bullet for him. Jac Nasser has 10 guys around him who'd like to put a bullet in him."

The turmoil took a toll on Ford's bottom line. The auto industry has high fixed costs for factories, machinery, employees, and dozens of other items. It's critical to keep the factories running at full speed and costs under control, but Ford was losing ground on both fronts. Nasser's revolving-door executive suite was incapable of spotting the situation in time, much less addressing it effectively. The company followed Chrysler into red ink, losing $752 million in the second quarter of 2001, when General Motors *earned* $477 million.

After that Ford announced it was restructuring its executive suite (again) to form a new Office of the CEO that would include both Bill Ford and Jac Nasser. "This new structure will allow both me and Jac to work hand in hand to lead the company," Bill Ford stated in a press release. It was a polite way of saying he was trying to keep a tighter rein on Nasser.

As the summer of 2001 gave way to fall, speculation began that Nasser was on his way out. Both men denied it and insisted that, in fact, they had "a very easy relationship," as Bill put it. But the drumbeat of bad news from Ford continued. On September 11, America suffered the shocking terrorist attacks on the World Trade Center and the Pentagon. In response, Ford cut car production and slashed its quarterly cash dividend 50 percent because it expected the economy to nose-dive. The 9/11 attacks weren't Nasser's fault, of course, but many of Ford's wounds were self-inflicted. In October the company posted a third-quarter loss of $692 million—its first back-to-back quarterly losses in a decade.

For months, quietly and discreetly, Bill Ford had been consulting with the board of directors and with members of his extended family to drum up support for ousting Nasser. In September Ford's board approved a rich severance package for the CEO, just in case. That had to be disconcerting to Nasser, but he marched blithely onward.

In October he tried to recruit Jim Holden, sitting on the sidelines since being bounced from DaimlerChrysler nearly a year earlier, to join Ford as head of sales operations. Wary about executive suite infighting from his DaimlerChrysler days, Holden asked to meet with some Ford directors to get their assurances that Nasser's job was safe. Nasser agreed to arrange it, but things never got that far.

On Tuesday, October 30, the ax fell. Ford fired the fifty-three-year-old Nasser and ended his meteoric career with the company, making him the latest example of the hubris that had plagued Detroit for decades. He had been CEO for less than three years, during which time Ford had descended from record profits to widespread disarray with stunning speed. When forty-four-year-old Bill Jr. walked into the company auditorium to be introduced as the chairman *and* CEO of the company his great-grandfather had founded, an overflow crowd of employees desperate for a new beginning greeted him with a standing ovation. "Gee, it's like the Lions won a game," the new CEO quipped with endearing self-deprecation. Now Prince William really did have his monarchy back. But this wasn't to be a happily-ever-after fairy tale.

When Rick Wagoner was named CEO-designate of GM on February 2, 2000 (the actual transition wouldn't occur until June 1), he was a couple weeks shy of his forty-seventh birthday and thus potentially positioned to run General Motors for nearly twenty years. When reporters asked him about that, Wagoner brushed off their questions with easygoing modesty. "The question shouldn't be about me keeping the job for such a long time," he laughed, but about "whether I can perform in a way to keep the job a long time." The self-effacing response would prove more appropriate than Wagoner, or anybody else, could have realized.

One of his first goals was to expand GM's international operations, where he had a potential game-changing move in the works. On the weekend of March 11–12 he and GM's departing CEO, Jack Smith, flew to Milan to negotiate with Italy's Fiat, whose small diesel engines were popular in European cars and needed by GM Europe. Fiat Automobile was financially troubled, but it was also the center-piece of a sprawling Italian conglomerate controlled by the Agnelli family, and it was the pride and joy of the family's aging patriarch, Gianni Agnelli.

The GM executives knew this well as they settled into the Four Seasons Hotel Milano, a converted medieval convent, for talks with Paolo Fresco, Fiat's chairman. Fresco was a veteran deal-maker from his decades at General Electric, where he had risen to become Jack Welch's second in command before Agnelli recruited him to help fix Fiat. Like Wagoner himself, Fresco was tall and outwardly relaxed; the two had developed such a close rapport that Fresco's Fiat under-lings called him "Rick's older brother." But like any good negotiator, Fresco knew he needed alternatives—or at least he needed to make the other guy *believe* he had alternatives. Not by chance, the apparent alternative was camped out in another suite in the Four Seasons in the person of Jürgen Schrempp.

One might think that the troubles at Chrysler would have sup-pressed Schrempp's appetite for acquisitions, but lions never get tired of wildebeest. Schrempp offered to buy Fiat Automobile outright for 13 billion euros, an incredibly generous price for a company that was a money-losing mess. The problem, however, was that selling Fiat to the Germans would offend the pride not just of Gianni Agnelli but of the entire Italian nation.

Schrempp didn't know it, but that weekend his role in this opera was to play the foil for Fresco, who engaged in corporate shuttle diplomacy by bouncing between the German and American suites in the Four Seasons. The wiley GE veteran emerged with the perfect deal, at least from the Fiat perspective.

General Motors would acquire 20 percent of Fiat Automobile by paying Fiat $2.5 billion in GM stock—enough to make Fiat the largest single shareholder in GM (albeit with only 5 percent of the shares). The transaction would give GM access to Fiat's diesel engine technol-ogy, saving GM the huge cost of developing new diesels on its own. Fiat also got a highly unusual "put" option on its stock that would allow the Italians to *force* General Motors to buy the remaining 80 percent of Fiat Automobile anytime between 2004 and 2009. The price would be determined by a formula, but Fiat would remain free to find another buyer (well, sucker) who might pay more.

Wagoner balked at the "put" provision, but Fresco insisted it was a sine qua non. He figured that Fiat Automobile would have to be sold at some point, and that allowing the Italians to control the timing and the process would salvage the pride of the Agnellis and the nation. Around midnight on Sunday, when the deal finally was struck, Wagoner, Fresco, and their colleagues popped open a bottle of champagne and phoned Gianni Agnelli, who was celebrating his seventy-ninth birthday.

The guy who should have been celebrating was the jilted Jürgen Schrempp. For the apparent winner, General Motors, the Fiat deal would be a bridge to nowhere. A few years hence the deal would unravel in a way that would help Fiat mount a remarkable turnaround. And before the decade was out, after the Germans had retreated to lick their wounds, the Italian company would mount its own takeover of Chrysler. Indeed, irony would be piled atop irony as a result of the Milan Four Seasons negotiations in March 2000, in ways that nobody did or even dared predict.

Wagoner, meanwhile, returned to Italy in triumph that June oblivious to the woes his "victory" eventually would create for GM. In the lake district town of Brescia he hosted financial analysts and journalists for three days of briefings on the future of General Motors. The young CEO presented the Fiat deal as the centerpiece of a new strategy of global alliances with foreign car companies. Wagoner was the personification of openness, striding through the group during question-and-answer sessions with a wireless mike and declaring, "Our position around the globe is enviable."

In December, back in Detroit, Wagoner made another big move: the stunning announcement that GM would close its 103-year-old Oldsmobile division, one of the original building blocks of the company. The move was long overdue because Olds sales had plunged nearly 75 percent in the preceding fifteen years, but GM watchers were impressed, and rightfully so. Wagoner was tackling Oldsmobile's decline head-on instead of just ducking it, as GM had done for years.

He soon pulled off a surprise coup by reaching outside GM to hire

John Devine, the former chief financial officer of Ford, as GM's new CFO. The move shocked GM's finance staff veterans, who regarded themselves as the company's elite, but it delighted Wall Street, where respect for Devine was high. Even more dramatic, in August 2001 Wagoner lured sixty-nine-year-old Bob Lutz, whose vehicles had so dramatically revived Chrysler in the mid-1990s, to become GM's product czar.

After the 9/11 terrorist attacks, Wagoner made yet another daring move with ramifications far beyond the auto industry. While Ford was cutting production in anticipation of a sales slump, Wagoner acted to spur car sales by offering interest-free financing on every car and truck in GM's lineup. The program, called "Keep America Rolling," sent Americans pouring into GM showrooms to buy cars, thus keeping GM's factories running and keeping money flowing to parts suppliers, dealerships, ad agencies, and virtually every corner of the economy.

The gambit proved successful and made Wagoner a symbol of America's determination not to shrink in the face of adversity. GM executives began sporting lapel buttons that read "29," symbolizing their determination to keep 29 percent of the U.S. car market. All the moves reflected a corporate self-improvement program that Wagoner called "Go Fast," to speed up decision making at the notoriously sluggish company. And in the eyes of the business press, it seemed to be working.

A *Forbes* headline declared "Time to Praise GM." *Fortune* wrote that despite being slow to launch new trucks, GM was scoring big with the Chevy Avalanche, which converted from a pickup to an SUV like an adult Transformer toy, and the Cadillac Escalade EXT (as in Extreme), a $50,000 SUV on steroids that attracted professional athletes just as, well, real steroids were doing. "Expected to operate as a play-it-safe leader," *Fortune* stated, "Wagoner instead is making GM move faster and do better."

The praise seemed eminently justified. But one can always tell skill from luck by its duration. And behind the scenes, developments were occurring that would undermine the duration of GM's apparent gains.

.   .   .

In mid-2001 an internal "deep dive" analysis at GM concluded the company had far too many U.S. brands, too many dealers, too many factories, and too many workers, all of which added huge layers of unnecessary costs. The report recommended taking action, while times were good, to cut the excess baggage in every one of those categories. But when the recommendations were presented to Wagoner, he waved them off.

The decision to close Oldsmobile was proving unexpectedly difficult for GM, because America's car dealers command considerable political clout. There are dealers in virtually every state legislative district in the country, and they contribute generously to candidates from both parties. Over the years the dealers had parlayed their power to get stringent state franchise protection laws. Any car company that wanted to drop a brand had to compensate dealers, who had considerable leverage in negotiating a settlement because of the franchise laws.

As a consequence, the cost of killing Oldsmobile was running past $1 billion. The stories of aggrieved dealers were hitting Wagoner emotionally, because of Oldsmobile's long heritage at GM. The result: the pain of closing Oldsmobile doused discussion of eliminating more GM brands, just as the 1998 Flint strike had made talk of confronting the UAW strictly off-limits. Wagoner's "Go Fast" was becoming, in effect, "Don't Rock the Boat."

After only a year as CEO, Wagoner was moving to a more deliberate and cautious approach to solving GM's fundamental structural problems. Instead of broaching sensitive issues with the UAW, GM would use attrition and retirements to trim its hourly workforce over several years. And instead of closing more brands outright, GM would slowly consolidate three of them—Pontiac, Buick, and GMC truck—into a multibrand franchise that dealers would sell under one roof.

It seemed a play-it-safe strategy designed to minimize the threat of strikes by angry unionists and lawsuits by aggrieved dealers. But by rejecting decisive action, Wagoner was betting that GM could rely on steadily growing profits to meet its cash-flow obligations for years. And to produce the profits, he placed some risky bets—one of which had nothing to do with cars.

Between 2002 and 2006 America was enjoying the greatest housing boom in history. GM's financial arm, GMAC, was betting big on what looked like a golden opportunity: augmenting its core business of financing GM dealers and car buyers by expanding its lending for home mortgages. The strategy was producing spectacular financial results.

In 2002 GMAC proposed moving into commercial lending as well. In the boardroom discussion, one director objected, saying that further growth in mortgage lending would be a better bet, because at least GMAC had expertise there. The director was Stan O'Neal of Merrill Lynch, who a few years later would approve Merrill's own entry into the mortgage business. Before the decade was out, mortgages would blow up on both Merrill and GMAC, and on many other financial firms. O'Neal would be axed, and Merrill Lynch, a company as symbolic of America as General Motors itself, would be sold.

Meanwhile, Wagoner's second big bet was that profits from gas-hungry SUVs and pickup trucks would continue. That bet assumed that gasoline would stay priced where it was in 2003 and 2004—around $1 a gallon, even less in some states. Wagoner's *mañana* strategy, in effect, was a big bet on continued cheap oil.

By coincidence, in June 2004, *National Geographic* magazine carried a cover story titled "The End of Cheap Oil." One GM executive showed the story to Wagoner and suggested GM might be relying too heavily on trucks and SUVs. Wagoner retorted that the same faulty thinking had made GM the last company in Detroit to cash in big on the truck boom, and he wasn't about to repeat that mistake. As usual, GM was slow to sense where the market was heading. Wagoner wasn't about to hedge his bet on gas prices staying low.

In the fall of 2003, meanwhile, Chrysler's "butts in seats" marketing strategy gave way to a new sign of desperation: locker-room humor. One television commercial for the new and longer Dodge Durango SUV showed two men using side-by-side urinals and talking about their, um, vehicles.

"It's seven inches longer; my girlfriend loves it," said one man to his friend. "You should drop by tomorrow; I'm going to wax it." Another commercial showed a woman in sexy lingerie discovering that she had a Dodge Ram tattoo on her cheek. Yeah, that cheek. The commercials grabbed more attention than Chrysler's cars. The first new vehicle launched since the merger, an SUV crossover called the Chrysler Pacifica, was proving to be an overweight and underpowered flop.

Chrysler lost nearly $550 million in 2003, causing overall earnings for DaimlerChrysler to plunge 91 percent. In April 2004 Jürgen Schrempp sounded a brave note at the company's annual meeting in Stuttgart. "When the going gets tough," he told his restive shareholders, "running away or changing a winning strategy isn't the right course of action." Germany had its own particular brand of executive hubris.

By the summer of 2004, however, Schrempp's perseverance appeared to pay off. Dieter Zetsche, after parachuting into Auburn Hills three and a half years earlier, had slashed costs, sacked veteran Chrysler executives, and revamped the entire product plan. Dodge belatedly launched a new minivan with a fold-flat third-row seat, just like the Honda Odyssey, but the surprise hit was the new Chrysler 300C. It was a rear-wheel-drive sedan, with a mawlike front grille, that could be bought with a special engine: a 340-horsepower V8 Hemi (the term referred to the hemispherical cylinder heads).

Car and Driver and the other automotive-enthusiast magazines lavished praise on the 300C, even though it got only fifteen miles a gallon—not much more than some of Chrysler's SUVs. Zetsche, like Wagoner, was doubling down his bet that cheap gas would continue, but at least ailing Chrysler finally had a hit on its hands. In September 2004 the 300C alone outsold every Cadillac model combined.

In Maine, Gene Benner finally started to think that "things were getting on the right track" at DaimlerChrysler, as he put it. Like other dealers, his major interest was in getting a steady stream of good products to sell, and the disarray of the merger's early years had been a big disappointment. But his dealership had held its head above water. And if the 300C was a portent of more new cars to come, Benner thought, maybe the merger's early promise finally would be fulfilled.

After billions in losses between 2001 and 2003, Chrysler was starting to make money again. Its earnings jumped 48 percent in the third quarter of 2004 and more than doubled in the fourth. That should have made Schrempp a happy man. But Chrysler's revival was relative; the American subsidiary still was producing less than one-third of the annual profits that Daimler had projected before the merger.

Worse yet, just as Chrysler was showing signs of life, the flagship Mercedes division took a tumble. In 2003 and 2004 *Consumer Reports* removed all Mercedes-Benz models from its recommended list because of quality glitches. Earnings at the Mercedes division tanked too, partly because management was fixated on fixing Chrysler. The press began asking whether Schrempp, whose contract lasted until 2008, might be fired and replaced by Zetsche.

In Dearborn, at the same time, Bill Ford was learning that it isn't always good to be king. Ford Motor regained profitability in 2003, albeit barely. Late that year Standard & Poor's downgraded Ford's debt to triple-B-minus, just one notch above junk-bond status. The CEO sent an e-mail to employees, saying the move "does not accurately reflect the state of our business." His message seemed to be borne out when the company earned $3.5 billion in 2004, but that was still less than half of what Ford had earned in 1999. Ford wasn't making much money for a company of its size, and it was spending nearly $3,700 on buyer discounts for every vehicle it sold.

Hefty as it was, that amount actually looked good compared to General Motors, where rebates and discounts were averaging a staggering $4,500 on every car and truck. The company was continuing to lose market share despite the best efforts of Bob Lutz, who was finding it difficult to focus his efforts and resources in a company that, even after killing Oldsmobile, now had eight brands: Chevrolet, Pontiac, Buick, Cadillac, GMC, Saturn, Saab, and the latest addition, Hummer. The new Pontiac GTO, a reborn version of the iconic 1960s muscle car, wrapped a hot engine inside a body that resembled an insurance adjuster's fleet car. The decision to stick with plain-vanilla styling was a classic GM cost-cutting move, but it backfired when the car flopped.

Reducing rebates was simply out of the question, however, because it would mean selling fewer cars, and General Motors needed every sale it could get. By 2003 the company had more than 460,000 retirees and spouses, who outnumbered active employees by nearly three to one. All were collecting pension and healthcare benefits, and UAW members—active workers and retirees alike—still didn't have to pay annoying deductibles or co-payments for doctor visits.

General Motors had to keep the factories running just to pay for this crushing burden. But the company wasn't yet desperate enough to seek better terms from the union, even though the ever-combative Yokich had retired. He had been succeeded, in 2002, by fifty-eight-year-old Ron Gettelfinger, a short, wiry man with a modest mustache who didn't drink, had quit smoking, and only rarely cursed—qualities befitting the younger brother of the Most Reverend Gerald Gettelfinger, the Roman Catholic bishop of Evansville, Indiana.

Ron Gettelfinger had started at Ford's factory in Louisville, Kentucky, in 1964, earned a degree from Indiana University while working, and climbed through the union's ranks. No gregarious glad-hander, Gettelfinger owed his ascent to mastering the details of contracts and the art of negotiation. After becoming UAW president, he banned the regular Friday afternoon golf outings between union officials and their management counterparts because the coziness offended his sense of propriety. "I don't like saber rattling," he once told *The New York Times,* "but if people think that cooperation means capitulation, they'll be in for a surprise." In his own way, Gettelfinger was wedded to UAW dogma.

Facing this landscape, in 2003 GM launched a massive sale of thirty-year bonds to fund its retiree obligations by spreading out the repayment period. It was much like a homeowner refinancing mounting credit card debt with a new thirty-year mortgage. GM put a rich yield on the bonds, and investors proved so eager to buy them that GM sold $17.6 billion worth, far above its original $13 billion goal. It was one of the largest corporate bond sales in history, and enough for GM to fully fund its pension obligations—at least for the moment.

About the only people on Wall Street who weren't impressed were the debt analysts at Standard & Poor's. They figured, correctly, that GM was just substituting one kind of financial obligation for another. To them GM, like Ford, was edging closer to junk-bond status.

GM earned $6.50 a share in 2004—which would prove to be the company's last profitable year. Nearly seventy cents of every dollar came from GMAC, which was writing home mortgages more profitably than the parent company was selling cars. Wagoner nonetheless called the results "solid" and added: "We strongly believe the auto business is a growth business." Like many at GM, Wagoner had talked himself into believing that he and the company were on the right track.

There actually was growth in the U.S. car business, but it was coming from the import brands instead of the Big Three. Toyota surprised everyone, including the other Japanese car companies, with the amazing success of its gas-electric hybrid, the Prius. The Prius's breakthrough engine used only electricity at speeds below thirty miles an hour, and then switched to a tiny gasoline engine at higher speeds. The result was fuel economy upward of forty miles a gallon in city driving, which was unheard-of in a car big enough for a family. Even though Toyota made plenty of gas-guzzling SUVs too, the Prius gave the company's reputation a shiny green glow.

By the end of 2004 the import brands had grabbed more than 41 percent of the U.S. market, an incredible increase of nearly 10 percent in just five years. The losers were GM, Ford, and Chrysler, whose collective market share had fallen below 60 percent. Just a few years earlier the Japanese had seemed stalled out in the United States, but no more. They were on a renewed winning streak led by their own Big Three—Toyota, Honda, and an amazingly resurgent Nissan.

TEN

THE HURRICANE THAT
HIT DETROIT

When 2005 began, Detroit's car companies remained America's Big Three, clinging tenuously to the position they had held in their home market for eighty years. But Toyota was closing the market-share gap on Chrysler, which remained barely ahead, 14 percent to 12. Detroit's dominance was about to disappear like taillights in the haze of a humid summer night, perhaps the taillights of the new Nissan 350Z. The speedy, sexy "Z-car" was a reborn version of the sleek Japanese roadster that had first appeared in the fall of 1969. Nissan had abandoned the car, however, in the late 1990s as the company teetered on the brink of bankruptcy.

In its nadir year of 1999, Nissan had sought salvation in desperation. After DaimlerChrysler backed away from a deal, Renault had swooped in to buy 37 percent of Nissan. The French company then had installed Carlos Ghosn (it rhymes with *cone*), whose nickname inside Renault was *"le cost killer,"* at the helm of Nissan. Like Jac Nasser, the forty-five-year-old Ghosn was an ethnic Lebanese; he had been born in Brazil, was a French citizen, and spoke four languages, though none of them was Japanese.

Nonetheless, he arrived in Tokyo like a man on a mission, quickly closing five factories and axing 15 percent of Nissan's workforce in a country where lifetime employment was about as sacred as the emperor. He also set about revamping Nissan's bland-as-bread product lineup with the hot 350Z and other stylish new models.

The year after Ghosn's arrival Nissan stunned the business world by surging back into the black with profits of $1.6 billion for the first half of its fiscal year, its best financial performance in a decade. Within a couple more years the company wiped out its crushing $20 billion debt load, defeated a UAW effort to organize its factory in Tennessee, and reintroduced the Z-car. It also started building a second U.S. assembly plant.

This remarkable turnaround happened because Carlos Ghosn had embraced just the sort of take-no-prisoners approach that might have helped, say, General Motors—except that GM was mired in battles that Nissan didn't have to fight. In the spring of 2005, for example, GM tried to ban smoking on its assembly lines, as was done in the Japanese and German "transplants."

Assembly line smoking was bad for all sorts of reasons. It pushed up GM's health insurance costs, and it caused the occasional cigarette butt to be flicked onto the seat of a new car. But the UAW, some of whose members lived in a different reality, mounted a spirited defense of the "right" of its members to smoke on the job. Yet again General Motors backed down. In the rights-versus-responsibilities balance, the union often stood for the right to be irresponsible, and the company accepted the ridiculous.

Rick Wagoner had opted for measured methods to resolve GM's issues, including the mounting cost burden of its retirees. The company's actuarial tables showed that its ranks of retirees, with their pensions and healthcare bills, would start shrinking in 2008, when time and the grim reaper would take their toll on people who had retired decades earlier, in the company's peak-employment years. Meanwhile the $17.6 billion of bonds that GM had sold in 2003 would provide bridge financing.

Thus GM hoped to meet its retiree obligations—which the company called "legacy costs"—without cutting benefits and risking a damaging strike by the UAW, like the Flint strike of 1998. As for GM's other "legacy" issues—too many brands and too many dealers—Wagoner would address them gradually too. He remained steadfast in refusing to relive the Oldsmobile experience by paying more billions to more dealers to eliminate more brands.

Gradualism had its own costs, however. The ranks of retirees might start dropping in 2008, but meanwhile their cost to GM was soaring. The company's healthcare expenses rose by $1 billion in 2005 alone. The "legacy cost" burden wasn't just a UAW issue. Retired GM executives didn't have to choose between a 401(k) or a fixed-benefit pension plan: they had both.

As for excess brands, the math was sobering. At the end of 2004 General Motors had 27 percent of the market (down from 33 percent a decade earlier), but nearly half came from just one brand: Chevrolet. The other seven brands each had an average of just 2 percent of the market. This meant that GM's product development and marketing dollars were spread thinly, like the troops of a fading empire that couldn't keep enough garrisons to defend its territory. The practical result was that many Pontiacs and Chevys and Saturns tended to be close imitations of one another.

Within GM these cars were known as "look-shares." Perhaps the most glaring example was the 2005 Saab 9-2X, which was basically a gussied-up version of the Subaru WRX, which GM could produce cheaply because it owned 20 percent of the Japanese company that made Subarus. But Saab's entire brand image was built around being quirky and different—the car with the key in the floor beloved by Shakespeare scholars with tweed jackets and leather elbow patches. The Saab 9-2X quickly became derided as the "Saabaru," part of a lineup of aging models and look-shares that were sending Saab sales into a tailspin.

Other GM brands were ailing too. Internal marketing surveys showed that many GM brands didn't even make the "consideration list" of young shoppers. GM tried to lure them anyway by boosting rebates, on the theory that it could outspend Ford and Chrysler. But Chrysler and Ford didn't back down, and Detroit's costly rebate war escalated.

At least GMAC's car lending wasn't as lax as its mortgage lending. Some GM dealers in Southern California were taken aback when customers bristled at being asked to fill out a GMAC credit report for a car loan. They hadn't needed a detailed credit report to get a mortgage from GMAC on their new home, they complained, so why should they need one for a new car? But mortgage lending, which by now was providing most of GM's profits, was a ticking time bomb.

All this was occurring when the SUV profit bonanza—which had propped up GM, Ford, and Chrysler for a decade—was on the wane. The Japanese belatedly launched a salvo of attractive new SUVs, including the Honda Pilot, the Toyota Sequoia, and the funky Nissan Murano, which looked like it was descended from a moon buggy. By mid-decade Americans could choose from among nearly seventy different SUVs, more than double the number of a decade earlier. If, that is, they were inclined to buy an SUV.

A backlash was brewing against big SUVs, led by groups ranging from the Sierra Club to the Evangelical Environmental Network, a Christian group that launched an anti-SUV ad campaign that asked, "What would Jesus drive?" (Scripture, alas, isn't explicit.) Detroit figured the backlash would fade, or at least that its effects would be uncertain. But the impact of rising gas prices was becoming clear.

In March 2005 crude oil hit a then-record price of $57 a share, and gasoline soared to an average of $2.11 a gallon, 21 percent higher than a year earlier. Little wonder, then, that sales of full-size SUVs plunged 19 percent in the preceding two months.

Nonetheless GM's single biggest new-product initiative that year was a new line of full-size SUVs that would be launched early in 2006. Wagoner maintained that SUV sales were just suffering a temporary dip, and that GM would make up for any overall decline by increasing its market share. He had bet on continued strong sales of SUVs, and it was too late to turn back. Fifty years earlier one of Wagoner's predecessors as CEO had declared: "General Motors must always lead." As 2005 unfolded, General Motors would indeed lead Detroit's car companies—to the brink of the abyss.

The year's first maelstrom hit where Wagoner had held his CEO coming-out party five years earlier: Italy. In early 2005 Fiat was staggering under $10 billion in debt and more than $3 billion in losses over the previous three years. The company brought in a new CEO, Sergio Marchionne, an attorney by training and a hard-nosed negotiator by nature. He was a hyperactive blue-collar sort of CEO who chain-smoked and never wore suits—though he carried multiple BlackBerries and an iPhone and drove a Ferrari, Fiat's most prestigious marque. To Marchionne, the contractual "put" option that could force GM to buy Fiat, which had cemented the companies' alliance five years earlier, was potential money in the bank.

He threatened to invoke the option unless GM paid Fiat $2 billion in a corporate divorce settlement—on *top* of the $2.5 billion GM had invested in Fiat to begin with. Owning an ailing Fiat and all its liabilities was about the last thing GM wanted. So GM lined up lawyers to make the legal case that Fiat had invalidated the "put" provision by making financial-restructuring moves that GM had not approved.

But Wagoner, just as Marchionne had figured, wasn't willing to run the risk of litigation; instead he agreed to pay up. GM had $24 billion in cash and could easily handle the $2 billion, but the settlement marked an ignominious end to Exhibit A of GM's global-alliance strategy. The two companies parted, and Fiat disengaged from Detroit—though it was destined to return.

A month later General Motors dropped another bombshell. The company canceled its forecast of $5-a-share earnings for the year and said profits would top out between $1 and $2 a share because of "a significant full-year loss" in North America. The surprise announcement caused the Dow Jones Industrial Average to plunge 112 points, at a time when that sort of drop still was considered a big deal.

GM's stock tumbled 14 percent, more than it had dropped after the Fiat debacle, and for good reason. The Fiat partnership could be viewed, albeit charitably, as a one-off deal that went bad. But the new earnings forecast exposed GM's more fundamental issues: softening sales of SUVs and too many mouths to feed—excess factories, workers, managers, retirees, brands, and dealers that added billions of dollars to the company's costs.

"GM's big retiree handicap and lower-cost competition has prompted some speculation [about] bankruptcy," wrote *Business-Week*. But the magazine quickly pulled its punch by adding: "No one who seriously follows GM's finances sees that as an option, though."

Well, maybe not yet.

For years GM had been ratcheting up the rebates on its cars to keep its sales machine churning. Those moves allowed the company to pay pensions, benefits, and salaries—and to keep its brands alive (except for Oldsmobile) and dealers afloat. There was even a little left for shareholders, the people who, after all, owned the company. At the Monday morning meetings of the Strategy Board, the company's ruling council, members would pound the table in atta-boy approval when an executive announced that the factories had exceeded the previous week's production target, because the extra "units," as vehicles were called, meant more revenue.

But just because GM could *build* more cars didn't mean it could *sell* them. By the late winter of 2005, the onset of the industry's spring selling season, GM dealers had 1.3 million unsold vehicles crammed onto their storage lots, and many balked at ordering more despite the pleading and table-pounding of the company's regional sales managers.

As it happened, the 1.3 million unsold vehicles equaled analysts' assessments of GM's excess production capacity—meaning the company had eight or nine extra assembly plants and all their attendant costs. Put another way, General Motors had the capacity to produce enough cars for 35 percent of the U.S. market but was selling only enough cars to account for 25 percent. The chances of getting back to a 35 percent market share, or even to GM's 29 percent goal, were virtually nil. The "29" buttons that GM executives had begun wearing three years earlier quietly disappeared.

With eight brands to nurture and promote, GM was developing lots of mediocre cars as opposed to a few outstanding ones. Even its best new models, such as the sporty Cadillac CTS sedan, had to make do without features that were common on competing cars, such as the optional all-wheel-drive on the BMW 3 Series. Likewise, the CTS and other potential winners got caught in the clutter of GM's model overload, competing for advertising dollars against such yawners as the Buick LeSabre and the Pontiac Bonneville.

All those factors, in turn, spelled further declines in sales and market share, adding to the overhang of excess factories and employees that General Motors couldn't afford. The company might have broken this perverse downward spiral by dropping five or six brands and shedding enough employees for GM to be comfortably profitable with 20 to 25 percent of the U.S. market. But that would mean fighting battles with the UAW and with dealers that Wagoner was determined to avoid.

So in the spring of 2005 he made other moves. GM canceled plans for a new line of sedans so the company could accelerate the development of new full-size SUVs and pickups. They were GM's most profitable vehicles, but the move only added to GM's bet on gas prices not going higher. In early April Wagoner reshuffled GM's executive suite and took direct command of the company's North American operations, which was tantamount to declaring a state of emergency. It soon became clear why. Two weeks later GM posted a $1.3 billion loss for the first quarter, its largest such deficit in more than a dozen years. The company also canceled *all* financial forecasts for the year—disavowing its reduced earnings estimate of only a month earlier. GM stock was hovering just above $25 a share—only one-third of its price when Wagoner became CEO five years earlier.

That was bad news, of course, if you had owned the stock for Wagoner's entire tenure. But it could be good news if you liked to buy a stock when it was cheap, agitate for moves to increase its value, and then sell when the price went up—you know, buy low and sell high. That was the modus operandi of Kirk Kerkorian, the eighty-seven-year-old investor who had cashed in big on Chrysler stock when Daimler-Benz bought the company. And of Jerome B. York, the man who had helped him do it.

The sixty-six-year-old "Jerry" York had been trained at West Point and MIT; he spoke with a soft Southern accent that betrayed his boyhood in Tennessee. He had worked at Ford and General Motors before joining Chrysler in 1979 and rising to become chief financial officer, where his relentless focus on cutting through the "bullshit," a word he invoked often, had helped to fuel Chrysler's comeback in the mid-1990s.

York wasn't there to enjoy it, however, because his work had gained the attention of Lou Gerstner, the CEO of IBM, who lured York to Big Blue in 1993 to help revive the ailing computer giant. There York and Gerstner spotted all kinds of wasteful bull-stuff, including the twenty telephone staffers whose sole job it was to call company phone numbers at random to make sure IBMers changed their voice-mail messages daily. Those twenty people, and 45,000 others, were axed during York's first eight months on the job, helping to produce a corporate turnaround even more dramatic than Chrysler's.

In September 1995 York had made another job switch, departing IBM to become vice chairman of Kirk Kerkorian's holding company, Tracinda (named after his daughters, Tracy and Linda). There York used his knowledge of Chrysler and the auto industry to pepper the company's management with advice and encouraged the merger that formed DaimlerChrysler in 1998. Having made one fortune in Detroit, Kerkorian figured he wasn't too old to make another.

On May 4, 2005, Tracinda disclosed it had acquired about 4 percent of GM's stock and would make a public offer to buy another 5 percent—an investment of $1.7 billion, enough to make Kerkorian GM's largest individual shareholder. GM shares jumped 18 percent, their largest one-day increase in years. That normally would have been great news for Wagoner, except that backseat driving from Kirk Kerkorian and Jerry York wasn't what he wanted.

The very next day Wagoner and GM got another jolt. Standard & Poor's took a step that was once unthinkable but was now inevitable: it downgraded GM's debt to junk-bond status. In effect, S&P was telling investors it was safer to lend money to Poland or Russia than to General Motors. The consequences were far more serious to GM than wounded corporate pride; the downgrade threatened GMAC and its home mortgage division, Residential Capital. GMAC and ResCap, as it was called, made money by borrowing from the credit markets and lending at higher rates to car dealers, car buyers, and home buyers. With GM in junk-bond territory, GMAC and ResCap would face higher borrowing costs that would pinch profit margins severely.

Fiat. Record losses. Kirk Kerkorian. Junk-bond ratings. Things seemed to be unraveling at General Motors with amazing speed. And as if those hot potatoes weren't enough, up popped another one: Delphi, GM's former car-parts business. With $35 billion in annual sales, Delphi Corporation was the largest components company in the world. General Motors thought it had shed Delphi, and its problems, when it had spun off the company to GM shareholders in 1999. But now Delphi was coming back to haunt its former parent company, like some corporate Ghost of Christmas Past.

In the spring of 2005, when GM was tumbling into the red, Delphi posted a first-quarter loss of $460 million and the auditors uncovered problems with the company's past earnings reports, some of them involving transactions with GM. The Delphi board placed an urgent call to corporate America's crisis go-to guy—Steve Miller.

Sixty-three-year-old Miller had been a compatriot of York's at Chrysler during the Iacocca years. After leaving Chrysler in 1992

Miller had made a career of coming into troubled companies as CEO, making the tough decisions that previous management had ducked, and moving on to clean up another mess elsewhere. Sometimes it had worked; other times the company was beyond saving.

The situation at Delphi was bleak when Miller became CEO on June 1, 2005. Delphi's workers were making an average of $70 an hour, including wages, benefits, and payments to retirees—the same amount made by workers at General Motors. But workers at other car-components companies, even those organized by the UAW, were making less than half that amount, because those companies had different wage scales than GM.

The wages of Delphi workers were way out of whack because the UAW always had insisted that all GM workers be paid the same, whether they were assembling cars or making door handles. Honoring that pay-parity principle had been the union's condition for allowing GM to spin off Delphi without making trouble.

Delphi also was paying about four thousand idled workers nearly $100,000 apiece in wages and benefits—or $400 million a year—through the Jobs Bank, yet another obligation the company had inherited from GM. Delphi had muddled through the first six years of its existence despite these burdens, partly because its overseas business was handsomely profitable. But Miller wasn't willing to muddle through anymore.

"We have a problem," he told the union, "and unless we solve it, we're going into chapter." *Chapter* was CEO shorthand for Chapter 11 bankruptcy, like *hoodie* is kid shorthand for a hooded sweatshirt. Miller delivered the same message to Wagoner, adding that if Delphi did file, GM would be on the hook for at least $7 billion—and perhaps much more—in payments to workers that the company had guaranteed in the spin-off agreement.

When both company and union officials offered sympathy, Miller was pleased—until he found that sympathy was all they offered. GM told him to get concessions from the union, the union told him to get payments from GM, and both parties suggested he plead with Delphi's bondholders to reduce the payments owed them. Miller was getting a classic runaround, and everybody just *knew* he had to be bluffing about taking Delphi into Chapter 11.

What it all boiled down to was that two former Chrysler guys, Miller and York, were riding back into town in the spring of 2005 with the temerity to tell GM—*General Motors!*—how to manage its affairs. GM executives had looked down their noses at Chrysler for decades. York and Miller were like the geeks in Detroit's version of *Revenge of the Nerds*. Of course, when that movie ended, the nerds were on top.

In June Wagoner tried to regain the initiative by publicly threatening to cut the UAW's healthcare benefits unilaterally. That's exactly what GM already had done with its white-collar workers—who weren't covered by a union contract. He had raised their co-pays and deductibles to 27 percent of their overall healthcare costs, but UAW members paid hardly anything.

That situation was just fine with the union. "I don't consider it a problem," said Ron Gettelfinger, adding that any unilateral benefit cuts would jeopardize seven years of labor peace. That return threat got the company's attention. The June 30 deadline came and went, leaving GM's hapless PR people to explain that, upon reflection, the company had decided that dialog would work better than deadlines. To nobody's surprise, Wagoner and General Motors had retreated once again.

U.S. car sales were cruising toward 16.99 million vehicles for the year, almost an all-time record, but GM was careening toward the largest full-year loss in its history. If GM was losing billions in this kind of market, could the company *ever* make money? It was the right question, and Wagoner's reply seemed to signal his resolve to turn things around. "Nobody wants to be the guy who runs General Motors," he said, "when it goes out of business." In due course he would find out how it felt to be that guy.

After a disastrous first half of the year, could the second half possibly be any worse for Wagoner and GM? The unfortunate answer came on August 29, when Hurricane Katrina smashed into New Orleans and the adjacent Mississippi Gulf Coast, creating damage and anarchy that stunned the nation. Detroit is 1,070 miles north of New Orleans, but Katrina's fury struck there nonetheless—not physically, but psychologically. By mid-September gasoline prices had spiked to nearly $3 a gallon in many places, up from $1.75 a year earlier. Any doubts that the halcyon days of big SUVs had ended could be put to rest. Ford administered automotive euthanasia to the Excursion, killing its SUV behemoth after five years on the market. But the situation was more complicated for GM.

The company's revamped line of big SUVs—the Chevy Suburban, Chevy Tahoe, and GMC Yukon—were scheduled to launch in January 2006, thanks to Wagoner's orders to accelerate their development. It was a logical decision, if one ignored the market's shift away from SUVs. The vehicles were GM's only source of domestic profits, because there was no way to make money on small and midsize cars without getting concessions from the UAW that everybody knew were impossible.

Car companies need three to four years to develop new vehicles, and GM's big new SUVs were just three or four months away from being introduced. General Motors had no choice but to charge ahead with a product plan more suited to 1995 than to 2005.

On Saturday, October 8, another storm struck. Shortly before noon a group of lawyers walked into federal bankruptcy court in lower Manhattan and put Delphi Corporation—the nation's sixty-third largest company, according to *Fortune*—into bankruptcy. The UAW had rebuffed Miller's demand to cut wages and benefits and scrap Delphi's Jobs Bank. But Miller, it turned out, had been dead serious about "going into chapter."

The day before Delphi filed, Miller had granted two-year severance packages for twenty-one top Delphi executives, as an incentive for them to stay with the company despite the bankruptcy. It wasn't the best PR move. But what followed next illustrated the bitter labor-management divide that, more than a century into its existence, still plagued Detroit's auto industry.

"Once again, we see the disgusting spectacle of the people at the top taking care of themselves at the same time they are demanding extraordinary sacrifices from their hourly workers," the UAW declared. At that point the time-honored Detroit script would have been for Delphi to shut its corporate mouth, take its lumps, and move on. But Miller was playing a different game.

Instead of sweetening their severance packages, he said, maybe he should have put Delphi's executives into the Jobs Bank, where they would have to be paid forever instead of just for two years. With that tart statement hanging in the air, Miller then flew to New York for a series of briefings with *The New York Times*, *The Wall Street Journal*, the major news magazines, and the television networks.

At each stop he delivered a sympathetic but sobering message: the era of high-paid but low-skilled jobs was over. U.S. companies could no longer pay uncompetitive wages, nor pay pensions and medical benefits to people who would spend more years in retirement than they spent working. "Behind all this financial drama are the lives and livelihoods of thousands of our loyal and dedicated workers," Miller told the journalists. "These are honest, hard-working human beings who played by the rules and cannot be blamed for pursuing the American dream by taking a job at GM or Delphi. They expected us to live up to our promises, but we have been caught by fast-changing global economics."

Delphi, he added, was the canary in Detroit's coal mine. "Beyond Delphi, things are going to get messy for the Big Three. The current labor agreements expire in 2007, and it will be a historical collision point for all these social and economic forces that are at work." Delphi's Chapter 11 filing "significantly increases," Miller added, the chance that General Motors itself would wind up in bankruptcy.

Miller had stood up for his position in a public way that the Big Three always had avoided—a reticence that had prevented honest discussion of the issues that had threatened Detroit for decades. Gettelfinger was not happy. "Our people are irate about the approach that has been taken," he fired back. "They resent very, very much that Mr. Miller has taken his case to the public." Well, of *course* they did. Under Detroit's traditional rules of engagement, public criticism of the UAW was corporate suicide.

Though the union was angry with Miller, it quietly hired Wall Street bankers to assess whether GM's position was really as weak as the company claimed. The bankers replied that it was even worse. On October 17, the same day that GM posted another massive quarterly loss of $1.6 billion, the UAW agreed to modest healthcare cost reductions. Medical benefits for active workers would remain free, but union retirees would start paying monthly health insurance premiums and deductibles for doctor visits, just like other Americans.

The annual savings to General Motors would be just $1 billion— less than the company had lost in the latest quarter alone—and they wouldn't begin for another year. But Wagoner portrayed the union's concession as a vindication of his policy of patient negotiation, and he was careful to reassure the union that he wouldn't press too far, too fast. "Our plans do not include anything radical like eliminating the Jobs Bank," he said. "We'd like to do that, but I don't think that's a realistic assumption." At the time GM was paying $800 million a year to workers in the Jobs Bank—enough to develop new engines or transmissions or to build a modern new factory.

In 2005 the weaknesses in GM's crumbling foundation had been fully exposed. In describing the disastrous year, Wagoner was philosophical. "It started out bad," he said, "and it got worse." Actually, much worse was yet to come.

One car company CEO had his head on the block in 2005, but his name wasn't Rick Wagoner. It was Jürgen Schrempp. By then DaimlerChrysler's total stock market value stood at just $47 billion, down from the combined value of nearly $85 billion that Daimler-Benz and Chrysler had enjoyed as separate companies before the merger. In late March the company announced the recall of 1.3 million Mercedes cars, the largest recall in history—by a long shot— for Germany's legendary nameplate. A few weeks later the Mercedes division reported a first-quarter loss of more than $1 billion, its first such loss in a decade.

It was easy to understand, then, why many of the eight thousand shareholders who gathered in Berlin on April 6 for the company's annual meeting were disenchanted. "Shareholders' patience is exhausted," a German investment manager griped at the meeting. Schrempp, never a man to admit a mistake, replied that Chrysler's recovery under Daimler management had proved the wisdom of the merger. The fund manager shot back: "Do you have to shoot yourself in the foot first to apply first aid?"

The very un-German public criticism went on for hours. Even the famously tone-deaf Schrempp got the message that, despite the two years left on his management contract, it might be time for him to go. Key members of the company's supervisory board—akin to a board of directors in the United States—were concluding the same thing. In the last week of July, after a tumultuous decade at the top, Schrempp agreed to retire at the end of the year.

His successor, ironically, would be the man whom Schrempp had dispatched to Detroit to fix Chrysler, Dieter Zetsche. On Thursday night, July 28, the day after he got the good news, Zetsche flew from Stuttgart back to Detroit on a company Gulfstream V. The next morning, at Chrysler's headquarters in suburban Auburn Hills, hundreds of employees gathered in the atrium to applaud the man who had earned the trust and respect of many by reviving Chrysler's fortunes. Some employees even fought back tears when Zetsche promised that, despite his promotion, "I am, and always will be, a Chrysler man."

Chrysler would register a slight gain in market share in 2005, the only Detroit company to post an increase. The hated Jürgen Schrempp was out. Chrysler seemed to be recovering, not to its pre-Daimler glory, but enough that the future looked promising once again.

Rick Wagoner might have been philosophical at the end of 2005, but Jerry York and Kirk Kerkorian weren't. GM's stock was trading under $19 a share, which meant that Kerkorian had lost some 30 percent of his $1.7 billion investment. The company's total market value was just over $11 billion, even though GM had $19 billion of cash in its coffers—a sure sign that investors expected the cash drain, running at $2 billion each quarter, to continue.

Bankruptcy rumors surfaced, prompting Wagoner to send an e-mail to employees denying them. Yet the UAW Jobs Bank, with its $800-million-a-year outlay to idled workers, remained an off-limits topic with the union. On a smaller scale, the company was spending hundreds of thousands of dollars to sponsor college football's GMAC Bowl featuring Toledo versus Texas–El Paso—with all the ratings potential of, say, the Bulgarian weightlifting finals. To Kerkorian and York, GM wasn't acting like a company whose very survival, along with a healthy chunk of Kerkorian's money, was at stake. It was time to step up the pressure.

On January 10, 2006, York addressed the Society of Automotive

Analysts in Detroit, beginning in a low-key, aw-shucks tone. "Now my wife and I, we moved back to Detroit a year and a half ago, and I didn't have a clue that I was once again going to become immersed in the auto industry," he said. "I'm sitting there in my home office a year ago, and I see General Motors heading south, below 40 bucks a share, so I started doing a little digging. One day the phone rings. I pick it up and Kirk Kerkorian is on the line. He says, 'Jerry, have you seen what's going on with GM stock?' And I said, 'Kirk, I almost called you yesterday.'"

Thus, York recounted, he began a six-week "deep dive" analysis of GM, which he summarized in a fourteen-page memo to the billionaire. General Motors was in a heap of trouble, he wrote, but it also had enough cash to fund a turnaround effort. The key would be management's willingness to act urgently by eliminating dozens of near-duplicate models, dumping unneeded brands, making realistic sales assumptions, and negotiating a better union contract.

He described the tough measures that had produced the turnarounds at Chrysler and IBM in the 1990s, and then presented a sobering statistic about GM. The company was burning through $24 million of cash each and every day. At that rate General Motors actually would *run out of cash* in one thousand days, or about three years. (In the end York would be astonishingly close to the mark.)

In light of this, he asked, "Why does GM still own Saab? It's been a pretty consistent money loser, so why not just get rid of it?" He also recommended selling Hummer and cutting the $2-a-share annual dividend by 50 percent to conserve cash—even though that would cost Kerkorian $56 million a year. York added that GM should cut the pay of board members ($200,000 a year), senior executives, and other managers down the line to create shared sacrifice, and it should ask the UAW to cut the company's healthcare costs further. "This situation calls for the company going into crisis mode," he said, "and adopting a degree of urgency that recognizes if things don't break right, the unthinkable could happen."

He concluded: "The cynics, of course, will say it can't be done, that there is no solution here given the 70-year history of mistrust in management-labor relations. But for my part, I believe we can prove them wrong. Can't all of us who are involved in this just grab hold of that steering wheel and get this industry headed down that right path in the road?"

It was an emotional appeal that people hadn't expected from the no-nonsense York, but it hit home. When corralled by reporters after the speech, Fritz Henderson, GM's new chief financial officer, said he agreed with much of what York had to say, and that he personally already had entered "crisis mode."

It was, for sure, the right mode. On January 26 GM reported an $8.6 billion loss for 2005, including $4.8 billion in red ink for the fourth quarter alone. A week later GM's directors cut the dividend in half, cut executive pay, and eliminated bonuses for Wagoner and other managers, just as York had suggested. They also went further and elected York to the board.

York's first board event was the monthly director's dinner on Sunday, March 5, at GM headquarters in Detroit's fortresslike Renaissance Center—which had been built, ironically, by Henry Ford II. York sat at a table with Wagoner, Bob Lutz, and George Fisher, the company's lead outside director. Fisher was inherently sympathetic with an underperforming CEO because he himself had been one—twice.

During his tenure at Motorola the company had been outflanked by competitors in the cell phone market. Then Fisher moved to Kodak, which he led to laggard status in the digital photography revolution. Fisher's corporate governance philosophy, as he often said amiably but adamantly, was to support management, period.

But he didn't argue over dinner when York observed that GM looked like a "good bank," consisting of Cadillac, Chevrolet, and the international operations, and a "bad bank," comprising pretty much everything else. And he agreed to York's suggestion that Wagoner update GM's strategic plan to take a realistic look at future market share. The next day's meeting was a little less comfortable, with York asking polite but pointed questions.

The real jolt came ten days later. On Thursday, March 16, GM disclosed that its actual loss for 2005 wasn't $8.6 billion, as first reported, but a whopping $10.6 billion. Further, GM had delayed filing its annual report with the SEC because ResCap's mortgage transactions had raised questions from the auditors. To top it off, GM announced it was restating its earnings for a five-year stretch, between 2000 and early 2005, because of a whole series of *additional* accounting missteps that previously had gone undetected—and now were being investigated by the SEC.

The disclosures were incredible for a company that forty years earlier had been the gold standard for corporate accounting, and it left GM's directors stunned. Losing money and market share was one thing. But faulty financial reports and SEC probes raised the specter of lawsuits, fines, and even potential personal liability for the members of the board.

The next day the board convened a special conference call to demand how all this could have happened. Fritz Henderson said he didn't have all the answers yet but would get them quickly. Rick Wagoner said little. He had dialed into the call from Asia, where he was visiting GM's local operations. The bad news had caught him totally unawares—not a good thing for a CEO. Inevitably, board members began questioning Wagoner's performance.

Events then began to move quickly. On March 26 the board held a special meeting in New York to discuss Wagoner's proposal to sell 51 percent of GMAC. The buyer would be Cerberus, a little-known New York firm that had outflanked the big boys of private equity—notably Kohlberg, Kravis & Roberts—to emerge as the preferred bidder for one of the largest financial institutions in the United States. Wagoner had harbored doubts about Cerberus, but they were assuaged by assurances from Citigroup, the nation's biggest bank.

The deal would kill two birds with one stone, Wagoner told the board. Selling control to Cerberus would open the way for GMAC to be freed from the junk-bond ratings of GM itself, which was making it expensive for GMAC to raise funds. What's more, the deal would replenish GM's shrinking cash coffers with a $13 billion payment from Cerberus that GM could use to finance its turnaround effort.

A couple of directors asked whether GM should simply sell GMAC's mortgage business and keep full control of the core business of automobile financing. But Wagoner said the move would yield GM just $2 billion to $3 billion. That wouldn't help much with a turnaround that was looking increasingly expensive, he explained, because the strategy update York had requested showed GM's market share would drop from 26 to 20 percent during the next five years. *That* was a scary number.

One director who didn't gulp, however, was George Fisher, Wagoner's chief supporter, because he wasn't there. He had recused himself from the GMAC discussion because of possible business conflicts. The others took advantage of Fisher's absence to call an executive session to discuss a subject that was getting hard to avoid: whether Wagoner should be replaced. There was some talk of naming Fritz Henderson CEO, with York as executive chairman, at which point York left the room. The directors concluded that they needed another executive session of the full board and asked Fisher to schedule it for Sunday, April 9, in New York.

Fisher fervently believed Wagoner shouldn't be blamed for GM's problems. The CEO's hands were bound, he reasoned, by a recalcitrant union, punitive dealer-franchise laws, and other chains. There was some truth in that, of course. But other CEOs, notably Carlos Ghosn, had rejected the conventional wisdom about what couldn't be done.

Not so Wagoner. GM had refined the art of avoiding the tough, fundamental changes—such as confronting the union and killing more brands—that actually would make a difference. With those steps automatically deemed off-limits, the company always settled for half-measures or worse. Somewhere along the way Wagoner's explanations had morphed into excuses. GM was like a football player frantically running from sideline to sideline but never moving up the field toward the goal line.

But Fisher was a blind believer in boardroom loyalty—meaning loyalty to management, as opposed to the shareholders whom the directors were elected to represent. It's a common, though rarely acknowledged, attitude on corporate boards, especially when board members get red-carpet treatment and, in the case of GM's directors, a new car to drive every few months. But Fisher's dogged loyalty in the face of GM's decline would prove exceptional by any standard.

He viewed the request for an executive session as the road to rebellion, a potential replay of the boardroom coup that had ousted

Bob Stempel as GM's chairman thirteen years earlier. And Fisher resolved to stop the rebellion in its tracks.

The board, he told fellow directors, had conducted Wagoner's annual performance review just five months earlier, so there was no reason to depart from procedure and go through that exercise again. When several board members insisted that the recent jarring events warranted another look, he bowed to their wishes. But he also gave Wagoner a heads-up on the special meeting.

It was jolting news to Wagoner. He had got his big career break in the 1992 revolt against Stempel, but now he was on the other end of things. On Thursday, March 30, he joined GM's general counsel and its PR chief in a headquarters conference room. Both men told him that he, Wagoner himself, had become the issue, and that he had to fight back.

He couldn't keep "paying the price like a punching bag," the advisers said, by letting the hits against him go unanswered. The advice didn't sit well with Wagoner, who wanted to "put a few points on the board," as the ex-athlete put it, before speaking out in his own defense. The trouble was, his aides retorted, things were moving so quickly that he might get fired before he had time to score.

The board convened again on April 2 to approve the GMAC deal, and when that business was done, Wagoner said he had another issue to raise. He had lived through a couple of grueling weeks, he said, and the planned meeting on April 9 to evaluate his performance threatened to undermine all his efforts to get General Motors turned around.

Without a solid show of support from GM's board of directors, Wagoner continued, he could not be an effective CEO and would resign immediately. Wagoner's calm and deliberate tone belied the high drama and high stakes of the moment. He was issuing an ultimatum to his board in a way that he had never managed to do with, say, the UAW or the dealers who distributed GM's bleeding brands. Having thrown down the gauntlet he left the call, so the directors could talk among themselves.

They were panicked. It was never clear just how many might have voted to fire Wagoner on April 9, but the board wanted to control the timing, the method, and everything else about the decision. The directors weren't ready to act on the spot, but Wagoner had left them no other choice.

As if on cue, the ever-loyal Fisher came to their rescue. He had prepared, he said, three different drafts of a statement of support for Rick. They were like the old Sears catalog model of "good, better and best," with the best, in Fisher's view, expressing the board's "unanimous" support for Wagoner.

A couple directors fretted that if they showed support for Wagoner now, they might have to reverse themselves and fire him later. But Fisher pressed the point, arguing that the board should act "in the best interest of GM right now." So the board caved, approving a statement of support for Wagoner that wasn't unanimous—Jerry York wouldn't go for that—but was strong enough. Fisher then clinched his victory by canceling the April 9 discussion about Wagoner's performance because the meeting, he said, had become "moot."

The next morning, Monday, April 3, GM announced the sale of 51 percent of GMAC, a corporate crown jewel founded in 1919 that had provided most of the company's earnings in recent years. The deal brought GM $13 billion, but it also meant GM would no longer control the pipeline of credit to its dealers and car buyers. It was a watershed moment, but buried in the press release was even bigger news. "While there is still much work to be done," George Fisher stated, "the GM board has great confidence in Rick Wagoner, his management team and the plan they are implementing to restore the company to profitability." That was a watershed moment too.

With the board publicly behind him, Wagoner launched into a series of press interviews. He told *Face the Nation:* "I wouldn't be in this job if I didn't think I was the right guy to do it." In a more self-deprecating tone, he told other reporters: "I appreciate support from the board, our workers, my wife—anybody I can get it from these days." Wagoner also struck a contrite tone about the accounting miscues. "While I will not offer excuses," he wrote to GM's shareholders, "I do apologize on behalf of our management team, and assure you that we will strive to deserve your trust."

Wagoner was like the winner on *Survivor,* eating a bit of crow along the way but coming out alive. Kerkorian and York were amazed and dismayed. In their view, General Motors was hemorrhaging cash, losing market share at an alarming rate, and reeling from sloppy accounting—all indications that management didn't have a grip on the business. And the company had responded with . . . a PR campaign.

At five P.M. on Friday, May 5, York hopped into his private Gulfstream III jet and flew from Detroit to London. He spent the weekend there to be fresh for a Monday meeting with someone he had long wanted to know: Carlos Ghosn. By now Ghosn was CEO of both Nissan and Renault and basically lived on a corporate jet as he trekked between Paris and Tokyo and visited other parts of the two companies' far-flung empires. Nissan, which Ghosn had run for six years, was earning eight cents on every dollar of revenue—the highest profit margin of any major car company in the world. In contrast, GM was *losing* five cents on every dollar.

At one-thirty P.M. that Monday, York and Ghosn lunched in a private room at the Dorchester Hotel. They talked about turnarounds, strategy, and the workings of the alliance between Nissan and Renault. It really was pretty simple, Ghosn explained. Whenever either company contemplated a new model, it invited the other partner to make it a joint project. That produced enormous economies of scale by eliminating the expensive duplicate engineering that would be required to develop a similar car separately.

Neither company was required to participate in the other's projects, but senior management pushed for as much cooperation as possible. And because Ghosn himself happened to be the *most* senior manager at both companies, he had unique leverage to make the arrangement work.

York was enthralled. A system like this, with a leader like Ghosn, could work wonders for General Motors, he thought, just as it had revived Nissan. Might the Frenchman be interested, York asked, in adding a U.S. partner to the Nissan-Renault alliance? Absolutely, replied Ghosn, under the right conditions, which would include a genuine commitment from General Motors. After two hours of conversation Ghosn headed back to Gatwick Airport for the next stop on his corporate jet journeys. That afternoon, back in Detroit, GM made a major announcement.

The first-quarter loss of $323 million that the company had reported three weeks earlier suddenly had morphed into a *profit* of $445 million. It was really just an accounting change—allowed by the SEC at GM's request—related to the prior year's healthcare deal with the UAW. GM's publicists, nonetheless, said the profit provided proof that the company's turnaround was "gaining traction."

York didn't believe it. As a former CFO at two major companies, he knew that earnings reflected all sorts of accounting assumptions, but that cash flow—which excluded calculations for depreciation of equipment, product development costs, and a host of other things— was a purer measure of corporate performance. GM's cash flow remained negative, and York figured that *gaining traction* was a synonym for *bullshit.*

On June 15 at seven-thirty P.M. York and Ghosn met again, this time for dinner in Ghosn's suite at the Vanderbilt Hotel in Nashville, home of Nissan's North American headquarters. They were joined by a third person, Kirk Kerkorian himself. As the evening progressed, lubricated by fine red wine, a meeting of the minds emerged. Kerkorian and York viewed a tripartite alliance as a way to get Wagoner off the dime, and Ghosn saw it as a way of extending his global automotive empire.

The delicate part, though, was what to do next. York and Kerkorian knew full well that they were violating corporate protocol in a big way. Proper procedure would have meant York raising the idea at a GM board meeting and asking the board to direct Wagoner to evaluate it. But York figured that after the GM board had caved in to "Riskless Rick," as he had taken to calling Wagoner, the company would continue dallying toward disaster unless somebody applied a corporate cattle prod. So he made an appointment with the CEO.

At three P.M. on June 22—his sixty-eighth birthday—York was ushered into Wagoner's office in the Renaissance Center's 300 Tower, with a commanding view of the Detroit River and the Ambassador Bridge to Canada. He described the lunch in London, the dinner in Nashville, and the idea of an alliance and said that, by the way, maybe

Rick should call Kirk to hear from his largest individual shareholder directly. Wagoner appeared surprised but outwardly calm. His pique was evident, however, in his conversation with Kerkorian the next day.

Billionaires tend not to like being scolded by people who work for them. But Wagoner peppered Kerkorian with questions. Why had he acted on his own? Why didn't he bring the alliance idea to management and the board first? Why didn't he have faith in the turnaround plan that Wagoner and his team were implementing—and that already was showing results? Kerkorian was angry with Wagoner's message and, especially, with his tone. "Fuck that son of a bitch," he barked at York, when he called him to report on the conversation. "If we have to, we'll hang a fucking 8-K on him." And so on Friday, June 30, Tracinda made a public regulatory filing, called a form 8-K, with the SEC, disclosing that Kerkorian wanted GM to explore a Nissan-Renault-GM alliance. All hell broke lose.

GM's stock jumped 9 percent. The company's board convened an emergency conference call. PR people at all three companies found themselves besieged with phone calls. GM's lawyers in Detroit, New York, and Washington parsed every word of the 8-K filing. They concluded that if GM's board rebuffed an alliance out of hand, it would be vulnerable to being sued by Kerkorian for breach of fiduciary duty. Wagoner groused that York hadn't acted like a loyal board member, but the directors bowed to the inevitable and issued a statement saying they would study Kerkorian's proposal. On cue, Nissan and Renault said they stood willing to consider the idea. The dance had been scripted with exquisite precision.

The choreography continued on Friday, July 14—Bastille Day in France—when Ghosn whisked into Detroit for an afternoon press conference and departed shortly afterward for a secret meeting. At seven P.M. he arrived at the Renaissance Center for a private dinner with Wagoner. The two CEOs (well, three, because Ghosn was CEO of two companies) agreed to set up study teams to evaluate synergies and potential cost savings from any alliance. They also agreed (and this was critical to Wagoner) to refrain from public comment until the evaluations were completed. The next morning, before he left town, Ghosn met privately with York to fill him in on the previous night's dinner.

Kerkorian and York appeared to have seized the upper hand, but appearances were deceiving. The real key would be who was going to evaluate the potential benefits of an alliance. They wanted the GM board to hire independent consultants, but Wagoner and Fisher argued back that the study should be conducted by management. Their position got sympathy from the other directors, who were already annoyed that York and Kerkorian were pushing them around in public. "Who does this guy from Las Vegas think he is, telling us what to do?" snapped one director at the board meeting on August 1. The board sided with Fisher and Wagoner.

York could guess what was coming, and his fears were confirmed by a most unexpected source. He found a mole in GM's inner sanctum, who slipped him—through an intermediary—some revealing numbers. The initial analysis showed that by coordinating their purchasing operations, GM, Renault, and Nissan could save between 8 percent and 10 percent on the price of some components—an enormous number in an industry that strives to shave pennies per part.

But those savings were discounted in the analysis because GM assumed its own cost-cutting efforts would save nearly 10 percent on the same parts without any alliance. In other words, a projected alliance savings of 10 percent was being counted as zero, because GM assumed it could equal that alone. In late September York got, also surreptitiously, a GM study forecasting savings of more than $6 billion a year from an alliance. But when Wagoner presented the forecast to the board on October 2, the forecast had shrunk to $2 billion.

York couldn't object because that would betray his "Deep Throat," but a clear pattern was emerging. All the analysis was being skewed toward killing the deal. Wagoner wasn't doing anything illegal, because GM's management was perfectly within its rights to exercise judgment in projecting possible savings. In fact, conservative assumptions might be considered prudent, considering all that was at stake.

But Wagoner had a personal motive as well. It was clear that in any alliance with Nissan and Renault, the top dog would be Carlos Ghosn. He had engineered one of the most remarkable corporate turnarounds in history, while Wagoner had engineered, well, GM's plunge into record red ink. Wagoner had been raised in an era of GM hegemony, and he couldn't let go of that. "GM sells more than nine million vehicles a year globally," twice as many as Nissan and Renault combined, he reminded journalists at the Paris auto show. "It's not logical or responsible to say we must have a partner to recover." He didn't mention a less convenient statistic: GM had lost $10.6 billion the previous year selling all those cars, while Nissan and Renault had earned a combined $8 billion in profits by selling half as many cars.

Nonetheless, at GM's board meeting of October 3, Wagoner took the offensive. He told the board that the advantages of any alliance were so tilted toward Nissan and Renault that those companies should pay General Motors several billion dollars up front as the price of doing any deal. In other words, the profitable companies (Nissan and Renault) would benefit more than the money-losing company (GM).

Bizarre as that sounded, it was a brilliant tactic. Had he simply opposed an alliance outright, Wagoner would have been acting too blatantly in his own self-interest. But he portrayed his request for a multibillion-dollar "equalizing contribution" from Renault and Nissan as fairness for GM's shareholders—including Kerkorian himself. Predictably, Ghosn took a different view. In a telephone conversation the day after GM's board meeting, he and Wagoner agreed, inevitably, that they remained too far apart for a deal. Wagoner had fought his way off the ropes again; the tripartite alliance was dead.

York knew he was beaten, outmaneuvered one more time by a man whose wits and resilience continued to surprise and dismay him. On October 6 he faxed a letter GM's general counsel. "The company has made excellent progress in several areas . . . [but] I have grave reservations concerning the ability of the current business model to successfully compete in the marketplace," he wrote. "To get to the crux of the matter, I have not found an environment in the board room that is receptive to probing much beyond the materials provided by management . . . That environment has been a puzzle to me." With that he resigned from the board, and two months later Kerkorian sold all his shares in General Motors. He pocketed a profit of about $100 million—which by Kerkorian's standards counted as a disappointment.

It had been a remarkable two years for Rick Wagoner, the onetime

Duke hoopster and GM "high pot" who had ascended to the corner office as if by destiny. His company was suffering from record losses, accounting snafus, and a relentless erosion in market share (nearly two points in 2006 alone), all of which had occurred on his watch. A multibillionaire had become GM's largest individual investor and tried to sweep him out of a job. At one point, indeed, Wagoner had been on the very brink of being fired. And yet he had convinced GM's board that he, and only he, understood GM's culture, systems, and delicate dealings with the UAW well enough to fix the company. The press began referring to Wagoner as "Teflon Rick."

While Wagoner was saving his job during 2006, another Detroit CEO would give his own up voluntarily. Bill Ford, Jr., had begun the year by dismissing comparisons between his company and the ailing GM. "We're profitable this year," he told *Automotive News*. "We have tremendous liquidity, which is not borrowed liquidity. It's real liquidity." He did, however, concede that "we're an insular company in an insular industry in an insular town." It was an unusually frank remark, and the coming months would prove him depressingly accurate.

Despite Ford's $2 billion profit in 2005, the company lost nearly $1.6 billion in its core North American auto operations. Ford's planners had forecast a decline in SUV sales, but by 2006 sales had plunged to levels that Ford hadn't expected to see until 2010. In late January, Bill Ford announced a corporate overhaul called "The Way Forward," under which Ford would close factories and shed tens of thousands of employees, both salaried and hourly. The Way Forward was housed in a special "war room" (a clichéd corporate favorite) with a sign that read "Culture Eats Strategy for Breakfast."

The trouble was, a culture of chaos was eating a strategy of confusion. In a baffling series of moves, the company dropped the venerable Lincoln Continental name in 2006 and gave Lincolns alphabet-soup monikers like MKZ and MKX. Then Ford said MKZ should be pronounced *Mark Z*, only to retreat from that and revert to *M-K-Z*. It was a too-smart-by-half episode of marketing groupthink that occurs when no one has the temerity to say it's a dumb idea. *The New York Times* called the flip-flop "the first recall of car pronunciation." Even worse was what Ford did with the Taurus. After neglecting the car for more than a decade, while Honda and Toyota had been steadily improving the Accord and the Camry, Ford now decided to drop the car entirely. The company was squandering twenty years and hundreds of millions of dollars' worth of precious brand identity.

Bill Jr. was bright, engaging, and well educated, but he had gotten the top job at Ford Motor because he was a Ford. It was the fastest way to the top, but in many ways it was the worst possible preparation. Growing up Ford meant seldom hearing the word *no* (at least outside the family) or having to bang heads to get things done. Since Bill Jr. had become CEO, Ford's executive suite had been spinning faster than a multivalve engine as winners ousted losers in corporate power struggles while the young heir remained above the fray. By the spring of 2006 Bill Jr. was telling some of his board members he needed help. Ford needed a major corporate overhaul, he explained, and maybe somebody else would make a better CEO to lead the company through it. It was just the opposite of Rick Wagoner's attitude at GM.

But Ford had no suitable inside candidates for CEO. As for candidates from other car companies, Bill Ford had sent feelers to Carlos Ghosn and Dieter Zetsche, but they were understandably wary. Ford hadn't hired an outsider as president in forty years, and that man—a former GM executive—had been axed after just eighteen months. Bill Jr. asked a few directors to make discreet inquiries with their corporate contacts, to see if anyone from outside the auto industry might fit the bill.

One name that surfaced was Alan Mulally, who at Boeing had presided over precisely the sort of makeover that Ford now needed. An engineer by training, Mulally laced his speech with terms like "Way cool!" and "Aaaabsolutely!" that were as corny as Kansas, from where, in fact, he hailed. After thirty-seven years at Boeing he was running the commercial airplanes division, which he had turned around by cutting the workforce to 50,000 employees from 120,000, and by slashing the time it took to build a big jet by nearly half. Some of his inspiration had come from Ford itself—ironically, from the special-team approach used to develop the original Taurus in the 1980s.

In July, around the time Ford posted a second-quarter loss of $123 million, Bill Ford and Mulally started talking, first by phone and then in person. The courtship continued on Sunday, August 6, when Mulally met with a couple of Ford's outside directors in Aspen, Colorado.

The directors broached what they thought might be a sensitive question: Would Mulally insist on being both chairman and CEO, or would he accept just the CEO post if Bill Ford wanted to continue as chairman? Mulally, to their pleasant surprise, replied that he would *insist* that Bill remain as chairman and wouldn't come to Ford otherwise. Because Bill was a Ford, Mulally explained, he could represent the company and work with the family in a way that no non-Ford could do.

The directors were sold, and so was Bill Ford. But the next few weeks brought only radio silence from Mulally, who was having second thoughts. He had a secure career and deep emotional ties to Boeing after nearly four decades there. In late August Mulally called Bill Ford, who was visiting his parents at their Long Island estate, on his cell phone. Reception was so bad that Bill had to bike to a public beach a mile away to take the call. And there he heard from Mulally that the answer was no. Faced with continuing as CEO of a company that was deeply troubled, Bill Ford was deflated.

What happened next, however, was a surprise. Mulally found himself deflated too. He was sixty-one years old, and if he wanted to run a company himself, this would be his last chance. So he reconsidered his refusal and resumed his discussions with Ford. On Friday, September 1, in a conference room at Chicago's Midway Airport, Mulally inked his new contract as president and CEO of Ford Motor. For years the Boeing executive had adorned his signature with a little airplane drawn next to his name. This time he did not.

The next week, when the announcement was made, Detroiters were shocked that Bill Ford basically had fired himself, drawing an unavoidable contrast to Wagoner's insistence on staying put. "I have a lot of myself invested in this company," Ford explained, "but not my ego." Any humiliation from admitting that he wasn't the right man for the job might have been cushioned by the fact that, as a Ford, he would remain chairman. Still, stepping aside required a portion of courage and self-awareness seldom seen in the corner offices of

American companies. Changing the CEO would prove to be the move that saved Ford Motor, while sticking with the CEO would be the decision that doomed GM.

Three months after Mulally's arrival, Ford borrowed $23.6 billion from banks to finance its turnaround effort. For the first time ever, the company had to pledge assets as collateral—including patents, real estate, factories, and even the blue-oval Ford logo, perhaps the most recognized trademark in the world. Executives characterized the deal as a giant "home improvement loan," and it quickly became clear why the money was necessary. Ford lost $12.6 billion in 2006— a horrific number that exceeded even GM's record loss from the year before. Mulally had arrived just in time.

During 2006, General Motors and Ford had racked up most of the big headlines, unfortunately for them, but toward the end of the year Chrysler began to play catch-up. In October, when DaimlerChryrsler released its financial results for the third quarter, the Chrysler division lost $1.5 billion—its first quarterly deficit after three straight years of profits.

It was a remarkable reversal of fortune for a company whose apparent emergence from the corporate repair shop had vaulted Dieter Zetsche into the top job at DaimlerChrysler. But the recovery had proved ephemeral. Sales of the flagship 300C sedan, with its gas-chugging 340-horsepower engine, had evaporated when gas prices resumed their post-Katrina climb, and Chrysler had responded by making a monumental error. Instead of cutting production in the summer of 2006, the company kept building cars that hadn't been ordered by dealers—and then trying to cajole or coerce the dealers into taking them.

Dealers often resent the practice, which they call "channel stuffing," but they usually try to go along. Gene Benner ordered extra cars, even though his sales were slowing, when Chrysler offered him wholesale discounts of $1,000 a vehicle. He figured the discount would defray the cost of carrying the extra inventory until he could sell it. But he soon learned that other dealers who had waited until Chrysler got more desperate were being offered discounts of $3,000 to $4,000 per car, putting him at a disadvantage.

Benner was angry, along with like-minded dealers who had tried to help the company from the get-go, and the result was all-out rebellion. Dealers refused to order more cars, and Chrysler resorted to parking 100,000 unsold vehicles in overflow lots near its factories—airport parking lots, fairgrounds, and any other empty surfaces the company could rent. It was a rerun of the "sales bank" that almost had killed Chrysler back in 1979.

The Jobs Bank, meanwhile, also was getting lots of use. Because of it Gene Young was making good money in the factory at Belvidere, despite Chrysler's woes. He stayed on the job while Chrysler was building cars that it couldn't sell, and whenever his shift was shut down, he was bounced back into the Jobs Bank, building no cars but making 95 percent of his take-home pay. He and other workers were insulated from the struggles of DaimlerChrysler, or so it seemed.

With Chrysler back in the red, Zetsche placed a call to Ron Gettelfinger at the UAW. The union had agreed to reduce healthcare costs at General Motors and Ford, Zetsche noted, and now Chrysler needed similar help. This wasn't exactly what Gettelfinger wanted to hear. The latest union concessions, at Ford, had passed the union's rank and file with a razor-thin majority, and the UAW president wasn't eager to risk defeat at the polls.

Even though Chrysler itself was losing money, Gettelfinger told Zetsche, the parent company, DaimlerChrysler, remained profitable overall, so the union couldn't agree to cut benefits. Zetsche was flabbergasted. He stormed out of his office and said, "What do we have to do? Lose $10 billion to get a level playing field?" A few weeks later Zetsche quietly directed his people to start exploring the sale of Chrysler.

The trick would be to find a buyer. When 2006 ended Toyota surged ahead of Chrysler in U.S. sales for the first time—with 2.5 million vehicles to Chrysler's 2.1 million. The Big Three were no longer the biggest three in their home market. *Automotive News,* which had coined the term *Big Three* eighty years earlier, started calling the companies the "Detroit Three" instead.

ELEVEN

CHAPTER 11?

*A*t the beginning of 2007 General Motors, Ford, and Chrysler were like big rowboats careening down the Niagara River, heading toward the falls and the terrifying plunge toward bankruptcy. They couldn't see the precipice. Indeed, hardly anyone could foresee the financial crisis that would hit America twenty months later, with devastating effects on Detroit. But the companies could sense danger, like an ominous but unseen roar in the distance. So they kept throwing extra baggage overboard by laying off employees and closing factories to lighten their loads. Still, the water kept washing over the sides faster than they could bail. They could only watch their Japanese, Korean, and German competitors (except for troubled DaimlerChrysler) with envy. The foreign companies had better boats, more cooperative deckhands, and abler pilots. They were far upriver, perhaps facing a few rapids, but well out of danger.

Detroit's car companies had one last chance—just one—to reach safe harbor. But getting there would require choosing the right path, shedding still more weight, and rowing with all the might they could muster. Ford had taken aboard a new pilot to steer a fresh course, and Chrysler was about to do the same. Not so General Motors, which viewed its boat as too big to sink and was determined to stay the course. In the end, just one of the three rowboats would make it, while the other two would tumble over the edge and into the depths below.

When the hundredth Detroit auto show opened to the press on January 8, 2007, there was little outward sign that General Motors was in danger. Automotive journalists voted the Chevrolet Silverado pickup the Truck of the Year, and they named the Saturn Aura sedan Car of the Year, prompting fist pumps from Saturn executives worthy of Tiger Woods at the Masters. But the best news for the company was the acclaim for a prototype car called the Chevy Volt. It was a "next-generation" hybrid that would leapfrog the Toyota Prius because, Rick Wagoner explained, the battery could be recharged from an ordinary electric outlet and might get more than a hundred miles a gallon, at least twice as much as the Prius.

Bob Lutz, the executive in charge of the Volt, couldn't resist quipping: "A GM electric vehicle is an inconvenient truth." So much for Al Gore's movie, and another one called *Who Killed the Electric Car?*, about GM killing its EV1 electric vehicle a decade earlier. When the film's director saw the Volt, he said: "My next project may be called *Who Resurrected the Electric Car?*" Never mind that sitting just a few feet away from the Volt was another new Chevrolet that was rather less eco-friendly and was already on the market—the 638-horsepower Corvette ZR1. (Gas mileage: Don't ask.)

As a business proposition, as opposed to an environmental statement, the Volt bore some inconvenient truths of its own. The battery technology was unproven, the car wouldn't be launched for at least three more years, and the price tag would be around $37,000, some 50 percent higher than the Prius. GM was counting on buyers getting tax rebates from the government to broaden the Volt's appeal beyond well-heeled granola-lovers, but the car still was likely to produce more publicity than profits. And after nearly $13 billion of losses over the prior two years, GM badly needed profits.

On that score, after unveiling the Volt, Wagoner retreated to a private General Motors booth on the show floor to confront Mike Jackson, CEO of the AutoNation chain of car dealerships. "You are causing me more trouble with my board than any man alive," Wagoner snapped, turning red with pent-up anger. Jackson had stepped out of line, Wagoner continued, by publicly criticizing GM for trying to boost profits by building too many cars and foisting them on reluctant dealers. Jackson would do best to cut the public complaints, Wagoner added, and to air any problems in private.

It was the sort of dressing-down from the chairman of General Motors that would have frightened any dealer thirty years earlier, when Wagoner started his career with GM. But this was 2007, not 1977, and Mike Jackson wasn't just any old car dealer. AutoNation was the nation's largest publicly owned automotive megadealer, with shares traded on the New York Stock Exchange and some three hundred dealerships nationwide. Jackson wasn't about to back down to guys from "the factory," as the car companies were called.

"I'm being a lot nicer than I could be, Rick," Jackson shot back. "What you're doing is bordering on earnings manipulation in a public company. Your people are shipping us cars we haven't ordered, sending us the bills, and then refusing to take the cars back." Wagoner himself surely hadn't directed this, Jackson acknowledged. But with GM dealers choking on more than a million unsold cars and trucks on their lots that January, the pressure on the company's salespeople to push more cars onto dealers was intense. Jackson was fed up. "You're a public company, I'm a public company, and we can't do this," he told Wagoner. "Stop stuffing my stores!"

Mike Jackson passionately denounced "channel stuffing," which he viewed as a perverse treadmill. The companies built too many cars to keep their factories running. Dealers balked at buying them. The companies pressured them with sticks (cutting their allotments of the hottest models) and carrots (wholesale discounts of up to $4,000 per car). The deep discounts, on top of the rebates to buyers, killed profits and devalued the reputation of Chevrolet, Dodge, Ford, and other once-venerable brands. So sales would drop further, discounts would get bigger, and losses would grow. The cycle, in Jackson's view, was putting the Big Three—well, the Detroit Three, now that Chrysler's sales trailed Toyota's—on the road to bankruptcy.

Bankruptcy? That couldn't really happen, could it? Especially not to General Motors, which had built America's industrial might, helped win its wars, and shaped every aspect of its culture from sexual mores to popular music to shopping habits. In early 2007 it seemed as far-fetched as, well, an African American president of the United States. Detroit's executives got annoyed at the mere mention of the word. "I don't care which junior analyst on Wall Street or two years out of Harvard B-school says, 'General Motors is inevitably headed for bankruptcy,'" Lutz had declared. "That's a crock. It's not going to happen."

To most Detroit executives, it didn't matter that every major U.S. airline had made at least one trip to bankruptcy court to take a big corporate shower, washing away layers of debt and union contracts to emerge with a cleaner cost base. Cars weren't like airline tickets. They were a typical family's second-largest purchase, after their house. People expected to own their cars for years and would want warranty service and, possibly, spare parts throughout that time. Surely Americans wouldn't buy cars from a company that might not be around to provide all that. The last big car company to declare bankruptcy was Studebaker in 1966, and nobody was buying Studebakers anymore.

Besides, Wagoner maintained, GM was on the mend. "Our entire GM team rose up to meet the collective challenges we face," he wrote to his shareholders in the spring of 2007. "Our performance was validation that we have the right strategy, and it's working." As evidence, Wagoner cited GM's narrower loss for 2006—$2 billion, compared to the prior year's loss of $10.6 billion. The company would have been profitable, he added, without special restructuring charges for layoffs and plant closings.

Of course, another way of looking at the same numbers was that, entering the seventh year of Wagoner's chairmanship, General Motors had posted yet another loss in yet another year of near-record car sales, and it had incurred so many special charges that they didn't seem special anymore.

Wagoner's public optimism wasn't echoed by Dieter Zetsche. In 2005, before he had left Auburn Hills to become CEO of Daimler-Chrysler, Zetsche had vowed he would "always be a Chrysler guy." But when he returned to Auburn Hills in February 2007 for a meeting of the DaimlerChrysler supervisory board, it was getting hard to be a Chrysler guy. Once again the American company was mired in multi-billion-dollar losses. More than 70 percent of Chrysler's sales consisted of SUVs, pickup trucks, and minivans, which Americans were turning away from as hybrid cars supplanted SUVs as the new sign of cool.

Chrysler's small cars, meanwhile, had harsh rides and cheap-looking interiors because of cost cuts ordered by Zetsche himself. But the company couldn't make money on the cars anyway because its cost structure included some $18 billion in unfunded pension and healthcare obligations. The restiveness among DaimlerChrysler shareholders that had cost Jürgen Schrempp his job was spreading, and unless Zetsche did something about Chrysler, his own job would be at risk. The meeting of the supervisory board he convened on February 13 would last nearly all day. The next day would go down in Chrysler's history as the "St. Valentine's Day Massacre."

The company announced a sweeping new restructuring plan, called "Project X," to cut 13,000 employees—out of its total of 83,000—and close a couple more factories. The goal was to shed enough ballast to make Chrysler profitable by 2008, although the internal projections called for minuscule profits, at best, even then. At a press conference that day, when Zetsche was asked whether he might sell Chrysler, he replied: "In this regard we do not exclude any option to find the best solution." He might as well have climbed to the top of the big headquarters tower that displayed the Chrysler Pentastar logo and hung out a giant For Sale sign. DaimlerChrysler stock jumped 8 percent when his words crossed the wires and finished the week up 14 percent. The shareholders were voting, in a landslide, for selling Chrysler, and Zetsche could read the returns. He was so eager to be rid of the American company that he was ready to give it away.

General Motors couldn't resist taking a sniff. Wagoner and his executives thought they could whack out huge chunks of Chrysler's costs by eliminating its legal, financial, and administrative staffs and by cutting duplicate products. The latter was a step GM should have taken within its own operations, but Wagoner couldn't bring himself to do that. When he brought the Chrysler idea to GM's board, however, the directors asked why a money-losing company with eight brands and difficult dealings with the UAW would buy another money-losing company with three more brands (Chrysler, Dodge, and Jeep) and still more difficulties with the UAW. Common sense prevailed, for once, and GM backed away.

Interest in Chrysler also came from foreign car companies, ironically including Nissan—which DaimlerChrysler, under Jürgen Schrempp, had considered buying a decade earlier. But the union issues and Chrysler's billions of unfunded liabilities for retiree healthcare proved too scary. Kirk Kerkorian, who had made a fortune on Chrysler once before, weighed in as well, offering the UAW partial ownership of the company to satisfy part of the unfunded liabilities.

But Ron Gettelfinger said no thanks. The UAW would rather milk Chrysler than own it—though two years later, the union wouldn't have a choice.

That left private equity firms, the new powers on the American corporate landscape. They raised pools of money from investors, leveraged the money by borrowing heavily from banks, and used the funds to pay bargain prices for troubled companies. Then they installed new management, ruthlessly cut costs, turned losses into earnings, and sold out for huge profits to "strategic buyers"— typically, public companies looking for a quick way to boost their own earnings.

Private equity firms believed that, unlike the managerial bureaucrats that ran most public companies, they could fix anything. So Chrysler looked intriguing to the firm that had emerged from obscurity a year earlier to buy GMAC: Cerberus Partners LLP. It was named for the three-headed dog of Greek mythology that guarded the gate to the underworld. That was appropriate, because Chrysler would become Cerberus's deal from hell.

Cerberus's founder, forty-eight-year-old Stephen Feinberg, drove a Dodge Ram pickup truck and liked to hunt, with guns. Cerberus was headquartered on Park Avenue, but the upscale address didn't prevent Feinberg from decorating his office with the mounted head of an elk that he had shot himself, and a scale model of a Harley-Davidson motorcycle, just like the real one he had at home. Meetings there rarely began before eleven A.M. because Feinberg worked late and didn't want to get up early.

He saw Chrysler as a chance to combine patriotism (saving an iconic American company) with profits, though not necessarily in that order. He figured there *had* to be synergies between GMAC (now controlled by Cerberus) and Chrysler's own lending arm, Chrysler Financial. In fact, if Chrysler's auto operations could just get to break-even, Cerberus still could make tons of money on automotive financing. Besides, Feinberg knew that Zetsche had come to view Chrysler as a millstone that would drown him, and possibly even Daimler itself, unless he got rid of it somehow. Feinberg loved dealing with desperate sellers. And on May 14, after weeks of negotiations, he and Zetsche reached a deal.

Nine years after paying $36 billion to buy Chrysler, the Germans sold 80.1 percent of the company (enough to get Chrysler off their books under the accounting rules) for only $7.4 billion, or 20 percent of what they had paid. But that wasn't all. Virtually all of the $7.4 billion would be paid not to Daimler but to the new holding company created to own Chrysler, which meant that Cerberus would be paying itself.

The deal was lubricated by some of America's biggest banks—JPMorgan Chase, Citibank, and others—who bought $10 billion of Chrysler debt that was secured by the car company's assets. The banks planned to resell the debt to investors and pocket a profit for their trouble. Cerberus's one concession was agreeing to retain Chrysler's $18 billion of unfunded retiree healthcare liabilities, which the Germans wanted to get off their balance sheet. Under almost any scenario, however, Cerberus figured it wouldn't get stuck holding the bag for that money. Zetsche had gone way beyond discounting the price of cars; he had discounted the price of an entire car company.

It was a humiliating retreat for Daimler and, by all appearances, a sweet deal for the banks and for Feinberg. With control of GMAC and now Chrysler, the once-obscure private equity firm had emerged in little over a year to become one of the dominant forces in the American automobile industry. Cerberus celebrated the deal with a party for Chrysler employees. Acrobats rappelled from the roof of the headquarters in Auburn Hills, and daytime fireworks streaked across the sky.

"People say, 'How can you turn this around and [others] can't?'" remarked John Snow, the former U.S. Treasury secretary who had become Cerberus's chairman and public spokesman. The answer, he said, was patience, the inherent advantage of private equity ownership. "It might take a couple of years to really show the results. And public companies don't have two or three years." There was plenty of hubris on Wall Street as well as in Detroit.

Not that Cerberus was willing to wait years, or even weeks, to make money from its new prize. On August 3, 2007, the same day Cerberus completed the transaction, a company called Auburn Hills Owner LLC bought Chrysler's headquarters—the nation's second-largest office building, behind only the Pentagon—for the bargain price of $325 million. Auburn Hills Owner then mortgaged the property and leased it back to Chrysler, which would use its cash flow to pay the rent.

The lease terms, which weren't public, were easy to negotiate because Auburn Hills Owner, like Chrysler, was a subsidiary of Cerberus. So Cerberus could collect rent money on Chrysler real estate while waiting to make money on Chrysler's cars. It was all perfectly legal and clever—rather too clever, in fact, for an ailing car company that needed to devote its cash flow to filling its anemic pipeline of new products. But financial finagling is what private equity firms did. Why wait for automotive engineering when financial engineering was faster?

As for the banks that helped to finance the deal, unlike Cerberus, they really would have to be patient. Contrary to their plans, they couldn't find buyers for the $10 billion of Chrysler debt they had agreed to accept, so they were stuck with holding it for a while. The loans would come back to bite the banks in a way they couldn't imagine.

Despite the celebrations at Chrysler's headquarters, workers at the factory in Belvidere watched the company's sale to the moguls on Wall Street with worry. The workers were delighted to see Daimler go. While they didn't know much about Cerberus, they did know, as Gene Young put it, that private equity firms "break companies up into little pieces and sell them off." Young and his co-workers described the sale to Cerberus with a special acronym: BOHICA. It was pronounced *bo-hee-cuh,* and it stood for "Bend Over, Here It Comes Again." Belvidere workers had been nervous under the Germans; now they were frightened, but also frozen in their tracks.

Belvidere's workers were making such good money that few started looking for another job, BOHICA or not. In 2007, the year Cerberus bought Chrysler, Young would make $72,000, his best year so far. (He didn't know it would be his best year ever.)

He was forty years old and had worked at Chrysler eight years, living a Ping-Pong work life as he bounced back and forth between the assembly line and the Jobs Bank. During his Jobs Bank stints he volunteered for community service projects, including painting his church. Other times he hung out at the union hall, helping his fellow "bankers" repair their computers, until an inverse layoff or an increase in production would bring him back to work.

The Jobs Bank was just part of the UAW's elaborate safety net that included "thirty and out" retirement, guaranteed pensions, nearly free healthcare, and more. The system fostered a "So what?" attitude that was reinforced by management's professed dedication to quality, which seemed to disappear every time production fell behind schedule.

Sometimes when workers pointed out defects, they were ordered to ignore them, because "it's just a Mexico car"—that is, bound for the Mexican market. Once when Young suggested a more efficient method for installing windshield wipers—the sort of suggestion the Japanese welcomed in their factories—he was rudely rebuffed by his supervisor. After that he pretty much kept his mouth shut.

This workplace culture was part and parcel of what Cerberus was getting when it bought Chrysler, but the Wall Street guys didn't have a clue. Their analysts and bankers pored over every number in Chrysler's financial reports, but none of the braniacs on the due-diligence team bothered to head to downtown Belvidere for coffee with Young to talk about BOHICA, inverse layoffs, and other realities of life in the trenches. The guys from Cerberus were flying at thirty thousand feet, and Belvidere was in the fly-over zone.

Nor did anyone talk to Gene Benner in South Paris, Maine. By 2007 his sales volume had plunged to just half of what it had been two years earlier, and his initial belief that the problem was just a cyclical slump was fading fast. By focusing on trucks and SUVs, Chrysler had left him without an attractive lineup of smaller cars at a time when demand for those vehicles was increasing. The Chrysler 300C's initial success had been a flash in the pan. And those people who still wanted an SUV could choose from among an increasing array of Japanese vehicles, such as the redesigned Toyota 4Runner or, for hard-core off-roaders, the Nissan X-Terra.

The initial promise of DaimlerChrysler had long since faded. But car dealers are, by nature, optimists. Benner was hoping that the new owner for Chrysler would mean better days ahead because private equity firms, he figured, were sort of like car dealers—people who put their own money on the line. Surely, he figured, the Cerberus people understood the need to invest in better products. "Any new owner will be better than Daimler," Benner would say. "Right?"

In July 2007, while Cerberus was working to finalize the Chrysler deal, Ford announced second-quarter earnings of $750 million, its first quarterly profit in two years. A few days later General Motors weighed in with earnings of $891 million for the second quarter. Cost cutting seemed to be working at both companies, and normally the return to modest profitability would have been good news. But the summer of 2007 wasn't normal in Detroit. Good news, in this case, was really bad news.

The same month that they posted their second-quarter profits, GM and Ford, as well as Chrysler, began negotiations for a new national contract with the UAW. The talks offered a potential safe harbor for the corporate rowboats careening downriver: the chance to jettison some of the healthcare costs for UAW retirees, similar to the reductions the companies had imposed on retired managers. But the chances for convincing the union to go beyond the modest concessions of 2005 hinged on the companies' ability to prove that they were in dire straits. The second-quarter profits were, well, not helpful, especially because GM couldn't resist citing them as further evidence of its turnaround. Then again, other facts painted a darker picture.

GM's unfunded healthcare liabilities had swollen to $51 billion. The 450,000 U.S. hourly workers the company had in 1985 had shrunk to under 74,000. Yet GM continued to provide generous healthcare benefits for 340,000 UAW retirees and their spouses. It was now a ratio of nearly five retirees for every active worker—an increase from the three-to-one ratio of a few years earlier, because the company continued to shrink. GM's numbers were unsustainable, like a preview of might happen to the U.S. Social Security system thirty years in the future. Except this was now—and GM, unlike the federal government, couldn't print money to pay its retirees.

The burden added more than $1,600 to the cost of every car and truck that General Motors made. In contrast, Toyota spent less than $200 per vehicle for retiree healthcare because it didn't have many U.S. retirees, and the ones it had paid co-pays and deductibles for doctor visits, just like most other Americans. Thirty years earlier, ironically, Detroit had demanded the Japanese build factories in America to "level the playing field." Now there were more than two dozen U.S. transplants, and Detroit and the UAW were fingering them for giving the Japanese an unfair advantage.

At Chrysler and Ford, the retiree-cost numbers were a little better than at GM, but not much. After decades of delaying the pain of a solution, the system had reached the breaking point. All three companies wanted to toss their retiree healthcare baggage overboard by creating a VEBA (*vee-buh*). The name was being heard so often in Detroit that one might have thought the Ford VEBA was a new car.

Instead it was a Voluntary Employee Beneficiary Association (though it wasn't exactly voluntary), a trust fund to be financed with company payments capped at a fixed amount, but controlled by the UAW and union-appointed trustees. The trust would dispense healthcare benefits however the trustees decided—setting deductibles, co-payments, and benefit levels—at whatever the fund could afford. A VEBA's benefit to the car companies was obvious: The funding cap would get them off the hook for unlimited, and constantly rising, healthcare expenses.

There actually was an upside for the UAW too. Without a VEBA trust, healthcare benefits for union members could be wiped out if the car companies ever did file for bankruptcy. By mid-2007 that possibility was quietly beginning to enter the UAW's calculations. Just to be sure, the union again hired some number-crunching Wall Street bankers, who confirmed that it damned well should be considered a possibility.

Whatever the logic, however, a VEBA wouldn't be an easy sell to the union's rank and file. When the 2007 contract discussions began, union activists started handing out leaflets saying VEBA stood for Vandalizing Employee Benefits Again. It was better than BOHICA, but not much.

The man in the middle was Gettelfinger, a tough negotiator who wasn't about to sleep with the enemy—or even with the enemy's pillow. In mid-September, when the national contract negotiations with GM turned into an around-the-clock marathon, Gettelfinger took to sleeping on the floor in a company conference room. But the man who had banned company-union golf outings archly refused the pillow offered by GM negotiators, opting instead to use a plastic bag filled with shredded documents from the talks. A man with such a stiff backbone, and neck, wasn't about to go down easily. The pillow was a symbolic act of defiance that presaged a bigger one just ahead.

At eleven A.M. on Monday, September 24, just as a new national contract with a VEBA appeared imminent, Gettelfinger ordered GM workers to walk out of their factories and take to the picket lines. It was the first national contract strike against General Motors in thirty-seven years. "We've done a lot of things to help that company," Gettelfinger told a crowded, hastily called news conference. "But look, there comes a time when you have to draw a line in the sand."

The GM negotiators were stunned, and the news media entered hyperventilation mode. National Public Radio described the move as the union's "bold gamble that it could get a stronger contract by shutting down an already weakened company." In truth, the strike wasn't a line in the sand or a bold gamble or any other such cliché. Instead it was calculated political theater, intended to last just long enough to let UAW members blow off steam and convince the rank and file that their leader had fought the good fight. Just two days later, exactly as planned, Gettelfinger ended the strike and declared a historic victory for the UAW. He was right about the historic part, but not about the victory. The new contract marked the end of seventy years of steady, virtually uninterrupted UAW gains.

For the first time ever the union accepted a two-tier wage system, with lower pay for new hires at Detroit Three factories. It also agreed to a VEBA, completely absolving the car companies of their responsibility for retiree healthcare, which instead would fall to the trust fund. GM agreed to cover its $51 billion of unfunded retiree health liabilities with a payment of $35 billion in cash to the trust—about seventy cents on the dollar, a pattern that Ford and Chrysler would follow.

The money would be paid in installments over three years, although there was one big catch. The companies wouldn't realize any cost savings on retiree healthcare until 2010, so reaping the fruits of their historic breakthrough would require some delayed gratification. GM's shareholders, at least, didn't seem to mind. On October 12 the company's stock hit $42.50 a share, its highest price in three years. One retired GM executive who had been ready to cash in his stock options decided to wait, because his contacts on Wall Street advised him the company's stock was sure to go higher. It would be like waiting for Godot.

Just three weeks later GM's third-quarter financial results unveiled some ugly surprises. ResCap, the mortgage-lending arm of GMAC, had racked up $1.8 billion of losses on "subprime" loans to deadbeat borrowers. At least the good news there, relatively speaking, was that Cerberus was stuck with 51 percent of the losses.

The real stunner was GM's decision to write off $38.6 billion in tax credits it had accumulated over the prior three years—more than eclipsing the company's $34 billion in earnings between 1996 and 2004. The "reversal of tax-loss carry-forward" was an accounting charge that, GM quickly explained, didn't impair the company's actual cash condition. Which was true, but quite beside the point.

The accumulated tax credits could have been used to reduce taxes on the company's future profits, but there was a time limit on their use. By writing off the credits, GM was conceding that it didn't expect to make any profits in the next few years. It was a shocking admission for a company that had been proclaiming its turnaround and had just cut a deal to shed $51 billion of healthcare obligations to retired hourly workers. On top of the accounting charge GM lost another $400 million in the quarter from its operations.

Now the stock went into reverse. Over the next few weeks GM shares plunged nearly 40 percent to close, on November 20, at $27— lower than when Wagoner had launched his first restructuring effort three years earlier. Despite all the plant closings, layoffs, contract concessions, and cost cuts since then, the company's profitability picture really hadn't changed. General Motors was rowing hard but going nowhere, and the boat was slipping farther downstream.

Nonetheless, in January 2008 Wagoner's annual presentation to Wall Street analysts was an upbeat update on the state of GM, with nearly fifty PowerPoint slides covering everything from the "Revitalized Sales and Marketing Strategy" to GM's "Multi-Pronged Leadership Strategy" on fuel-efficient cars. *Revitalized. Multi-pronged.* No buzzword was left behind. The presentation was titled: "From Turn-around to Transformation." The message might have been disingenuous, but it wasn't duplicitous. Wagoner believed it so much that he delivered the same message a month later in Naples, Florida, to his old friends and former colleagues in the GM Executive Retirees Club, a group whose existence bespoke the continuing cozy insularity of GM's corporate culture. The old-boy attendees applauded appreciatively.

But four months later the company posted a first-quarter loss of $3.25 billion, which would have been shocking except that bad news from GM was losing its shock value. General Motors was heading for a transformation, all right, but not the kind Wagoner had in mind.

While Detroit's new labor deal was coming together, Cerberus was staffing Chrysler with an automotive all-star team, including some high-profile American executives it had lured from Toyota. The real headliner, though, was the selection of Bob Nardelli, no stranger to headlines, as Chrysler's CEO.

The son of a steelworker, Nardelli had climbed almost to the top of General Electric, where, like Jac Nasser at Ford, he so admired CEO Jack Welch that Nardelli was nicknamed "Little Jack." After losing the race to succeed Big Jack in 2000, Nardelli became CEO at Home Depot, where his cost cuts increased profits but also alienated employees and compromised service in the stores. In 2006 Nardelli told Home Depot's directors to skip the annual stockholders' meeting, which he decided to limit to thirty minutes anyway, because he deemed the exercise a waste of time. The resulting firestorm of criticism ended in Nardelli's departure, with an eye-popping $210 million severance package.

It made him America's poster boy for executive arrogance and excessive pay—"Mr. Golden Parachute," as the workers at Belvidere called him. Neither stigma, however, carried much baggage on Wall Street, where Cerberus couldn't resist hiring a CEO trained in hardboiled GE-style management.

After arriving in August 2007, Nardelli quickly dismissed another 10,000 employees (on top of the previous 13,000), killed slow-selling vehicles, and cut 100,000 cars out of Chrysler's production schedules to control inventories. He earmarked $500 million of the cost savings to upgrade the tacky interiors of Chrysler's cars, and he repaid $2.5 billion of Chrysler's bank debt. He also sought counsel from Jerry York, who told him that fixing Chrysler would be a thousand times harder than he could imagine.

To help with the effort, Nardelli brought in former colleagues from his previous companies. The new purchasing chief from Home Depot explored buying lower-priced components from India and China, only to learn that shipments of car batteries would lose their charge somewhere over the ocean. Meanwhile, consultants trained at GE started putting Chrysler managers through Six Sigma training to diagnose hidden operational problems. The managers groaned because as far as they were concerned, all their problems—lousy cars, burdensome factory work rules, etc.—were glaringly obvious.

The most problematic of Nardelli's imports, though, was Peter Arnell, a flamboyant brand-development guru who once had convinced Chrysler to hire singer Celine Dion to burnish the company's image—until her multimillion-dollar appearances flopped. Arnell's subsequent gigs included PepsiCo, where his twenty-seven-page memo on redesigning the soda can was derided by *Newsweek* as "so much pseudo-intellectual claptrap—references to the *Mona Lisa,* the Parthenon, the golden ratio, the relativity of space and time, magnetic fields, 'perimeter oscillations' of the Pepsi logo," and more.

Soon after Nardelli landed at Chrysler, Arnell was back, sticking his neck into design, marketing, and, well, other places. Once during a "walkaround" to evaluate a new design, a Chrysler manager felt an odd presence on his right shoulder. Arnell was resting his chin there, perhaps to examine the car's perimeter oscillations. His appeal to the no-nonsense Nardelli mystified many at Chrysler, but people who challenged him found themselves rebuked or, in at least one case, fired.

Amid all the internal jockeying for position, the real problem was that Chrysler remained a truck company in a market that was turning back to cars. The company's big new product for 2008 was the Dodge Ram pickup truck, available with a 5.7-liter Hemi V8 engine that got just thirteen miles a gallon in city driving. It was the wrong product at the wrong time—and with the wrong publicity stunt, as it turned out.

On January 13, 2008, journalists at the Detroit auto show were greeted by the sight of 130 longhorn steers parading through the city's downtown streets toward the Cobo Hall exhibition center. The herd had been trucked in from Oklahoma—in Chrysler's latest auto show scene-grabber—to provide a dramatic backdrop to the unveiling of the new truck. Nardelli presided over the show, gamely insisting that, despite the price of gasoline, there were plenty of pickup buyers still out there.

While he was speaking, however, some of the steers started to mount each other, with wide-eyed children watching and television cameras rolling. The film, which quickly appeared on YouTube, produced lots of publicity all right. Unfortunately, it was all about horny longhorns and snickering references to "Brokeback Pickup." Not long afterward Nardelli confided to Jerry York that he had lied: fixing Chrysler would be a million times harder than he had believed.

In March 2008, a couple months after Chrysler's cattle fiasco, Ford announced it was selling Jaguar and Land Rover to Tata Motors of India for $2.3 billion, about what Ford had paid to buy Jaguar alone nearly twenty years before. It was a drastic action, but these were desperate times. The sale signaled a shift of the tectonic plates beneath not only the auto industry but also the broader world of political economy.

Jaguar and Land Rover were the official purveyors of luxury cars and SUVs to the landed gentry of England—the "Rule, Britannia" types who had lorded over India as a colony for two hundred years. But by 2008 Tata had become an international business powerhouse. The former colonials had become the buyers and the bosses. It wasn't quite Cornwallis at Yorktown, but for the global auto industry, it was the world turned upside down.

It also was a sign of the new order at Ford World Headquarters in Dearborn. As an auto industry outsider, like Nardelli, Alan Mulally wasn't bound emotionally to Jaguar and Land Rover as veteran Ford executives had been. To Mulally the facts were simple and stark: Ford had lost billions on both companies since buying them, not only hurting the company's bottom line but also sapping resources that could have been used to develop new Fords and Lincolns.

Selling Jaguar and Land Rover was unfortunate but necessary, like tossing a couple of injured people off the rowboat so the other occupants could stay afloat. It was exactly the sort of brand-culling that Wagoner should have been doing at GM but didn't want to face. Mulally also lightened Ford's rowboat by continuing to close factories and cut employees. By the end of 2007 Ford's employment ranks had shrunk to 246,000 people worldwide, 100,000 fewer than at the beginning of the decade.

Unlike Nardelli, however, Mulally didn't bring a flock of high-profile outsiders into Ford. Instead he chose a course that seemed more plodding and pedestrian but was in fact more effective. Mulally refocused Ford's executive team on a single goal: revitalizing the flagship Ford "blue oval" brand, as it was called in the company. The key would be to develop new cars in one place and sell them globally—as opposed to Ford's traditional practice of wasting billions to develop similar cars in each region of the world.

It was a disarmingly simple idea that Wagoner might have emulated to focus on reviving Chevrolet, and it was a return to Ford's roots. A century earlier the Model T had been Ford's first "world car," engineered in one place (America) but built and sold everywhere. But subsequent "world car" efforts had fallen afoul of Ford's fierce regional rivalries and daunting internal politics.

One glaring example was the subcompact Ford Escort of the 1980s, which was supposed to have been the same car in the United States and in Europe. But it wound up being two different cars that looked identical but had only one part in common, because rival engineering teams on each continent insisted on doing it their way. Such nonsense never would have been tolerated at Honda or Toyota, and Mulally was determined to kill it at Ford too. He ordered that the new Ford Fiesta, a high-mileage subcompact being developed in Europe, be launched in China and the United States as well, virtually unchanged.

Mulally started monitoring the Fiesta and other product-development programs with a weekly BPR meeting, as in business planning review. Unusual issues were referred to an SAR, for special attention review. Attendees at BPRs and SARs often discussed such nitty-gritty issues as HMI—human-machine interface—which was basically the location and feel of the buttons and knobs on the dashboard of each vehicle. It was like a parody of alphabet-soup corporate jargon, but at least everybody was speaking the same language. The new CEO also predicted Ford would return to profitability by 2009.

Mulally was mostly on the right track, but that prediction was something he soon would regret.

In February 2008, while Ford was negotiating the Jaguar–Land Rover deal, a smaller but nonetheless compelling drama was unfolding at Bessey Motors in Maine. Gene Benner got a personal visit from Chrysler Financial Corporation, Chrysler's moneylending arm. Normally such visits were routine and friendly, because Benner was a good customer. But this time was different.

The visitors pointed out that Bessey Motors had begun losing money—which Benner, of course, already knew, but figured he could reverse over time. Then his guests dropped a bombshell: Chrysler Financial had decided to cut off his credit, effective immediately. Benner was shocked. Car dealers can't operate without credit, which is what allows them to stock inventories of new cars. The sudden cutoff, without any warning, could drive him out of business—and destroy everything he had worked so hard to build.

Benner angrily told his visitors to get out. Maybe Chrysler's new Wall Street owners, he thought, wouldn't be better than the Germans after all. He quickly got a new line of credit from a bank, then endured a couple weeks of sleepless nights. The result, after much thought and soul-searching, was a turnaround plan that he described on a single sheet of paper with a simple preamble: "With the economic environment the way it is and with new vehicle demand lagging," Benner wrote to himself, "I have centered my business plan on the one thing that I can control—EXPENSES."

He cut his own pay, and then convened his thirty employees over pizza and Pepsi to give them some bad news. He wouldn't cut their weekly wages, but he would cut bonuses and eliminate contributions to the 401(k) plan. He also raised the deductibles for employee health insurance, reduced advertising spending and inventory levels, and laid off one employee. All told, the moves would save $357,000 a year and cut his break-even point in half, from 400 new cars and 400 used cars each year to just 200 of each.

It was just the sort of quick, decisive action in response to a crisis that Detroit's automakers should have taken themselves years earlier. But Benner didn't have to deal with shareholders, boards of directors, corporate compensation committees, unions, or any of that stuff. The only person he had to convince to act was himself. His employees quickly offered their support, despite the hardship it would bring, because they knew their jobs depended on making the business profitable. It was a sharp contrast to the UAW's grudging recalcitrance in Detroit.

As it happened, Benner had acted just in time.

On March 17 the investment bank Bear Stearns collapsed under a mountain of financial derivatives, subprime loans, and other stuff that most Americans didn't understand. The government hastily arranged a fire sale to JPMorgan Chase, one of the country's biggest banks. The resulting headlines about turmoil on Wall Street were undermining consumer confidence, the engine that drives car sales. Meanwhile the price of gasoline on Main Street was going through the roof—surging past $3.50 a gallon by mid-May and heading toward $4. After three decades of periodic crises, Detroit teetered at the tipping point.

On May 18 Mulally convened a rare Sunday meeting of a few senior executives. It wasn't a BPR or an SAR. It was an all-out emergency. Sales of pickup trucks and SUVs in the first half of the month had plunged far below what Ford had forecast. Without immediate action, Ford would wind up being saddled with a Chrysler-style "sales bank" of unsold, and unsellable, vehicles, which would be disastrous.

Four days later Mulally slashed truck production and canceled his prediction of profitability in 2009. When a reporter asked whether that would hurt his credibility, the usually jovial Mulally uttered a terse "No comment." Within days Ford decided to dismiss another two thousand salaried managers, 12 percent of its total in the United States and Canada. But at least Ford's boat was afloat.

GM's boat, though, was leaking badly. By June 3, when Wagoner convened the company's annual meeting in Wilmington, Delaware,

General Motors had racked up $55 billion in losses since he had announced his plan to transform the company in 2005. But Wagoner wasn't about to concede that he had made a colossal error by betting the company on trucks and SUVs four years earlier, when even *National Geographic* was writing about the end of cheap oil.

Instead he told the shareholders that GM had "made significant progress on all fronts." Then he announced that, despite that progress, the company would close four truck factories, put new emphasis on small cars, and consider selling Hummer—just as Jerry York had suggested more than two years earlier. *The Wall Street Journal's* headline read, appropriately: "GM Shifts Its Strategy Into Reverse."

The CEO's message was surreal, even in the context of corporate spin control. On the one hand, Wagoner was praising the company's progress. On the other, he was scrapping the strategy that had produced the "progress." Even now, though, the new strategy was to be phased in over a few years, and there were lots of caveats about the specifics.

Shareholders rushed to unload their stock. The day after the meeting GM closed at $17.01 a share, its lowest level in twenty-six years. By the end of the month it would drop another 33 percent, to $11.50. On July 2 a Merrill Lynch research report said bankruptcy was "not impossible" for GM, prompting Wagoner to reply that it was still unequivocally "not an option." In Dallas he told an audience of businessmen: "We're still kicking. We have no plans whatsoever to ride off into the sunset."

The events at General Motors, Ford, and Chrysler—unfolding like a boat sinking in slow motion, which nobody seemed able to stop— were an eerie replay of the events of 1973. Back then the American companies had been making big cars and big profits, until the first oil shock hit, gas prices soared, and consumers lurched toward small cars.

Fast-forward thirty-five years to 2008, and the Detroit companies had graduated from big cars to big SUVs. Americans had embraced them for twenty years until the early days of May, when gasoline surged past $4 a gallon and the market turned on a dime. GM, Ford, and Chrysler were responding with plans to shift to small cars, but developing them would take three or four years and billions of dollars.

Ford at least had cash to finance the transition, thanks to the money it had borrowed. But not GM and Chrysler.

In mid-July GM announced new layoffs, suspended its dividend, and eliminated medical benefits for retired managers and executives over sixty-five. The company hired a consulting firm to help the retirees navigate the maze of Medicare, something they had never needed. One retired executive called the firm's toll-free number and spent two hours on hold before hanging up without getting through. It was a rude glimpse of how the other half lived.

Detroit's second-quarter financial results for 2008 showed the deepening crisis. Ford lost $8.7 billion, its largest quarterly loss ever. Chrysler, being private, didn't report its results, but they had to be terrible too. General Motors lost $15.5 billion, a stunning $181,000 per minute, twenty-four hours a day, between April 1 and June 30. Some of the the red ink was from operations, some from the latest restructuring charges, but all of it was awful.

George Fisher even used the word *appalling.* Not to describe the losses, to be sure, but to describe reporters' insistent questions about whether GM's board finally might be losing faith in Wagoner. To rebut any such suggestion, the ever-loyal Fisher proclaimed that the board "unanimously" supported the CEO. "This is not just a passive board sitting by," he added. "The losses are something nobody likes." Well, that was good to know.

Fisher was always calm, collected, and wedded to the clubby decorum of the boardroom. He admired Wagoner's respectfulness toward board members, which contrasted with the imperious attitudes of many other CEOs. Fisher was no more likely to lead a boardroom revolt than he would go bungee jumping off the Empire State Building. He had saved Wagoner's job, after all, when the board seemed poised to fire the CEO two years earlier.

A few other directors weren't so sure about Wagoner, but they lacked the stomach to buck the go-along, get-along atmosphere of the boardroom. They kept telling themselves that $4-a-gallon gas wasn't Wagoner's fault, and that anyway, nobody but Wagoner understood GM well enough to fix the company.

But by now even some senior GM executives were questioning that assessment, even though, like most people at GM, they just *liked* Rick Wagoner. They saw him as the perfect paint-by-numbers CEO: smart, serious, mature, and capable of absorbing disparate data and presenting it in a coherent fashion. As for integrity, Wagoner honorably—though certainly not wisely—took his annual bonus awards in stock instead of in cash. The decision cost him millions as GM's stock declined.

The doubters, however, believed General Motors needed creative daring as opposed to paint-by-numbers planning. While Mulally had quickly disposed of Jaguar and Land Rover, Wagoner had resisted selling loss-plagued Saab and was just now starting to think about, maybe, selling Hummer. The list of failures on Wagoner's watch was astounding: the Fiat debacle, $70 billion of losses since 2005 (counting the latest quarterly results), and GM's endlessly eroding market share. And all of it, except for the very latest losses, had preceded $4-a-gallon gas by years. But the executives' doubts remained private. Public disloyalty would have been career suicide. Besides, it just wasn't the GM way.

The GM way of loyalty became evident, in poignant fashion, in early August, just days after the company announced the enormous second-quarter loss. It was time for the board to convene its traditional yearly meeting at the company's proving grounds in Milford, Michigan, an hour outside of Detroit, so the directors could test-drive the latest cars. The event was part board meeting, part hot-rodding (civilized, to be sure), and part family reunion, because retired General Motors executives—the same guys who usually wintered in Naples—were invited.

One attendee was a long-retired senior executive who liked the new cars and also liked what Wagoner said about his plans to fix the company. At around $12 a share, the retiree figured, GM's stock was a bargain. He bought some, and then headed to his summer retreat in northern Michigan, where he convinced some other retired GM executives to buy some too. Loyalty was a big reason why they had risen to the senior ranks of General Motors, and they weren't about to lose that trait now.

But they were about to lose their money.

On Sunday, September 14, Merrill Lynch, the once-solid firm that had brought Wall Street to Main Street, sold itself to Bank of America to avert financial collapse. Merrill was reeling under the bad mortgage investments incurred under CEO Stan O'Neal. He was the former GM director—and by now, the deposed chairman of Merrill Lynch—who had encouraged expanding the mortgage business at GMAC, with equally disastrous results. Over the same weekend, insurance giant American International Group begged for a bailout because its mortgage lending too had gone awry.

Worse still, Lehman Brothers, a once high-flying investment bank burdened by similar bad debts, filed for bankruptcy and plummeted toward liquidation. This time around the government declined to ride to the rescue, as it had with Bear Stearns. "The stunning series of events [on September 14] culminated a weekend of frantic around-the-clock negotiations, as Wall Street bankers huddled in meetings at the behest of Bush administration officials to try to avoid a downward spiral," wrote *The New York Times.*

It was futile. The next day—Monday, September 15—the Dow Jones Industrial Average dropped 500 points. Two weeks later, after much congressional wrangling, George W. Bush signed the last major law of his presidency, the Troubled Asset Relief Program (TARP), to inject up to $700 billion into ailing banks to prop up confidence in the financial system. But by late October the stock market plunged another 3,000 points, a total of 30 percent in five weeks. It was worse than the Crash of '29 and wiped out billions of dollars of wealth that could have been used to buy vacations or clothes or . . . cars. Wall Street had come to Main Street in disastrous fashion.

At AutoNation's headquarters in Fort Lauderdale, Mike Jackson pored over sales records and was shocked by what he saw. No event since World War II—not the JFK assassination, not the attacks of 9/11, nor anything else—had caused such a quick collapse in car sales as the Lehman bankruptcy. For the first half of the month, sales were running at an annual pace of 14 million vehicles, which wasn't great but was bearable. But from September 15 onward the sales pace dropped another 30 percent, to under 10 million vehicles—the lowest level in nearly thirty years. Consumers were afraid to buy cars.

Bankers were just as afraid to make loans. The car companies couldn't cut costs fast enough to keep up. Even the Japanese and German automakers started hurting.

Hurting, however, was different from desperate, and it was desperation time in Detroit. Wagoner had put out merger feelers to Ford, only to get a polite no thanks. Ford was Detroit's only car company with its head above water, and it wasn't about to be dragged down by GM.

Then Wagoner turned to Chrysler. The GM board had nixed the notion a year earlier, but times had changed, and Cerberus now was eager to get out. It also was eager to get paid, but GM was running out of cash. And the same bankers who were balking at car loans weren't willing to finance a merger of two money-losing car companies.

In October GM's Washington lobbyists started asking—discreetly, of course—whether the government might pony up $5 billion or so to finance the merger. But this was political dynamite. Any government money used to buy Chrysler would have gone to the private equity moguls at Cerberus and to the big banks that still held Chrysler debt. Even if the deal made sense, which the government types found questionable, it would have made GM look like a bagman funneling more government money to Wall Street. Congress and the Treasury Department weren't about to bite.

To cope with the crisis, automakers and their suppliers launched into new rounds of cost cutting. In late October Nardelli said Chrysler would cut its management ranks by another 25 percent, or five thousand people, by the end of the year. Delphi made the decision to skimp on bathroom maintenance; the occasional toilet paper outage was unfortunate, but it took a strong stomach to work for a company in its third year of bankruptcy anyway.

On November 5, in the midst of the economic maelstrom and Detroit's meltdown, Barack Obama made history by being elected the first African American president of the United States. The American people, with their economy in tatters, had opted for change. Not so General Motors, where Wagoner insisted he wasn't prepared to resign, even in return for government aid. "I don't think it'd be a very smart move," he told reporters. "It's not clear to me what purpose would be served." Louis XIV had said pretty much the same thing three hundred years earlier, but at least *"L'état, c'est moi"* had an elegant French snootiness.

Five days after the election GM's stock sank to $3.36 a share, its lowest level since 1946. The stock that GM's loyal retired executives had bought in August had lost 70 percent of its value in just three months. Later in November both Chrysler and GM said they would run out of money by the end of the year. General Motors—once the richest company on earth, the originator of tail fins and muscle cars, the font of the organizational principles used by every modern corporation—was actually, and incredibly, going broke.

For GM and Chrysler, the waterfall threatening their corporate rowboats was no longer just a menacing but unseen roar in the distance. The falls were now in plain view. Everyone on board, from the pilots to the people doing the rowing, stood powerless to prevent the plunge over the precipice. The only hope was that somebody would throw a lifeline—in the form of cold, hard cash.

The usual lifeguards, America's banks, were nowhere to be found. They were too busy trying to save themselves to keep the car companies from capsizing. The only hope was for a lifeline of money from the U.S. government.

So the government had to decide what to do, but who in the government? The lame-duck President Bush, or President-elect Obama? GM and Chrysler were draining so much cash that they couldn't wait for Obama to take office. Wagoner continued to say, incongruously but consistently, that bankruptcy was "not an option" for GM. But gallows humor in the Motor City suggested otherwise.

One joke was about a man with financial problems who went to see his priest. The priest told him to bring a Bible down to the beach, let the wind ruffle through the pages, and when the pages stopped ruffling to look down. The first words he saw would tell him what to do.

A year later the man returned to the priest, driving a new car and flush with obvious prosperity. "What words from the Bible," the priest asked, "inspired you to solve your problem?"

The man replied, "Chapter 11."

TWELVE

AS THE PRECIPICE APPROACHES

On November 15, 2008, Bob Lutz and his wife attended a Saturday night performance of *Madame Butterfly* at the Detroit Opera. Patrons in the next box noticed he was furiously thumbing his BlackBerry right up until the opera began, and then again all during the intermission. Was Lutz, they wondered, exchanging ideas with Rick Wagoner and other GM executives on how to present GM's request for billions in government aid to Congress? Not exactly. The seventy-six-year-old executive was playing BrickBreaker. Just three days before Wagoner would give testimony to the Senate Banking Committee that might decide the fate of General Motors, the company's vice chairman was fully absorbed in a video game.

It was just as well, actually. Any distraction would be welcome in the days to come.

Washington was tricky terrain for Detroit, especially during the interregnum between Bush and Obama. Both the outgoing president and the new one, it was quite clear, wanted the other guy to deal with the car companies. In Congress, Republicans were historically sympathetic to business. But the party's free-market types were skeptical about "corporate welfare," especially after the public backlash over the $700 billion bank bailout.

As for Democrats, the party's power base was shifting. The UAW had helped Obama win the election and still packed political clout. But blue-collar barons such as Representative John Dingell from Detroit, whose wife was a GM executive, were giving way to bicoastal suburbanites who championed the fuel economy and environmental regulations that Detroit had long resisted. Long the car companies' protector in chief, Dingell was being ousted as head of the House Energy and Commerce Committee by California's Henry Waxman, a leader of the ascendant greens. It was a sign of the times.

So was, in its own way, the e-mail blast that GM sent to its 100,000 U.S. employees just days before the congressional hearings The company urged them to contact their congressmen and provided a fill-in-the-blanks script to help them do it. "Hello, Senator/Congressman _____, my name is _____ and I have been an employee of [GM plant, city, and state] for _____ years," the instructions began. Leaving little to chance, the script continued: "Add personal detail here."

It was easy to imagine someone saying just that—"Add personal detail here"—to some puzzled congressional staffer. To clarify one sensitive point, the company told its employees it was "not asking Congress for a bailout, but rather a loan to be repaid." *Bailout,* like *bankruptcy,* was a b-word that GM executives didn't want to hear. If the message seemed a little heavy-handed, well, GM was never known for being subtle, and the company's very survival was at stake.

Meanwhile the halls of Congress were filled with supplicant car dealers, including Gene Benner from Maine. At the behest of the National Auto Dealers Association and Chrysler, Benner dropped by the office of Senator Olympia Snowe, a Republican, whom he had known since their high school days. Benner was still steaming from the way he had been treated by Chrysler Financial earlier in the year. But he had a lot to lose if Chrysler went out of business and took his dealership down along with it, so it was a time to set his anger aside. He and thousands of other car dealers were a potent political force and were pulling out all the stops, just like the car companies themselves.

On Monday, November 17, the day before the hearings, Banking Committee staffers summoned the Washington lobbyists for the automakers and the UAW to review some questions in advance. Would the $25 billion that the companies were seeking really be enough, or would it be just the first installment? How would it be divided among the three companies? What was the UAW doing to help Detroit get competitive?

The questions were predictable, but the lobbyists couldn't provide clear answers. That surprised the staffers, who told the lobbyists—in no uncertain terms—that their bosses should come prepared to provide clarity tomorrow. As it happened, however, Wagoner was getting just the opposite advice from a high-powered Washington consulting firm, which GM had hired to prep him for the hearings. The consultants advised Wagoner to keep his answers general and broad and to avoid being pinned down on specific numbers wherever possible. Wagoner, unfortunately, would take the advice to heart.

The Banking Committee convened at three P.M. Tuesday in room 538 of the Dirksen Senate Office Building, which was so crowded that Chairman Chris Dodd quipped that the panel should be meeting in RFK Stadium. Wagoner took the lead for the Detroiters. "What exposes us to failure now is not our product lineup, or our business plan, or our long-term strategy," he said in his prepared remarks. "What exposes us to failure now is the global financial crisis." It was the "not our fault" argument stated with conviction, because that's what Wagoner really believed. Mulally and Nardelli chimed their agreement. The problem, however, was that the senators didn't believe it.

Around six P.M., after three hours of long-winded questions and winding answers, Democrat Robert Menendez from New Jersey vented his frustration. "Part of the problem here is a credibility issue," he said. "In the 1970s all automakers argued that fuel efficiency standards would force them to make nothing but subcompact cars. Well, we did it, and we were flooded with sport-utility vehicles . . .

"I'm inclined to be helpful, but I've got to have a fundamental understanding of why this [$25 billion] number wasn't just picked out of the sky. I just don't see how the $25 billion is finite." Time would prove him remarkably right.

Menendez had cut to the two questions at the heart of the matter. Could anything Detroit's car companies said be believed, after their track record of missteps and blown opportunities over the last thirty-five years? And if they got the $25 billion, would they burn through it quickly and come back begging for more? The CEOs hemmed and hawed.

Then Bob Corker, a Tennessee Republican, asked how the $25 billion would be apportioned among the companies—the same question his staff had asked the lobbyists the day before, without success. "I just want the numbers," he said to Wagoner.

WAGONER: "Senator, sir, I think you have to be fair and look at it."

CORKER: "I just want, of the $25 billion, how much of it have you guys decided is going to GM?"

WAGONER: "We felt that, if we get our proportionate market share of that . . ."

CORKER: "Well, just give me the number."

WAGONER: ". . . which would be in the $10 billion to $12 billion [range] of that—that we would have . . ."

The exchange fit the tone for the entire day. Senators would ask the same question three or four different ways, but the CEOs seemed unprepared to answer. So did Gettelfinger.

"I find it very difficult [to believe] you're asking for $25 billion," Corker asked him, "when you have an agreement in place to pay 95 percent to workers who are not working . . . for how long?"

GETTELFINGER: "I'd have to look at the contract."

CORKER: "You got to be kidding me."

The answer, of course, was forever, which was why Gettelfinger deemed evasiveness better than telling the truth. Nonetheless, this was the moment when Congress and the American public were formally introduced to the insanity of the Jobs Bank. It had existed nearly twenty-five years in Detroit, so long that people just took it for granted. But politicians in Washington, and the public at large, were shocked.

As bad as the Senate hearing was, the next day was worse. As the House Financial Services Committee's hearing was concluding, an ABC News reporter buttonholed Wagoner and Mulally at the witness table to ask a question. How could they plead poverty, he wanted to know, when they had flown to Washington on their luxury corporate jets?

The CEOs bolted like a Corvette peeling away from a stoplight, which only made the damage worse when their hasty retreats were replayed on the evening news. ABC reported that the corporate jet flights had cost the companies $20,000 each, compared to the price of $200 for a commercial airline ticket.

The congressmen, predictably, pounced. "There's a delicious irony

in seeing private luxury jets flying into Washington and people coming off them with tin cups in their hands," snapped one Democrat.
"It's like seeing a guy show up at the soup kitchen in high hat and
tuxedo."

Obfuscation and obtuseness. All the stereotypes about Detroit
being removed from reality—in everything from products to public
policy to PR—came to life in two days before the television lights in
the Capitol. It was Detroit's worst drubbing in Washington since the
hearings about GM's spying on Ralph Nader more than forty years
before. The three CEOs and Gettelfinger, like errant schoolboys,
were dismissed to do their homework and come back for another
round of hearings with better answers.

As they retreated to lick their collective wounds, executives at all
three companies kicked themselves, belatedly, for the corporate jet fiasco. No one even had considered the potential danger. Corporate
jets were as integral to executive life in Detroit (and at many other
companies too) as the free cars, free car washes, and free gasoline in
the company parking garage.

In the damage-control meetings that followed, some executives
consoled themselves by saying that, had anybody tried to flag the
issue beforehand, he or she would have been brushed off. They probably were right. Detroit executives justified their jets as productivity
tools—even though Honda, no slouch in the productivity department, didn't have any corporate jets. Detroit's fundamental problem
wasn't jet-set but mind-set, one that seemed woefully out of touch
with the American public.

The hearings debacle proved irresistible to the comedy writers on
Saturday Night Live, who penned their own version of round two for
broadcast TV. "I would like to apologize to the committee for the fact
that we arrived in Washington so late," intoned the actor playing Rick
Wagoner, with mock dignity. "As many of you know, instead of flying, the three of us decided to, um, *drive* here from Detroit. (*Snickers.*)
But we had car trouble. (*More snickers.*)

"I was going to drive my 2009 Cadillac XLRV, a model that we at
GM are *very* proud of. But every time I tried to start it, I just got a
powerful electric shock and the upholstery would catch on fire. (*Rip-
ples of laughter.*)

"Bob here wanted to come in his new Chrysler 300. But the brakes, steering, engine, and transmission all went out. (*Pause.*) And also, I believe, the windshield came off. (*Roars of laughter.*) So we all piled into Alan's brand-new Ford Fiesta. Which worked out pretty well except that when you turned on the lights, the heater and the car alarm would come on. (*More roars.*) Plus the GPS system wasn't working too well, and we were just outside of St. Louis when we figured that out." (*Sustained roars.*)

Then he displayed a chart with the "revised" bailout plan: another $50 billion or so in government funding for the three companies, every three to six months, for years to come. "We *really* worked hard on this," said the fictional Bob Nardelli.

Detroit's beleaguered CEOs had become targets for the sort of ridicule once reserved for, well, members of Congress. Which was ironic, because Congress wasn't without blame in Detroit's downfall. The CAFE law (Corporate Average Fuel Economy) that counted only American-made cars toward the gas-mileage standard had forced the companies to build small cars at expensive UAW wage rates. The same congressmen who pointed to Europe's small cars as examples for Detroit to emulate didn't acknowledge that European taxes pushed gasoline to $8 a gallon, which provided a strong incentive for people to buy small cars instead of SUVs. But higher gas taxes were anathema to American voters, so few congressmen had the courage to support them. It was easier to write a law that required companies to build small cars, profitable or not.

Congressional hypocrisy aside, there were deep-seated reasons why the *Saturday Night Live* humor cut so deeply. Millions of Americans had endured real car problems, not altogether different from those parodied in the skit, and had given up on Chevys, Fords, and Dodges. Having voted with their wallets to buy cars from Toyota or Honda, they resented the idea of subsidizing Detroit's cars with their tax dollars. The corporate jets and the Jobs Bank sealed their hostility.

Detroit executives, though, were jolted by the nation's reaction. "Somehow, somewhere along the way we have crossed a line with the American public that we hadn't realized," said one GM executive who was trying to come to grips with it all. They hadn't realized it because they all lived in Detroit, where the reaction to the congressional hearings was different from that in the rest of the country.

The prevailing sentiment in Detroit was outrage at Congress for the "double standard" of bailing out the banks but beating up on the car companies. A local business magazine ran a cover story calling the Detroit bailout a "moral imperative" for the nation and hand-delivered a copy to each member of Congress. The home-team cheerleading, avidly joined by the local media, especially the radio talk shows, helped create the very insularity that had made Detroit executives and UAW officials oblivious to the sentiment elsewhere in America.

The combination of being a national joke and having a disastrous local economy sent Detroiters into a collective civic depression. One retired GM executive took solace by writing a limerick that he e-mailed to friends. It went:

> *Our cars made cash registers ring*
> *Our executives thought we were king*
> *But foreigners arrived*
> *And then markets dived*
> *So now to the Feds we do sing.*

> *In this time of our direst need*
> *The public recalls only dark deeds*
> *Engines don't start*
> *Cars fall apart*
> *We rebuffed fuel economy creeds.*

> *Bankruptcy's no option, we say*
> *We need just a few billion to stay*
> *Alive until when*
> *We can send once again*
> *Our fine products to once more lead the way.*

When the CEOs returned to Washington on December 4 to plead their case again, they followed the *Saturday Night Live* script—life imitating art, as it were—and really did drive from Detroit. Wagoner's dawn departure from his Bloomfield Hills home, in a Chevrolet Malibu hybrid driven by a GM chauffeur, was filmed by a Fox television news team, which was chided by GM's global security chief for driving up to the boss's house in a Toyota.

Wagoner, however, gamely agreed to an interview in the chill December darkness. Driving to Washington, he explained, "would be kind of a fun thing to do, to show off our new, in this case, hybrid vehicles." It was hard to believe it was fun, but at least Wagoner was playing his part.

So were Mulally, who traveled in a Ford Escape hybrid, and Nardelli. He rode in a Dodge Aspen hybrid SUV, a choice that showed how strained the whole green-groveling exercise had become. Just weeks earlier Chrysler had announced the Aspen hybrid would be discontinued because hardly anybody was buying it. But it was the only hybrid Chrysler had, and only a hybrid would do.

The second round of hearings produced less theater than the first but more news—mainly, Mulally's assertion that Ford really didn't want or need federal assistance after all. After the disastrous first hearing, Ford executives had regrouped. They decided that tethering their boat to GM's and Chrysler's, while those two were plunging toward the waterfall, might drag down Ford unless the company changed course.

Ford had done too much hard rowing, and had made the difficult decisions to jettison Jaguar and Land Rover, to risk getting swamped by the others. So Mulally steered away from GM and Chrysler. Ford, he told Congress, wouldn't mind having a guaranteed line of credit, just in case. But thanks to the $23.6 billion "home improvement loan" in 2006, he said, Ford wasn't facing a cash crisis and expected to make it on its own.

So much for "Solidarity forever," at least among CEOs. The dismay from Nardelli and Wagoner was almost audible. They had argued that their companies were helpless victims of the nation's financial panic, not of chronic mismanagement, and thus deserved government assistance. But if Ford could make it without a bailout—er, loan—why couldn't they? In the months to come, the disparity between Ford and the other two companies would raise that question time and again.

Only in early December did GM hire bankruptcy counsel, while Chrysler and even Ford had done so much earlier, if only as a standby measure. Wagoner had delayed because he insisted that even the hint of a possible bankruptcy filing would bring certain death to GM. The man who had bet the company on SUVs was betting it again on getting government money—in essence, giving Congress little choice but to open its wallet or to risk the economic consequences of a GM collapse.

And in truth, Congress was afraid to say no. Nobody knew the validity of the numbers Wagoner was throwing around about the consequences of GM filing for bankruptcy: three million U.S. jobs lost within a year, U.S. personal income reduced by $150 billion, and a government tax loss of more than $156 billion over three years. But nobody wanted to find out, either.

The fallout from the collapse of Lehman Brothers had frightened everyone in Congress, and not without reason. The economy was reeling, banks were collapsing, and the jobless rate was soaring. The Labor Department said the U.S. economy had lost 533,000 jobs in November, the highest monthly drop in thirty-four years. Things were getting scary.

The gathering crisis made unlikely bedfellows of the Bush White House and the Democrats in the House of Representatives, who had warred viciously for years over Iraq, the economy, and everything in between. On the weekend of December 6–7 the lame-duck Bushies and the House Democrats hammered out a compromise on Detroit: $14 billion in emergency loans to keep GM and Chrysler in business until March 31, during which time a new government "car czar" would help them craft a long-term restructuring plan.

Senator Corker, who had made a fortune in contracting and commercial real estate, was anal about doing his homework on issues that engaged him, and this was one. After the disastrous November 18 Senate hearing, he had gone to New York to meet with every automotive analyst he could find. He returned to tell his Republican colleagues that aid to Detroit without tough strings, as the White House was advocating, would be wasting money on companies that would just keep coming back for more.

On Wednesday, December 10, while the House was passing the

emergency loan measure, Bush dispatched his chief of staff, Joshua Bolten, and Vice President Dick Cheney to sell the idea to dubious Senate Republicans. They trooped to Capitol Hill for the senators' weekly policy lunch in the Capitol with Corker and his colleagues.

Cheney and Bolten ran into a buzz saw. The Republican president's deal with the House Democrats, far from shaping up as a bipartisan compromise, caused consternation among Senate Republicans, and they were further angered when Bush's two emissaries offered only a tepid defense. "If they came with ten votes," said Corker afterward, "they left with two." It set the stage for fifteen hours of high drama—along with very high stakes—the next day.

At seven-thirty A.M. on December 11 Corker's chief of staff called Fritz Henderson, GM's chief operating officer, on his cell phone. Corker, who was deputized to negotiate for the Republicans, got on the line and outlined a new plan with three points:

1. In return for the $14 billion, GM and Chrysler would have to cut their debt by two-thirds by getting their bondholders to agree to a stock-for-debt swap.

2. The UAW would have to accept stock in GM and Chrysler, in lieu of cash, for half the amount the companies owed the VEBA trusts.

3. The union would have to agree to achieving wage parity with the Japanese car plants in America in 2009.

Henderson, who was in New York, quickly accepted those terms, and at eight A.M. Corker called Gettelfinger, who said the union would agree to talk. Later that morning Corker visited Dodd and Harry Reid, the Senate majority leader, in Reid's office. They agreed to negotiate with the Republicans—who had enough votes to filibuster the White House bill—on the condition that Alan Reuther be included in the discussions. Reuther was a nephew of Walter and the UAW's chief lobbyist, a man whose very name harkened back to the union's glory days.

About two P.M. the Democrats, Corker, and Reuther convened, along with staff members, in the ornate Senate Foreign Relations Committee hearing room in the Capitol. Before long the group was joined by Steve Feinberg from Cerberus, who happened to be in Washington. The staffers, who had expected a loud, bombastic Wall Street type, were surprised that the private equity mogul seemed chastened that Cerberus had gotten in over its head. Feinberg said his investors couldn't put any more money into Chrysler; he seemed desperate to get out of Chrysler before the company collapsed.

As the negotiations continued, the Republican staffers summoned the lobbyists from the car companies, who frantically dashed to the Capitol, calling every few minutes to report their coordinates ("I'm stuck in traffic at Connecticut and K") en route. When the lobbyists arrived, however, they were told to cool their heels in the Foreign Relations Committee's anteroom, where Feinberg was also banished. The UAW had a seat at the negotiating table, but not the car companies themselves, even though their very futures were at stake. It symbolized how far the mighty had fallen.

Fritz Henderson, meanwhile, was at LaGuardia Airport, waiting to board a six P.M. Northwest Airlines flight back to Detroit, his new mode of travel in the post-corporate-jet era. Ken Cole, GM's chief lobbyist, asked him to stay on the ground and to stay on the phone as well, in case he was needed for quick consultations. So Henderson kept the phone line open and waited . . . and waited . . . and waited.

After three hours his phone ran out of juice, and Henderson himself was running out of gas. He booked a room at the LaGuardia Marriott and hopped on the hotel shuttle—just like your average corporate road warrior—arriving about nine P.M. and ordering a room service dinner. He turned on C-Span, to keep abreast of developments on Capitol Hill.

The negotiators had reached agreement on the debt-equity swap and the VEBA funding, but the sticking point was immediate pay parity with the Japanese transplants. There was little difference in hourly wages between the Japanese and Detroit factories, but the UAW's rich pension-and-benefits package for active workers and retirees created a big gap in total compensation: more than $70 an hour versus $50.

Corker offered compromise language. Instead of a pay package at "parity" with the transplants, he would settle for compensation that was "competitive" as defined by the secretary of labor, soon to be an Obama-appointed Democrat and therefore likely sympathetic to the union. But Corker insisted that getting "competitive" had to happen during 2009, no later. The Democrats and Reuther argued that the UAW had already given enough and wouldn't budge.

Around nine P.M., as Henderson was settling into his hotel, Corker and the Republicans caucused, while their staffers hovering nearby chewed gummi bears and sucked lollipops for dinner. The Republicans debated whether they should give in or hold firm and thereby risk being portrayed—as they had been throughout the financial crisis—as the heartless "party of no." They couldn't duck the issue, because Majority Leader Reid was insisting on a vote.

It came at 10:42 P.M., on the floor of the United States Senate. A few Republicans, including Senator Snowe from Maine, bolted their party. But mostly the Republicans held firm, and the White House bill died. Corker, with evident disappointment that the day's marathon negotiations had failed, said that the Republicans and the UAW had come within "one word" of reaching agreement. Harry Reid, in turn, said some nice things about Corker from the Senate floor.

The next day an angry Gettelfinger wasn't as generous. The UAW had made enormous concessions to the car companies in recent years, he said, and still the Republicans wanted to "pierce the heart of organized labor." But as the smoke cleared, the real reason the negotiations had failed became as clear as a high-beam headlight.

As the negotiations had neared a climax, White House staffers had quietly passed the word that if Congress wouldn't provide money to GM and Chrysler, President Bush would do it himself. Within days the president diverted $17.4 billion from the $700 billion bank-rescue package to keep the companies afloat for three months.

Bush's executive order required the two companies to submit new "viability plans" on February 17, outlining the measures they would take to return to profitability. George W. Bush, quite simply, wasn't going to preside over the bankruptcy of General Motors or Chrysler—icons of both American industry and American culture—during the waning days of his presidency.

A couple days later Gettelfinger tipped his hat to Bush. "Quite frankly, the White House has kept their word throughout this entire process," said the UAW chief, long a vigorous critic of the president. The praise must have felt strange to both men.

George Fisher, as GM's lead director, expressed relief. "We need these loans, and we're not particularly fussy about where they come from," he told *The Washington Post.* And to *The Wall Street Journal,* he lavished praise on the performance of a man he deeply admired: Rick Wagoner. "I am so proud of Rick for the way he handled himself through those discussions," Fisher told a reporter for the paper. "It is brutalizing to sit there in a Congressional hearing and have the world tell you that you've mismanaged or you're incompetent or whatever. Rick will go down in history as one of the great CEOs of GM and maybe of the auto industry. I will bet you on that one when this is all over."

True to his Tammy Wynette style, Fisher was standing by his man. His support for Wagoner was nothing new, so the *Journal* reporter decided to save the quotes for a future feature profile of Wagoner. But he would never get the chance.

In mid-November, not long after the election, thirty-one-year-old Brian Deese packed up his suitcases and his golden retriever and started driving from Chicago to Washington. En route he pulled off the Ohio Turnpike to sleep in his car—in the parking lot, as it happened, of the General Motors factory in Lordstown, home of the ill-fated Vega and birthplace of the blue-collar blues forty years before.

Deese was going to Washington to save the Detroit auto industry, unlikely as it seemed, which was very unlikely indeed. Neither an automotive enthusiast nor an expert, he was instead a policy wonk who had never set foot in a car plant.

After college at Middlebury in Vermont, Deese bounced around Washington think tanks, entered Yale Law School, and then took a leave to work on the Obama campaign. Instead of returning to Yale after the election, he accepted a job with the White House's National Economic Council. He was assigned to the president-elect's Automotive Task Force, which the new adminstration believed would be more effective than an individual "car czar."

For three months after the election Deese was virtually all there was to Obama's auto team. "When we call Washington," complained Steve Miller, Delphi's CEO, a couple weeks after Obama's inauguration, "nobody's home." Which was true, but even when somebody was home, Detroit didn't know how to ring the doorbell.

A comic example occurred in mid-January, when word leaked that Chrysler was negotiating an alliance with Italy's Fiat—which had staged a dramatic comeback after its divorce from GM four years earlier. Nardelli feared Chrysler would appear to be jumping the gun. So he shot off a frantic e-mail to Sergio Marchionne, Fiat's CEO, blaming the leak on an investment banker named "Phil Graham." Marchionne's people had to explain, politely, that "Phil Graham" was actually Phil Gramm, a former U.S. senator and political heavyweight, who was on Fiat's investment-banking team from UBS. Gramm had reached out to his former colleagues in the Senate to muster support for Fiat's negotiations with Chrysler. Nardelli, though innocently, was continuing Detroit's tradition of being clueless in dealing with Washington.

When others finally joined Deese on the task force in mid-February, many were a lot like him: wonkish whiz kids and junior executives on Wall Street who used *diligence* as a verb, as in "We've got to diligence that plan." (Translation: fully analyze a business plan and its underlying assumptions.) They didn't know a pound of potatoes from pound-feet of torque—if indeed they owned a car. Those who did often had a Honda or Toyota.

Their leaders, though older and more experienced, were cut from the same cloth: ex–Wall Streeters and private equity types just like, well, the guys at Cerberus who had fallen flat on their face with Chrysler. First among them was fifty-seven-year-old Steve Rattner, a former *New York Times* reporter who had left journalism to make a fortune in investment banking before cofounding a private equity firm. A trustee of Brown University (along with, of all people, George Fisher), Rattner was a smart, über–Rolodex schmoozer and big donor to Democratic candidates. He had backed Hillary Clinton in the primaries but then fell in line behind Obama and was eager to land a post in the new administration.

His alter ego was Ron Bloom, age fifty-three, a soft-spoken but hard-nosed idealist cut from the same cloth as Mike Bennett, the former UAW leader at Saturn. But Bloom, unlike Bennett, had a Harvard MBA and in 1996 had walked away from a lucrative Wall Street career to work for the United Steelworkers union. As the American steel industry collapsed in the late 1990s, Bloom helped the Steelworkers cope, partly by using his financial expertise to help restructure the companies and partly by insisting on sacrifices from the union itself.

Bloom described his style as "dentist-chair bargaining," in which the patient "grabs the dentist by the balls and says, 'Now let's not hurt each other.' " Rattner figured that Bloom, with his union background, could cover the task force's flank with the UAW and hired him. At four-thirty A.M. on February 17, the day GM and Chrysler would file their viability plans with the government, Bloom pulled out of his driveway in Pittsburgh to drive to Washington and report for work.

Rattner also brought aboard Harry J. Wilson, who had grown up in a depressed northern New York town where his mother had been laid off three times from dying textile mills. His father had fought in the Pacific in World War II and had refused to buy a Japanese car until he was eighty-three, when his new Dodge Neon broke down after just five thousand miles.

Wilson was the first in his family to attend college (Harvard), made millions in private equity, and retired at age thirty-six—the Wall Street version of "thirty and out." In late January, after reading that Rattner might lead the automotive bailout effort, Wilson sent him an e-mail, volunteering to sign up. "I do want to flag one issue," Wilson wrote. "I am a registered Republican, and I am a strong believer in free-market principles." Rattner met with him anyway and signed him up.

Wilson, in turn, brought others aboard the task force, though his recruitment effort wasn't exactly conventional. He sent some of his Wall Street contacts an e-mail that said: "The work is incredibly intense. The amount of work is massive, the timelines are tight . . . One should not expect this role to lead to a permanent position. Compensation = Government wages."

As if all that weren't bad enough, he added that a key qualification was the ability to tolerate bureaucracy. One of Wilson's task force colleagues who saw the e-mail said that nobody who read it would sign up. One applicant, a twenty-six-year-old just four years out of Harvard, was introduced to the federal bureaucracy when he arrived at the Treasury for a job interview and had to wait two hours for clearance just to enter the building. He enlisted anyway.

All during this time GM and Chrysler were staying afloat on short-term government funding that was soon to run out. What Detroit, in its desperation, saw as slow-motion movement was regarded as warp speed in Washington, where security clearances and background checks on new federal employees usually took weeks or months. Not until mid-March did the task force assemble its full, if sparse, contingent of fifteen members, supplemented by outside consultants and investment bankers.

The group's lack of auto industry experience provided grist for comedians. One TV comedy skit parodied a discussion of "that new-car smell" between young Deese and Larry King, both played by actors. "Awesome question, King-man," said Deese. "Essentially, it's an aerosol spray that uses nano-technology to give off a distinct odor of cleanliness." To which "Larry King" replied: "Can you make a corned-beef smell, too?"

Over the next three months, however, Deese and his task force colleagues would be like the fabled child who said the emperor has no clothes. They would ignore all Detroit's conventional wisdom about what couldn't be done and take their guidance from common sense instead of car sense.

That was fine with Rattner, to whom preconceived notions were a handicap. He wanted the government to approach the bailout like a private equity firm putting up its own money and that of its clients—but hopefully with more savvy than Cerberus's botched investment in Chrysler. This would require delving deeply and unemotionally into industry forecasts and corporate business plans, then deciding whether the prospects for GM and Chrysler warranted the investment of taxpayer dollars.

Political calculations would enter the equations at some point, he knew, but those could be left to the task force's two bosses: Tim Geithner, the Treasury secretary, and Larry Summers, chairman of the White House's National Economic Council.

For task force members, the last half of March would be like cramming for midterm exams (which many on the team were young enough to remember vividly). The interim funding that President Bush had approved for GM and Chrysler would expire on March 31, if not sooner. The waterfall was mere meters away, but at least the tugboat had arrived at the scene. The next few weeks would produce high drama, much of it hidden from public view, to decide whether two once-great American companies could be saved before they submerged.

The viability plans that GM and Chrysler filed as required on February 17 sought an additional $21.6 billion in federal assistance, on top of the $17.4 billion they already were getting. The amount would have been breathtaking, except that it paled alongside a $700 billion bank bailout and Obama's proposed $1.75 trillion budget deficit for 2009.

The word *bankruptcy*, likewise, was losing its ability to shock, at least among members of the task force. Although auto-industry insiders still viewed bankruptcy as certain death for GM and Chrysler, as opposed to a chance for a fresh start, Rattner and Bloom believed from the beginning that it might be the only option.

They saw straightaway that the companies were weighed down by enormous financial obligations to the UAW, debt-holders, and dealers. The whole purpose of U.S. bankruptcy laws was to provide relief from such burdens. They also concluded that, while the task force was dealing with a seemingly homogeneous industry, GM and Chrysler presented distinctly different issues.

In contrast to GM's global reach, Chrysler was smaller and narrowly focused on the United States and Canada, with hardly any business in Russia and China, the fastest-growing car markets in the world. Its pipeline of new products was virtually nonexistent, due to a decade of mismanagement by Daimler and eighteen months of directionless scrambling under Cerberus. And because Cerberus was refusing to put more money into Chrysler, the company lacked any funds to develop new cars. Chrysler needed a new partner or owner, but suitors weren't exactly lining up in the driveway. During 2008 Chrysler had scoured the world for potential partners, without success.

Ford was scrambling to save itself and wasn't interested. The task force reexamined the proposed GM-Chrysler merger, but quickly concluded it would be like tying two stones together to make them float. Gettelfinger and the UAW also hated the idea, figuring that the projected "cost savings" simply meant firing more workers. The only foreign car company interested was Fiat, which had held discussions with Chrysler in 2008 before backing away.

Fiat long had been derided as "Fix It Again, Tony," a sobriquet from the 1970s, when woeful quality had forced the Italian company out of the U.S. market. In 2009, however, a rejuvenated Fiat was building some pretty good cars, including the cute Fiat 500 subcompact that could be built in Chrysler's American factories. But there was one little problem: while Fiat wanted to own Chrysler, it didn't want to pay for the privilege.

Fiat's Marchionne, the tough-as-nails CEO who previously had stared down GM, wanted the U.S. government to put up the money to keep Chrysler alive until new cars, engineered by Fiat, could be launched in the United States. This was a novel proposition, even to a bunch of Wall Street types who thought they had seen every sort of deal possible. As the task force "diligenced" Fiat's proposal, the debate over Chrysler's future—and whether it even had a future—grew intense.

Wilson and several others believed that if Fiat was the only partner available, Chrysler should just be allowed to die. The chances that Chrysler would succeed under Fiat were slim, they figured, no matter how much money the government might provide. More important, they argued, keeping Chrysler alive could *destroy* even more American jobs than it would save. Both GM and Ford would have a much better chance to survive, they reasoned, if Chrysler, one of their chief competitors, went out of business. It was a grim argument that wasn't without logic.

Then again, Larry Summers and Tim Geithner were coming to the opposite conclusion, with support from Bloom and Brian Deese, who believed that simply letting Chrysler die would be too risky for a fragile economy. Geithner worried that the nation's economic crisis was getting worse and kept talking about the need to "spray foam on the runway." That's what airports did, he would explain, to dampen potential fires and avoid casualties when a plane seemed headed for a crash landing.

In late March there was a lot of talk in the West Wing and at Treasury about "spraying foam on the runway." Summers argued that Chrysler's collapse would, by itself, add a tenth of a percentage point to the nation's rising unemployment rate. Though the fraction was seemingly small, in macroeconomic terms it would have an enormous impact on the U.S. economy.

The other factor—largely unspoken but ever present—was the UAW. The union had spent enormous amounts of dollars and devoted thousands of man-hours to the Obama election campaign, especially in the battleground states of the industrial Midwest. Everybody knew the union wanted Chrysler alive.

The man in the middle was Rattner. He was outwardly self-confident, sometimes too much so, but he found himself torn over Chrysler, even as Summers asked him repeatedly, "What would you do if you were president?" Rattner danced around the question for days, which was uncharacteristic for him. The task force sent Obama a ten-page "decision paper" that, unlike most such documents prepared for the president, didn't make a recommendation one way or the other. With the task force and the president's advisers divided, the decision paper simply described the arguments on both sides.

On Thursday, March 26, Rattner was in the West Wing when Summers dragged him into the morning PDB meeting—the President's Daily Briefing—in the Oval Office. The discussion quickly turned to Chrysler, catching Rattner a little off guard, and Summers started to explain that saving Chrysler would require another $6 billion in government support.

"Larry, I read the memo," Obama said, cutting Summers off, and not looking terribly happy at the prospect of risking more money on the rescue effort. Then he said, "I need more time on this," and asked for another meeting later that day.

At six P.M. Obama walked into the windowless Roosevelt Room across from the Oval Office—with its painting of Teddy Roosevelt as Rough Rider hanging over the mantel—to decide whether to save the company of Walter Chrysler, the Dodge brothers, Lee Iacocca, the minivan, and the Jeep. His top advisers were there—chief of staff Rahm Emanuel, political guru David Axelrod, Summers, and others—along with task force members.

The president asked everybody, one by one, to go around the table and state their positions. Obama, clearly grasping the gravity of the moment, sat with his hands folded in front of his mouth as if in prayer while everybody spoke in turn. Rattner said he would "vote" 51 to 49 percent for trying to save Chrysler if the decision were up to him.

About an hour later, when everybody had spoken, the president asked, "Does anybody have anything else to say?" He seemed to mean it, but nobody in the room spoke up.

Now it was Obama's turn. "I've come to my decision," the president said. "It makes sense to try to move forward with Fiat."

It was a momentous decision, one that easily could have gone the other way. Turning to Bloom and Rattner, the president said, "I want you to be tough, and I want you to be commercial." Strictly commercial terms would have meant letting Chrysler liquidate, but short of that Obama wanted to drive a hard bargain.

Chrysler seemed to have more lives than a cat, proof of the remarkable resilience of car companies. The companies and their executives—witness Rick Wagoner at GM—had surmounted crisis after crisis when logic might have suggested otherwise. Such staying power would be a critical asset in the weeks to come.

Despite Obama's decision to broker a Fiat deal, Chrysler was hovering on the brink of the waterfall. Getting the UAW, Chrysler's debtholders, and Fiat to agree on a rescue plan would be complex and difficult. Not even the president of the United States could assure that all three groups would agree to terms that the government could accept. The task force had a lot of hard bargaining to do if the Chrysler rescue was to succeed. Meanwhile, during the debate over Chrysler's fate, hidden drama was revealing the depths of the dysfunction at General Motors.

Members of the Auto Task Force believed unanimously that General Motors, unlike Chrysler, couldn't be allowed to collapse. Even after decades of downsizing, the company was so big, and its outright demise would be so devastating to the economy, that the case for spraying foam on the runway—layers of foam, in fact—was compelling.

GM was a sprawling organism with nearly 100,000 U.S. employees, 6,240 dealers, and more than sixty different models, with eight brands in the United States alone. The company's legacy of dominance in its home market had fostered a culture of arrogance, though of a genteel, amiable variety, that still existed, despite decades of decline. Not even the recent experience of going broke had broken the belief inside the company that General Motors was, ultimately, indestructible. Inside the task force, though, the view was decidedly different.

Bloom, for one, had come to Washington suspecting that GM was hopelessly insolvent. His deep dive into the company's numbers did nothing to change that belief, even though he had discovered some unexpectedly pleasant pluses. Since 2005, when Wagoner had launched his first restructuring effort, the company had been moving in the right direction, albeit slowly and haltingly. And some of the company's new cars, notably the Cadillac CTS and Chevy Malibu sedans, were excellent.

The question was, how did those pluses square with GM's multibillion-dollar losses, continuing declines in market share, and a stock price that had evaporated to nearly nothing. The answer was that GM had a classic "brown pony problem," as Bloom told his task force colleagues. The restructuring was painfully slow and inadequate, and the company's good cars got lost among the mountain of vehicles that were mediocre or worse. Finding the good things at GM, in Bloom's analogy, was like trying to spot a little brown pony in a huge pile of manure.

There had to be a pony in there somewhere—heck, maybe even a few ponies—but their existence was obscured by all the surrounding brown stuff. And GM's efforts to clear away the crap always seemed too little and too late. It was a company, Bloom quickly concluded, whose culture specialized in developing reasons not to do something.

Exhibit A was the new viability plan that the company had given the government, as required, on February 17. It was GM's third such plan in just nine months, evidence of the company's penchant for incrementalism. The plan was another recipe for slow-motion self-improvement.

It said Pontiac would be relegated to being a niche brand. But that had been GM's intention for years. The plan also said Saab and Saturn would be subject to "strategic reviews—including their potential sale." But their "potential sale," after twenty years of mounting losses, stood in sharp contrast to Mulally's decisive action to dump Land Rover and Jaguar. More than likely, GM's "strategic reviews" of Saturn and Saab would unearth still more excuses for keeping them anyway.

The plan projected that GM's U.S. market share would stabilize, even though the company pledged (sort of) to cut brands and to curtail money-losing sales to car-rental companies—moves that surely would cause GM's market share to drop. It was a glaring internal contradiction. GM also said it didn't expect to repay the government's loans until 2017. By that time Barack Obama, if elected to two terms, would be leaving office.

Worst of all, the plan rejected bankruptcy as an option, based on Wagoner's bedrock belief that a Chapter 11 reorganization inevitably would lead to a Chapter 7 liquidation.

To Bloom, eliminating bankruptcy from the start was like throwing away your strongest weapon when the battle began. He regarded bankruptcy as a reckoning, a drastic step that absolutely forced a company to fix its problems. Dismissing it out of hand would give everybody—bondholders, dealers, the UAW, and the company itself—implicit permission to avoid the painful changes that would be necessary.

On March 9 Bloom, Rattner, and several task force colleagues visited Detroit, where their hope for a low-key look-see and quiet conversations was jolted by the reality of a city in panic. "Hear Us Out," shouted a front-page headline in the *Detroit Free Press*. "We're in Crisis."

While the team made the trek from Detroit Metro Airport to the GM Technical Center, TV news helicopters hovered overhead charting their every turn. It was like the choppers that had tracked the fleeing O. J. Simpson on the L.A. freeways fifteen years earlier, except that Rattner & Co. were government officials instead of celebrity murder suspects. The task force members were stunned.

When they reached the gated Tech Center, northeast of downtown Detroit, they had a working lunch with management—for which each task force member dutifully paid $11 in cash in accordance with the government's fussy ethics rules. Then the circus in the skies gave way to showtime on the ground.

GM trotted out an assortment of existing and experimental GM cars for the team to drive, including cars powered by hydrogen fuel cells and the vaunted Chevy Volt. It was exactly the sort of display that GM—and every car company in the world—had used for years to impress board members, Wall Street analysts, and journalists. But this time it backfired.

Despite all the hype and hope heaped on the Volt, Rattner and Bloom found it simply irrelevant to saving General Motors. With its likely $37,000 price tag and sales projections of only some ten thousand vehicles over the next three years, the Volt couldn't conceivably help a company that was running out of time. The more Wagoner touted the car, which he did at every turn, the more Rattner and Bloom became convinced he was removed from reality.

Shortly after the Detroit visit, Rattner sat down for a private chat with Wagoner. Besides reviewing GM's product and financial plans, Rattner told him, the task force wanted to assess the company's management team. Along those lines, he added, how did Wagoner see his own future?

Wagoner got the hint, not that it was terribly subtle. In contrast to his previous public statements, he replied that he would step aside for the good of General Motors, if necessary. But he believed he had several more good years to give the company.

The task force didn't believe that. Rattner was concluding that General Motors might be the worst-managed company he had ever seen. Bloom compared it to Bethlehem Steel, the quintessential industrial dinosaur that had collapsed in 2003 due to a cloistered management culture, crushing debt, costly labor contracts, and multiple retirees for every active worker. It had had problems, in short, not unlike GM's.

The two men passed the word to Geithner and Summers, all the way up the line to President Obama: removing Rick Wagoner would be good for General Motors and good for America. It wasn't exactly what Obama's political advisers wanted to hear. As a Democrat, they knew, the president would get lots of grief—editorials about "creeping socialism," and headlines about "nationalizing GM"—for sacking the CEO of General Motors. But GM's fate under Wagoner had been so clearly disastrous that Rattner got the green light from the White House, without much internal debate.

On the morning of Friday, March 27, Wagoner, Fritz Henderson, and GM's chief financial officer, Ray Young, walked into the anteroom of Rattner's spacious corner office on the first floor of the Treasury, across the street from the White House. At noon that day, GM's board would hold its regular weekly conference call, Rattner knew, and he wanted to discuss something with Wagoner beforehand. He asked Henderson and Young to head upstairs to a fifth-floor conference room while he had a private word with their boss.

"We'd like to take you up on your offer," Rattner said after closing the door, "to resign for the good of General Motors." As GM's banker by default, he added, the U.S. Treasury wanted Fritz Henderson to replace him as CEO, and one of the company's outside directors to become interim board chairman.

Wagoner paused, seeming not entirely surprised, but nonetheless shocked. "Are you going to get rid of Ron Gettelfinger too?" he asked Rattner.

Rattner was dumbfounded. He had expected anger, protest, anything but that question, which convinced him just how foreign the notion of CEO accountability was to the man running GM.

"Well," Rattner mumbled, "he doesn't really work for me." The implied message, of course, was that the CEO of General Motors did. With government money keeping GM on life support, Wagoner was backed into a corner.

Then the two men, who were almost exactly the same age, talked for a few more minutes. Wagoner said he wanted Rattner to know just how hard the job of running General Motors really was. Rattner said he appreciated that. Then Wagoner went upstairs to the fifth floor to tell Henderson and Young the news.

Henderson was shocked. At age fifty he was a GM lifer from a GM family. (His father had worked there, and his brother still does.) As an infant, Henderson had shared the same playpen with the children of other GM executives. He had attended the University of Michigan, the all-but-official academy for future GM executives. Armed with this pedigree, Henderson had emerged early as a GM "high pot," working for the company in key positions around the world. Henderson always had dreamed of running the company one day but had never expected it would happen like this.

After giving the GM people a few minutes to absorb the news, Rattner, Bloom, and Harry Wilson walked into the meeting room to deliver more disconcerting news. GM's February 17 restructuring plan was inadequate, they said, because it didn't go far enough or fast enough to save the company. The atmosphere was calm and businesslike—and therefore absolutely surreal. But it was nothing compared to what happened next.

At noon Wagoner convened the board's conference call and told the directors the news. They erupted in anger. The "Board of Bystanders" that had reacted with worried hand-wringing, but little real action, while General Motors plunged into penury, finally got its dander up.

They weren't angry at Wagoner, nor at themselves, at least not outwardly. They were angry at Steve Rattner. No government official, not even the president, had the right to fire Wagoner, they protested. Only the shareholders could fire him, and they—the directors—represented the shareholders. A boardroom revolt was brewing, not *against* the CEO, as in most such uprisings, but *for* the CEO.

That afternoon George Fisher called Rattner to register his anger about the ungracious treatment of Wagoner, a man, he noted, who had dedicated his career to GM. Rattner pointed out that the task force had tried to avoid humiliating Fisher himself, by allowing him to remain as GM's official "lead director." That title was meaningless now that another outside director was being installed as chairman, but the gesture helped mollify Fisher. If nothing else, peace would be preserved at future meetings of the Brown University board.

Rattner also fielded a call from the lawyer for GM's board, who registered the board's extreme dismay and asked Rattner to speak to the directors himself. That night Rattner joined another board con-

ference call and conceded that only the directors—not the government—had the power to fire the CEO. But then he cut them off at the
knees. Wagoner hadn't been fired, he noted; he had been asked to resign. Maybe the effect was the same as a firing, but from a legal standpoint the Treasury's action was altogether different. Wagoner could
refuse, or the board could decline to accept his resignation.

No one had to add that, should either of those paths be taken, the
Treasury could pull the purse strings, in which case General Motors
would collapse. The government might balk at doing that, but none
of the directors wanted to find out. The bald fact was that the board
that had presided over GM's downfall wasn't calling the shots anymore. GM's banker was in charge, and its banker was the United
States of America.

So it was that Rick Wagoner's meteoric rise to the top of General
Motors came to a bitterly ironic end. He had been vaulted to promi-
nence at thirty-nine by being named CFO in the 1992 boardroom
coup that was orchestrated by GM's outside directors. Now, having
survived for years despite successive corporate disasters, he was being
ousted in another boardroom coup, this one orchestrated by the president of the United States.

Wagoner had once been regarded as a Young Turk reformer, but
was ending his GM career as a symbol of a corporate culture that de-
fied reform. He hadn't solely caused GM's demise, which had begun
before he joined the company in 1977, fresh out of Harvard Business
School. But he had failed to take the risky but necessary moves—
cutting excess brands, dealers, work rules, the Jobs Bank, and all the
other baggage weighing down General Motors—to stem the company's slide as it accelerated dramatically during his years as CEO. Instead he had bet the company on mortgages, trucks, and SUVs, and
they had proved losing bets.

That Sunday, March 29, Wagoner formally resigned as chairman
and CEO of General Motors. After convening a scheduled five P.M.
conference call of GM's North American Strategy Board, he told the
group he was leaving, turned the meeting over to Henderson, and
signed off. It was his last official act as the chief executive officer of
GM.

As word of Wagoner's forced departure spread, the GM old boys' club reached out in support. One retired executive called to tell Wagoner he should take pride in departing with his integrity intact. General Motors, at its highest reaches, was like that. Members of the club circled the wagons in tough times. Times didn't get much tougher than this.

The next day in Washington, at 11:07 A.M., President Obama addressed the country on national television. "One of the challenges we've confronted from the beginning of this administration is what to do about the state of the struggling auto industry," he began. "Year after year, decade after decade, we've seen problems papered over and tough choices kicked down the road . . . Now is the time to confront our problems head-on." (Translation: I won't just throw money at Detroit, like George Bush did.)

He continued: "GM has made a good faith effort to restructure over the past several months—but the plan that they've put forward is not strong enough. I'm absolutely confident that GM can rise again, providing that it undergoes a fundamental restructuring. As an initial step, GM is announcing today that Rick Wagoner is stepping aside as Chairman and CEO. This is not meant as a condemnation of Mr. Wagoner, who's devoted his life to this company and has had a distinguished career." (Translation: I fired him, but I want to be gracious about it.)

"In this context, my administration will offer General Motors adequate working capital over the next 60 days. And during this time, my team will be working closely with GM to produce a better business plan." (Translation: Employees will take job cuts; investors will take haircuts on their investments.)

Then the president turned to Chrysler. "It's with deep reluctance but also a clear-eyed recognition of the facts," he said, "that we've determined that Chrysler needs a partner to remain viable." The best prospect was Fiat, he said, without adding that in fact the *only* prospect was Fiat. He committed the government to funding Chrysler for another thirty days while it tried to fashion an agreement with the Italian car company. If the negotiations failed, Obama said, "we will not be able to justify investing additional tax dollars to keep Chrysler in business."

Those were stark and sobering words. But before his listeners had a chance to digest them, Obama went further and said the b-word out loud, right there on TV. Saving GM and Chrysler, he said, "may mean using our bankruptcy code as a mechanism to help them restructure quickly and emerge stronger." (Translation: Without bankruptcy, these companies won't have a prayer.)

Obama didn't lay it entirely on the line: he didn't say that even if Chrysler cut a deal with Fiat, it would have to be propped up by tax dollars for a couple years until the Dodge Italianos, or whatever the new cars would be called, could start rolling off Chrysler's assembly lines.

He lavished praise on U.S. autoworkers without mentioning their shared complicity with management for bringing the companies down. He wasn't about to alienate his supporters in the UAW. Nor did he tip his hat to the nonunion workers in the Japanese, German, and Korean transplants in Ohio, Kentucky, Tennessee, and nearby states, who were every bit as American as the workers at GM, Ford, and Chrysler.

Still, it was an awfully good speech, especially for a president barely two months in office who had never run a business or even worked in one. On March 30 Barack Obama said uncomfortable truths about Detroit that many people had whispered for years but hadn't dared say out loud.

He offered not only lifelines to GM and Chrysler but also brand-new boats and a chance for a fresh start. But getting into the new boats almost certainly would mean going through bankruptcy. And that would mean tossing some workers, dealers, and investors overboard—because the new boats would be smaller, though hopefully more seaworthy, than their existing creaky craft. Chrysler had thirty days. GM had sixty. The rescue clock was ticking.

THIRTEEN

BAILOUTS, BANKRUPTCIES, AND BEYOND

The good news for Chrysler was that by the time President Obama started its thirty-day clock ticking, the company had already reached the broad outline of a deal with Fiat. The bad news was that actually getting a deal done would require many more parties to agree.

Among them were the Canadian Auto Workers union and the Canadian government, because Chrysler had factories and workers in that country. Then there were Cerberus, the United Auto Workers, Daimler (which still owned nearly 20 percent of Chrysler), and the creditors who held $6.9 billion of Chrysler debt. All were like a little flotilla circling around Chrysler and warily watching the tugboat, the president's Automotive Task Force, which would have to do the heavy hauling.

Getting all these boats to pull in the same direction would require reconciling different, and often conflicting, courses. The Italians wanted to board Chrysler's boat and run it themselves. The unions wanted to keep as many jobs, pensions, and benefits on board as possible, but even they were divided. The UAW wanted to keep American jobs, while the CAW wanted Canadian jobs.

The creditors' boat seemed to be holding the safest place in the water. This boat held the forty-six banks, hedge funds, and pension funds that had lent Chrysler money as part of its acquisition by Cerberus in 2007. The lenders had hoped to resell the debt instruments—originally $10 billion worth, but some had been repaid—for a fast and tidy profit but couldn't find buyers.

The creditors' boat was piloted by James B. Lee, Jr.—"Jimmy" to everyone on Wall Street—who might have been cast as Captain Hook, except that he was better dressed. As vice chairman of JPMorgan Chase, Lee was a big-time, hard-nosed moneylender known for the trademark suspenders he wore with his $3,000 suits. JPMorgan

Chase had the biggest chunk of the Chrysler debt, some $2.7 billion. Its fellow creditors included the biggest names on Wall Street: Goldman Sachs, Morgan Stanley, and Citigroup.

The debt they held was classified as "senior secured" and guaranteed by a first lien on Chrysler's assets. The lien was like a life preserver that assured they would be paid, the creditors figured, even if Chrysler crashed over the falls. Lee felt little inclined to participate in a rescue and kept his distance from the rest of the boats.

The flotilla had begun forming on January 2, well before the tugboat appeared, when a team of investment bankers from UBS, representing Fiat, waded into Auburn Hills. What followed was intense negotiating, in which the bankers made clear that Fiat didn't want to pay actual *cash* for Chrysler. But Fiat's small-car technology would save Chrysler billions in development costs, the bankers said, and therefore would replenish a new-product pipeline that had been depleted under Daimler and Cerberus. They were right on both counts.

Besides price, another sticking point was the fate of Chrysler Financial, the division that provided financing to Chrysler dealers and customers. Cerberus wanted out of the car company entirely but was eager to remain tethered to the financial company.

Three weeks later, after intense negotiations, the two companies and Cerberus agreed to a structure: Fiat would get 35 percent of Chrysler up front and an option for another 20 percent. Ownership of the rest was left to be determined, along with the fate of Chrysler Financial. Meanwhile Chrysler, Fiat, and Cerberus sought a truce with Captain Hook.

They wanted the banks to clear the path for the Fiat deal by reducing Chrysler's debt, preferably exchanging at least half of it for shares in Chrysler. Such debt-for-equity exchanges were common in corporate restructurings, but Jimmy Lee wouldn't discuss it—at least not for free.

He asked for tens of millions of dollars to serve as Chrysler's debt-restructuring adviser. It would be a blatant conflict of interest because, as Chrysler's biggest creditor, JPMorgan Chase couldn't possibly give Chrysler objective advice on restructuring its debt. Chrysler wisely hired a different adviser instead.

In late January one of Fiat's UBS bankers tried to open a channel to Lee by dialing into a conference call between the banks and Chrysler. It didn't work. "Fiat isn't a party to this discussion," Lee barked over the phone. "We have no interest in hearing from you." He ordered the banker to get off the call. Backed by the legal power of first-lien debt, Lee wanted payment in full for the banks. Period.

So despite all the frantic maneuvering, all the boats remained fixed in position, waiting for the tugboat to arrive and set the rescue course. Then on March 5 Sergio Marchionne went to Washington.

For his first meeting with the Automotive Task Force, Fiat's CEO wore his trademark black sweater and black slacks, the same thing he always wore to work as opposed to a jacket and, God forbid, a tie. (Well, he had made an exception a few years earlier, when he met the pope.)

The presentation began at ten A.M. in the ornate Diplomatic Room on the first floor of the Treasury. True to form, Marchionne didn't bring a large entourage. He was accompanied only by Andrew Horrocks, Fiat's investment banker from UBS, and a couple of others.

Marchionne began by describing Fiat's history and its dramatic turnaround since 2004, which had been helped in no small part, ironically, by the $2 billion "divorce settlement" that he had beaten out of GM. Then he provided his vision for the auto industry. Companies the size of Chrysler and even Fiat, he said, would be too small to survive independently. They would need larger economies of scale to support research on hybrid vehicles and other new technologies that would be critical to the cars of the future. Then he outlined why Fiat and Chrysler would make a good fit.

Fiat was strong in international markets, he said, but had little presence in the United States, which was Chrysler's citadel. Chrysler had strengths in trucks and SUVs, he added, while Fiat's strong suit was small cars. Without Fiat, Marchionne argued, Chrysler wouldn't meet future fuel-economy requirements under the CAFE law. But to his surprise, the task force members really didn't care. Their mission was to save jobs and the economy, not the environment.

Horrocks then launched into the proposed financial structure. Fiat would give Chrysler small-car technology and product blueprints, he said, that the Italians valued at $4 billion. Rattner and Bloom started picking away at that number—and at the fact that Fiat wouldn't put any cash into the deal. Marchionne replied that if the world's economic crisis intensified and Fiat found itself needing aid from the Italian government, the company would be crucified in Italy for having used cash to buy Chrysler.

The answer seemed to mollify the task force, at least somewhat.

There were dozens of other questions, polite but pointed, and Marchionne fielded them all—without the blue-suited supporting casts that his Detroit counterparts usually required. He impressed the task force with the depth of his knowledge and amazed his colleagues by going a full four hours without a smoke. The meeting ended at two P.M., and Marchionne quickly lit a cigarette on the steps outside the Treasury.

When the foursome sat down for a late lunch, Marchionne asked how the presentation went.

"It's hard to tell," replied Horrocks, who came away discouraged. He couldn't be sure that the task force wouldn't try to find another partner for Chrysler, maybe even reviving the GM-Chrysler deal yet again. "We did the best we could," he added, "but they didn't seem all that interested."

But that night, Marchionne got a phone call from Rattner, asking for more details on how Fiat proposed to integrate the two companies. Rattner also asked whether the Fiat team might be available to return next week, if the task force wanted more details.

Well, that was encouraging.

The task force was becoming convinced that a Chrysler rescue would probably require a trip through bankruptcy court—hopefully a quick one—but the question was how to get there with a workable restructuring plan. The biggest problem was financial, because Fiat was the high bidder for Chrysler, even though it was bidding *niente*.

And Chrysler was deeply in debt. Besides the $6.9 billion it owed the banks and other obligations, the company had pledged $10 billion to the VEBA trust fund to provide healthcare to retired workers. This was a big improvement over what Chrysler would have had to spend, without the VEBA, to pay the healthcare costs directly. But by now Chrysler's finances had deteriorated such that even the $10 billion was too much.

The bottom line was that the company didn't have enough cash, and wouldn't be getting any from Fiat or Cerberus, to pay either the VEBA or the banks, much less both. And Jimmy Lee was just as intransigent with the task force as he had been with Fiat. Lee felt confident in the knowledge that his debt was secured, while Chrysler's debt to the VEBA wasn't.

Throughout March, Rattner and Lee played hardball with each other. Rattner said that if the banks didn't renegotiate the debt, they could seize ownership of Chrysler and just run the company themselves. Lee retorted that if the banks did assume ownership of Chrysler, they would liquidate the company—a dare he didn't think the Obama administration would take.

Meanwhile, as it became clear that the task force was calling the shots, Chrysler executives chafed at being relegated to glorified observers to decisions about their company's fate. One Chrysler executive, in an e-mail to colleagues, referred to the Treasury Department as "God." In another, Nardelli himself wrote, "I guess the UST is running it!" The executives could do little more than grumble, however, because without tax dollars, they knew, Chrysler would be dead already.

The hurt feelings didn't deter Bloom, who was taking the lead for the task force in dealing with Fiat, Chrysler, and the UAW. Even while some of the president's advisers had been arguing for letting Chrysler die, Bloom was puzzling over how to save the company in the event Obama gave the go-ahead. On Wednesday, March 25, after another round of Fiat presentations to the task force, he approached Horrocks and said, "Can I speak to you alone?"

The two men walked back into the Diplomatic Room, where the ornate furniture had been temporarily replaced by cheap tables and folding chairs to serve as the task force's interim headquarters. "We've been looking at a lot of scenarios," Bloom said. "In one of them, the union's VEBA trust could have sizable equity in Chrysler. Maybe even a majority. Would that give you guys a problem?"

Horrocks thought for a minute. "As long as we get management control and a majority of the board," he replied, "I don't think it would be a problem for Sergio."

When Horrocks returned to Fiat's Washington office, Marchionne wanted to know what Bloom had wanted. When Horrocks explained, the Fiat boss replied that, yes, he could live with that. The very next day, at the momentous meeting in the Roosevelt Room, Obama gave the task force clearance to pursue the Fiat deal. The boats were lining up to take part in the rescue—except for one.

On the last weekend in March, just before the president spoke on television, Lee called Rattner. The banks wouldn't settle for partial payment of their loans, he reiterated, to help Chrysler reach a Fiat deal. "Pay me in full, and I'll get out of the way," he said. He wanted the entire $6.9 billion, he added, "and not a penny less."

But Lee's hardline stand wouldn't last long. On Monday, March 30, after watching Obama tell the nation that Chrysler really would be liquidated without a Fiat deal, Lee began to think the task force wasn't bluffing and called Rattner back. "We've got to talk," he said. The creditors' boat, it appeared, might be ready to change course.

On Thursday, April 2—three days after Obama's speech—Rattner and Bloom convened another meeting in a conference room on the fifth floor of the Treasury. Nearly forty people were there, including Ron Gettelfinger, Sergio Marchionne, Bob Nardelli, and Andrew Horrocks. For the first time they were joined by Jimmy Lee and other creditors.

All the banks had received TARP bailout money from the government, but that leverage had to remain unspoken because Rattner was under strict orders not to mention it. Still, he presided over the meeting with the confidence of a man who held the high cards.

"We want to give all of you an update," he began. "Here's how we see what a Fiat-Chrysler deal would look like." Lee interrupted to ask for cash-flow projections—he seemed accustomed to controlling the agenda of meetings—but Rattner cut him off.

In a Fiat-Chrysler alliance, he resumed, the UAW's VEBA trust would get 55 percent ownership of Chrysler in lieu of half the money owed to the VEBA. Fiat would get 20 percent ownership, with a chance to increase that to 35 percent, in return for contributing its product plans and technology—but without paying any cash. Nardelli and Marchionne made presentations, and then Rattner turned to the banks' claim for $6.9 billion.

"We have in mind for you a much lower number," he said. He paused and added: "$1 billion." The task force actually was prepared to pay more, but there was no use in leading with its best offer.

"What about equity?" Lee asked.

Rattner replied, "We didn't have that in mind."

Lee: "No equity?"

Rattner: "No."

Lee was stunned. "How can you justify an unsecured creditor getting more than 50 percent of the company," he asked, referring to the UAW, "while the secured creditors get nothing?"

"We're giving you the equivalent of what you would get in a liquidation" of Chrysler, Rattner replied. "That was your position, so you should be indifferent." Chrysler debt was trading at only eighteen cents on the dollar, Rattner added; $1 billion was nearly equivalent to that, so the banks would be getting market value.

"Why us?" Lee asked, in a newly plaintive tone. "The government has pumped billions into the banks to make them stronger, so why are you trying to hurt us?"

"Jimmy, when we asked you to participate in this, you said no," Rattner replied. "You said you would liquidate if you had to. We took you at your word."

Lee: "Well, something has changed since then."

Rattner: "How? What has changed?"

Lee: "The . . . White . . . House!"

Everyone sat silent for a moment, because Lee had just acknowledged that the president had called his bluff. But Rattner wouldn't budge on his offer, at least not then and there.

Jimmy Lee wasn't exactly a sympathetic character. Still, American law is supposed to protect unpopular people, even arrogant fat cats who wear suspenders. By law, when it came to getting paid, Lee and the other "senior secured" lenders stood in line ahead of the UAW and certainly ahead of Fiat, which wasn't a creditor at all.

That's the way it would come out in the news reports, but it really wasn't that simple. The loans the banks had made to Chrysler two years earlier had been reckless—analogous, say, to a neighborhood bank making a $100,000 "senior secured" loan on a three-year-old Dodge. The papers might say "senior secured," but the underlying value of the asset meant otherwise. As Bloom later would put it, standing up to the banks showed that "Uncle Sam wasn't going to be Uncle Sucker."

What's more, the UAW supplied Chrysler with a critical component, labor, that the company needed to keep building cars. Stiffing the UAW's claim, in Bloom's view, would be like refusing to pay a company that supplied Chrysler with steering wheels. No steering wheels, no cars. Likewise, no workers, no cars. Bloom believed a bankruptcy judge would approve payment to workers, and to the VEBA for retired workers, just like a payment to a steering-wheel maker.

Meanwhile, he had another problem. Ironically, behind the scenes, the UAW wasn't much happier than the banks.

Ron Gettelfinger didn't want 55 percent of Chrysler in lieu of $5 billion for the VEBA, any more than he had wanted to entertain Kerkorian's offer of Chrysler shares two years earlier. Chrysler stock, the UAW knew, might prove worthless, or at least might be valued so low that the VEBA would have to slash medical benefits to retirees. Just like Jimmy Lee, Gettelfinger wanted cash—cash that Chrysler didn't have.

On April 10, Good Friday, Fiat and the union arrived at the Treasury to hash it out. Bloom proceeded to squeeze the union as Rattner had the banks, only more politely. "Your VEBA claim is with a hopelessly insolvent company," he told Gettelfinger. "Getting stock is a good outcome for you."

If Gettelfinger blocked the Fiat deal, Bloom added, the alternative would be Chrysler's liquidation, which the UAW chief wanted to avoid even more than the banks did. The negotiations went back and forth for hours, during which Horrocks, the UBS banker, stepped outside for air, only to find that he couldn't get security clearance to reenter. Maybe the future of Chrysler was at stake, but the Treasury Department's security guards weren't about to bend. Bloom had to fetch him back inside.

Finally, at eight P.M., the UAW agreed to take Chrysler stock—nonvoting shares—in lieu of half the VEBA debt. Work rules and wages remained sticking points, but Horrocks was beginning to believe that his client's unlikely—well, brazen—bid for Chrysler might actually succeed.

He walked over to Gettelfinger and, referring to Marchionne, said: "If Sergio was here, he would want to shake your hand personally. Would you shake mine as his proxy?"

"I hope Sergio will come to Detroit one day," Gettelfinger replied, his voice tinged with emotion, "and see what it is like for ordinary folks who are losing their homes." Horrocks feared he had committed a faux pas and mentioned the incident later to Bloom. "You'll have to forgive Ron," Bloom explained. "That handshake you asked for was the undoing of seventy years of UAW bargaining."

He was right.

Since the 1937 Sit-down Strike at the GM factories in Flint, the United Auto Workers had successfully pursued the dream of achieving middle-class lifestyles for working-class people. That noble aspiration had lifted living standards for all Americans, provided healthcare for millions, and created college opportunities for working-class kids who otherwise would never have had the chance.

The dream had suffered temporary setbacks, such as the concessions the UAW had granted the car companies in the dark days of the early 1980s. But no days were darker than the ones of 2009. The UAW's dream was coming undone, a victim of the union's own excesses over the years, and of a global economy that was undermining the value of unskilled labor.

Gettelfinger, despite his penchant for prickliness, had represented the dream with more realism than any UAW president in the preceding quarter century. Partly that was because he had little choice; nonetheless he had risked his political position within the union to take courageous stands when necessary. And now, in his waning years of leading the UAW, he was making the tough decisions that his predecessors had ducked. He had a right not to celebrate.

Meanwhile the task force had more bargaining to do, because even some minor issues could become major hang-ups. The week before Easter, when Bloom was dealing with the UAW in Washington, two junior task force members flew out to Auburn Hills. They had to "diligence" the separate Chrysler and Fiat business plans to reconcile, among other things, the companies' different assumptions about the cost of rebates.

They convened in the Chrysler boardroom, the same place where Dieter Zetsche had decided to sell the company two years before. Fiat executives sat on one side of the table and Chrysler execs on the other, with the two young task force members at the head. They were at least twenty years younger than almost everybody else in the room. But they were in charge, and they admitted to themselves that they loved it!

When the young men returned to their hotel around two-thirty A.M., one of them promptly fell ill with food poisoning. But work resumed the next day anyway, because the clock was still ticking. Eventually the two companies' plans were reconciled, with a compromise projection that Chrysler's rebates would be $4,000 per car.

Kids running meetings. Late-night negotiations. Food poisoning. Compromises. Exhaustion. And still more work to do. The meetings in Auburn Hills captured virtually all the twists and turns of the quixotic effort to keep Chrysler alive.

And all the while new problems kept surfacing. After studying Chrysler Financial, the task force concluded that rescuing it would be far too expensive. Yet Chrysler needed the financial company—or some other financial company—to survive as an automaker. Some task force members began to question anew whether Chrysler could, or should, be saved.

Others too were having second thoughts. On April 14 one of Chrysler's outside advisers sent an e-mail urging the task force to ditch Fiat and reconsider General Motors as the prospective best owner for Chrysler. "We continue to believe that revisiting the combination/alliance discussion with GM . . . is the best alternative for all parties," he wrote. But the task force again decided that GM had enough problems of its own without taking on Chrysler's.

· · ·

That week, back in Washington, the UAW and Fiat reached agreement on wages and work rules. The union agreed that workers wouldn't get overtime until they worked forty hours in a week. That was considered normal in most of America, if not in Detroit.

Fiat also wanted workers' pay tied partly to Chrysler's performance, which the union stoutly resisted. The Italians settled for just a 5 percent performance component, hoping to increase that percentage over time. The union agreed to cut workers' breaks from forty-six minutes a shift to just forty, to suspend the paid Monday-after-Easter holidays and the cost-of-living allowances, and to dump, at long last, the Jobs Bank.

The task force, meanwhile, kept squeezing everyone and knocking off issues one by one. Cerberus agreed to hand back the deed to Chrysler's headquarters. Daimler willingly agreed to surrender its 19.9 percent stake in Chrysler and less willingly to pay $600 million in cash (yeah, cash) to the VEBA.

The Canadian Auto Workers consented to contract changes worth nearly $200 million in annual savings. Fiat acceded to performance measures—including selling Chrysler vehicles overseas and building a high-mileage car in the United States—as conditions for boosting its Chrysler stake to 35 percent over time.

The Italians also accepted the requirement that Chrysler repay its new government loans before Fiat could take majority control of the company. The U.S. and Canadian governments would get the 10 percent of Chrysler not owned by the VEBA or Fiat, at least until they could sell the shares.

Meanwhile, the big banks, including JPMorgan Chase, were losing their resolve. On April 20 Lee made a counteroffer to the task force. The creditors wanted a cash payment of $4.5 billion and would exchange their remaining $2.4 billion of debt for 40 percent ownership of Chrysler.

A similar offer two months earlier almost surely would have been accepted, or at least negotiated, but by now the task force wasn't about to give the banks the Chrysler stock that it already had earmarked for the UAW or Fiat. Lee's initial strategy of keeping his distance had backfired. A week later Rattner countered Lee's counteroffer, offering no equity but a sweetened pile of cash. "It's $2 billion." Rattner said. "Take it or leave it." It was, in fact, the amount the task force had intended to offer all along.

Just a day before Obama's April 30 deadline, Lee begged for another $250 million as a goodwill gesture. It was a last-ditch effort, he said, to get all the creditors to approve and to give Chrysler a chance to avoid bankruptcy.

Rattner reluctantly agreed but wanted an answer by six P.M. A flurry of frantic phone calls ensued, and Rattner extended the deadline till seven P.M. But more than a dozen smaller creditors—mostly hedge funds who had hoped to make a killing on Chrysler debt—still held out. They were used to scraping for pennies on the dollar, and that wasn't about to change. When the deadline passed, Chrysler's lawyers put the final touches on the bankruptcy filing. It was inevitable now.

There remained one last-minute issue that could scuttle everything—the fate of Chrysler Financial. The task force's solution was to fold Chrysler Financial into GMAC, which then would finance both GM and Chrysler dealers and their customers.

It seemed a reasonable solution, but by now nothing was simple. GMAC had itself been bailed out by the government by becoming a bank holding company. It couldn't swallow Chrysler Financial without separate agreements among Cerberus, Chrysler, Fiat, General Motors, GMAC itself, the task force, and—new to the party—the Federal Reserve Board and the Federal Deposit Insurance Corporation, which regulated the nation's banks. The FDIC, which was getting stuck with insurance expenses for a lot of failing banks, was especially reluctant. But eventually it relented.

It was after eight P.M. on Wednesday, April 29, before all the faxes with all the right signatures rolled into the task force offices. The final information was transmitted to the president, with a text of his speech for the next day.

On the morning of April 30 Chrysler's attorneys filed a Chapter 11 petition with federal bankruptcy court in Manhattan, listing $39 billion of assets but $55 billion of liabilities. The documents described

Chrysler's failed attempts to sell itself to Nissan, General Motors, and almost any other car company, and it portrayed Fiat as the company's last hope.

"Chrysler is seeking approval from this Court to consummate the only sale transaction that preserves some portion of its business as a going concern and averts a liquidation of historic proportions," the petition stated. "Liquidation would mean the end of an iconic, 83-year-old American car company . . . [and] would have impacts on the nation's economy and Chrysler's stakeholders that are grim."

The bankruptcy would be grim enough. Chrysler's plan called for dismissing 6,500 more employees, 20 percent of those remaining, while closing eight more factories and eliminating about 25 percent of the company's 3,200 dealers. In a federal bankruptcy court, the state franchising laws that required compensating those dealers didn't matter. Federal bankruptcy law trumped the state statutes, so Chrysler would owe the dealers nothing if the court approved its plan.

The taxpayers would feel pain too. The Treasury Department pledged to provide $8 billion to keep Chrysler going until Fiat could revive the company, on top of the $4 billion the government already had provided to keep the company afloat.

Along with those jolting numbers, the court filing also described the intricate mechanics of the bankruptcy process. Chrysler would transfer assets to "New CarCo Acquisition LLC," described as "an indirect wholly owned subsidiary of Fiat," a term only lawyers could love. And it would shut its factories for a couple months, while the dealers tried to work off the excess inventories sitting on their lots. UAW workers would get paid 80 percent of their wages during that time. In a way, it was the last remnant of the Jobs Bank before it disappeared.

Not since Studebaker in 1966 had a major American car company filed for bankruptcy. And for the last thirty years, ever since Chrysler's crisis in 1979, experts had been debating whether a car company could survive the process without customers simply walking away. Soon they would stop debating and find out.

At 12:08 P.M., for the second time in thirty days, President Obama went on television to talk about the auto industry. "Today, after consulting with my auto task force," he began, "I can report that the necessary steps have been taken to give one of America's most storied automakers, Chrysler, a new lease on life.

"Over the past month," Obama continued, "seemingly insurmountable obstacles have been overcome. I am pleased to announce that Chrysler and Fiat have formed a partnership that has a strong chance of success."

It sounded remarkably like a victory speech instead of an announcement that one of America's largest companies had gone bankrupt. In fact, the president didn't use the b-word until he was two-thirds finished, and then he made it sound like an achievement. Bankruptcy "is not a sign of weakness," he said, "but rather one more step on a clearly charted path to Chrysler's revival."

Some of the hedge fund holdouts, whom Obama had vilified as a "small group of speculators," quickly caved after the president's speech. But most opted to have their day in court. That was the right of every American, after all, even accused criminals. The hedge funds weren't exactly that. (In fact, some weren't even hedge funds, as it turned out, but public employee pension funds in the Midwest.)

In Auburn Hills, some Chrysler managers watched the president's speech with tears of joy, even though their individual fates remained unclear. Many employees stood to lose their jobs under the Fiat deal, but the alternative was worse: everyone losing their job in a quick corporate collapse.

In South Paris, Maine, Gene Benner concluded that Chrysler Financial's threat a year earlier to cut off his credit actually had been a blessing in disguise. It had forced him to make the painful changes that had kept his dealership afloat, even while Chrysler itself was tumbling into bankruptcy. He never would have made those moves, Benner admitted to himself, if he had avoided facing reality. His wake-up call had come in time, although it hadn't for Chrysler itself.

Obama's speech left Benner torn between relief and worry. Chrysler was still alive, which was good for his dealership. But would Bessey Motors make the cut when Chrysler culled its dealer ranks? And even if it did, would Chrysler's bankruptcy drive his customers away?

In Belvidere, assembly worker Gene Young was hoping it wasn't

BOHICA time again. The factory shutdown was supposed to be temporary, but despite what Obama had said, Young still wasn't feeling sanguine about his future. Nor was his father, Fred, who didn't know what further benefits, on top of previous reductions in health insurance, he might lose in retirement. "I'm seventy-one; where can I go get a job if I have to?" he asked plaintively. "I'm worried."

And Chrysler's bankruptcy, it was clear, was just the nation's warm-up for the main act: General Motors.

Unlike Chrysler, GM didn't have to convince the task force that it was too big to fail. Nor did GM have a potential buyer, like Fiat, requiring intricate negotiations and a complex transaction. But GM had other complications. It was a public company, for one, unlike Chrysler.

And it was enormous: more than ninety thousand U.S. employees (although the number was steadily shrinking), by now an incredible ten retirees or dependents for every active employee (that number, alas, wasn't shrinking), and $172 billion in liabilities—nearly as much as the national debt of Mexico. Beyond that, GM had operations in virtually every country on the globe, befitting the company that had long been called "the General" in Detroit. Its European operations, while not bleeding as badly as those in the United States, nonetheless were draining cash and facing likely sale.

Being worldwide, however, hadn't made GM worldly. In March, before Fritz Henderson replaced Rick Wagoner as CEO, Harry Wilson asked him what he thought of GM's culture. "I think it's fine," Henderson replied. He paused and added, "In reality, it's the only culture I know." That was true of GM's senior management, nearly all of whom were company lifers. At least Henderson recognized the problem. How could he or other GM executives find fault with practices that, in fact, were all that they knew?

The company's cash management system, for example, was so inexact that on any given day, GM didn't know its working balance within half a billion dollars. To Wilson, GM was like a guy who only occasionally bothered to balance his checkbook. That required keeping lots of extra cash in the checking account, just in case, but idle cash was wasteful.

Wilson, as the task force's point man for GM, knew that Wagoner's abrupt departure and Obama's sixty-day bankruptcy deadline had shocked the company. So he waited a few days after Obama's speech on March 30, to let things settle in. Then he reached out to Henderson and other executives.

"You started this turnaround in 2005 and you propose finishing it in 2014," Wilson told them. "I've been through a lot of restructurings, and they just don't work that way." GM had to move much faster, he said, pointing out that Nissan and Fiat had pulled off their dramatic turnarounds in just a couple years. GM's latest turnaround plan, he thought, was just another example of a culture of delay.

He suggested that GM and the task force collaborate, like partners, to develop a more aggressive viability plan that would go beyond GM's halfway measures of the past. Henderson quickly agreed (what choice did he have, really?), and task force members moved into conference rooms a few levels below the executive floor at GM's headquarters in the Renaissance Center.

Inevitably, their presence rankled some executives. In one meeting GM people and the Treasury team were sketching out product strategy on a white board, crossing out models with little profit potential and increasing spending plans for core vehicles that could actually make money. The task force members sensed increasing enthusiasm among the dozen or so GM people, when suddenly they all glanced at their BlackBerries and asked to be excused.

A few minutes later the GM executives filed back in together, obviously having held an impromptu caucus in the hallway. The options being discussed, they said, really weren't worth exploring after all. Somebody's sacred cow was being threatened, and plenty of those remained at GM, even though the company was keeling over.

In another meeting a GM executive pointedly asked the task force attendees how many of them had prior auto-industry experience. Not a single hand went up.

But experience had its drawbacks. GM executives had come to believe that solving their problems was impossible, and that living with them was inevitable. Despite the occasional flashes of resistance, however, Wilson and his colleagues kept asking fundamental questions that GM executives should have been asking themselves all along. When one executive praised a new model to be launched in

2011 as "a credible entry," Wilson asked, "Why shouldn't we have a compelling entry instead?" The GM man seemed surprised.

In the third week of April, the weather in Detroit was volatile, ranging from marble-size hail in midweek to eighty-degrees-and-sunny on Sunday. Events at General Motors were volatile too. On Wednesday, April 22, the Treasury loaned GM another $2 billion, on top of the previous $13 billion. With car sales remaining depressed and losses mounting, the company was once again running out of cash.

Five days later GM announced a public offering to exchange $27 billion of unsecured debt for GM stock. Because GM couldn't afford the interest payments, the task force insisted that the company get 90 percent of the debt off its books to retain any hope of staying out of bankruptcy.

But there were thousands and thousands of GM debt-holders, ranging from big mutual funds and pension funds to mom-and-pop investors. One eighty-one-year-old man in suburban Chicago had invested much of his life savings in 2004 to buy $270,000 of GM notes because of their 9 percent interest rate. The new stock GM was offering had little attraction for him. The face value of his investment would shrink to $10,000 or less, and the stock wouldn't pay a dividend, at least not initially.

There were plenty of others for whom the prospect of getting new GM stock had little appeal, even though the likely alternative would be taking significant losses in a bankruptcy. The bottom line was that getting 90 percent of the debt-holders to exchange their bonds for stock was virtually impossible. Henderson said he still hoped to avoid Chapter 11, but the already-slim odds were dwindling.

Investors' confidence was shaken further on May 7, when GM posted a horrific loss of $6 billion for the first quarter. The company's quarterly cash burn was even worse: more than $10 billion, or $113 million every single day—twice the rate it had been during the waning months of 2008. The company's first-quarter production plunged more than 40 percent, to just 1.3 million cars, which CFO Ray Young candidly conceded was "a staggering number."

The company that couldn't make money in good times was melting down dramatically as industry-wide sales plunged to thirty-year lows. In discussing the results with reporters and analysts, Young added: "We prefer to restructure outside of bankruptcy, but if we have to go in, we need to go in and out quickly."

The very next day GM got some unexpected relief, but only in the sense that misery loves company. Toyota, which had just supplanted GM as the industry's global sales leader, posted a loss of $7.74 billion for its fiscal fourth quarter (the same as GM's first quarter). It was a staggering loss, even greater than GM's, and enough to saddle Toyota with its first annual deficit in fifty-nine years.

For more than three decades the only direction Toyota had known was up—pretty much like, well, General Motors in the 1950s and 1960s. Despite the loss, Toyota had hefty cash reserves of $33 billion, as well as leadership in hybrid technology, and it remained the most formidable car company on the planet. But that only made the latest results more baffling.

The ironic truth was almost too simple. In its headlong rush to build new factories and become the world's largest car company, Toyota had succumbed to quality glitches and excess capacity, just as GM had done years earlier. Ford's cars now surpassed Toyota's in quality, *Consumer Reports* found.

What's more, Toyota's two-year-old pickup-truck factory in Texas was running at just half its capacity and was bleeding red ink. While Toyota didn't have the UAW or the Jobs Bank, it did adhere to a decades-old "no layoffs" policy that now amounted to the same thing: paying workers full wages for not building cars. That situation had rarely occurred during the company's decades of nonstop growth, but the global economic crisis that began in 2008 was leaving no automaker unscathed.

GM executives couldn't take much solace, however, in the troubles of Toyota or any other car company. They were too busy trying to convince the UAW to accept another 21,000 job cuts, on top of the 20,000 union jobs eliminated since the middle of 2008, and to deal with a host of other issues. As April turned to May, meanwhile, Fritz Henderson said GM was at a "defining moment."

May 14 began D-Days in America, as in dealer days. Nearly ten thousand General Motors and Chrysler dealers across the country got letters from the companies, telling them whether they would be kept or culled.

The logic for reducing the ranks of dealers was simple. Detroit's dealer networks were too big, relics of the companies' glory days of the 1960s, as opposed to reflecting the realities of the twenty-first century. In 2008 GM's dealers sold fewer than five hundred new cars on average, while the typical Toyota dealer sold more than three times that many.

The extra sales made Toyota dealers more profitable, with more money to invest in attractive showrooms, local marketing campaigns, and better service facilities. Dealer overload was another "legacy cost" to be eradicated. But one man's legacy cost is another man's living.

At ten A.M. on May 14 a brown UPS truck pulled into the parking lot at Bessey Motors in South Paris, Maine, with a letter from Chrysler. Benner had known a letter was coming that day—to him and to all the other 3,180 Chrysler dealers in America. Would it wipe out all he had worked for since he progressed from car salesman to car dealer over the last twenty-five years? "Dear Eugene N. Benner," the letter began in the stiff style of a mass mailing, which in fact it was.

"We are pleased to inform you on May 14th," the letter continued, "Chrysler designated your Sales and Service Agreement(s) to be assumed and assigned to a new company that is purchasing the primary assets of Chrysler. You can remain our dealer as we move forward with establishing a new company."

The man who had been cut decades earlier by the Cleveland Browns breathed thanks that he had made the cut with Chrysler. Small dealerships were bearing the brunt of the cutbacks, he knew, and with sales of only about two hundred new cars a year, Bessey Motors certainly was small.

Despite his size, however, Benner was the only Chrysler dealer in his area of rural Maine, and he had all three company brands—Jeep, Dodge, and Chrysler—under one roof. Plus he had taken his future into his own hands and made the tough decisions to return his dealership to profitability, despite the slump in sales. Those things made all the difference.

Benner got on the dealership's intercom system and said, simply, "We're good to go." Every employee knew exactly what he meant. A few exchanged smiles of grateful relief before turning back to their work.

In 789 other Chrysler dealerships, however, people weren't smiling. A dealer in Kentucky got a letter from Chrysler the same day saying he hadn't made the cut. The very next day he got a similar letter from GM, terminating the Chevrolet franchise his father had started half a century earlier. The back-to-back blows were "more than I can handle right now," he said.

Also that day the Chevrolet dealership in Belvidere—just a few miles from the Chrysler factory where Gene Young worked—got its termination letter too. The dealership had been run by the same family since 1924 and was displaying an eighty-five-year anniversary banner in its window when the bad news arrived.

In a two-day period, three of Belvidere's six car dealers got termination letters. The "new math" of the twenty-first century auto industry made six dealers too many for a town of 22,000, but the dealers were part of the fabric of Belvidere. For decades they had supported Little League baseball, youth hockey, and other civic causes. Those and other groups, not to mention the local tax base that provided everything from teachers' salaries to city services, were going to take a hit.

GM's timing surprised many dealers, because the company hadn't filed for bankruptcy. Without filing, the company would have to pay them damages, but they knew GM didn't have money for that. The letters were the latest clue that D-Days soon would give way to B-Day.

Meanwhile, bad news came to Gene Young via e-mail instead of a letter. At eleven P.M. on Tuesday, May 19, he got an automated message saying that the second shift at the Belvidere factory would be eliminated indefinitely, even after production resumed in mid-July. In years past Young, and the 991 other workers on the second shift, wouldn't have been unduly worried. They simply would have slid seamlessly into the Jobs Bank, waiting for an increase in production or an inverse layoff to bring them back to work. But now the Jobs Bank—like the DeSoto, Oldsmobile, and tail fins—was passing into automotive history.

At forty-two, with four children, two cars, and a mortgage, Gene Young faced a brutal choice. He could hope that the second shift would be restored before long and in the meantime scramble to find temporary work. Or he could take a buyout from Chrysler, hoping the money would tide his family over until he found a new occupation.

With a high school education and a good work record but no special skills, Young was under no illusions. Any new job was unlikely to command the compensation of his old one. "Everything we have has been financed with my Chrysler pay level," he said ruefully. "So what happens when I don't have a Chrysler pay level anymore?" But there was little use waiting around for a job that might never return.

On May 26, the day after Memorial Day, Young decided to bid Chrysler, the assembly line, the Jobs Bank, and (hopefully) BOHICA good-bye forever. Maybe he would find another job or start a small business of some sort. The days when he could finance a new car just by saying he worked at Chrysler were gone for good.

Detroit was ground zero of the car crackup of 2009. But the meltdown of the Motor City's corporate giants was slamming tens of thousands of people throughout America in little towns like Belvidere too—dealers, workers, suppliers, and all the doctors, drugstore clerks, and others who depended on them. Economic evolution was ending a way of life across America for many people who had depended on the auto industry. It wasn't clear what would take its place.

While Chrysler and General Motors struggled, Ford stayed out of the headlines, if not out of deep water. The company's decision to forgo federal funding had been admirable but not entirely altruistic. Declaring bankruptcy, company officials knew, would mean wiping out existing shareholders—including the Ford family, which would lose control of the company. Family control was as sacred as the blue-oval logo.

Nonetheless, going it alone was producing a peculiar set of problems for Ford. If Chrysler and GM should emerge from bankruptcy quickly, with far fewer dealers and much less debt, Ford could find itself at a disadvantage, like a family making full payments on its mortgage, while the folks next door got their payments cut.

So the company pursued an out-of-bankruptcy restructuring, in effect, to reduce its debt load and its dealer body on its own. Ford brokered mergers between dealers, wiped out $10 billion of debt by exchanging it for stock, and even managed to sell $1.6 billion of new shares to the public—something neither Chrysler nor GM had a prayer of doing. Ford also convinced the union to accept reduced cash payments for the VEBA trust, to end the Jobs Bank, and to negotiate better work rules.

All those measures mirrored what Chrysler and GM were doing—except that without taking government money and going through bankruptcy court, Ford couldn't move as quickly. But there was an offsetting benefit: Ford was getting an unexpected boost in the court of public opinion. Radio talk shows were filled with angry references to GM as "Government Motors" and with callers vowing that the only American car they would buy henceforth would be a Ford.

Ford started to gain market share, in contrast to the continuing declines at GM and Chrysler. The company still faced some heavy rowing to keep from being swamped. But its decision to steer an independent course, away from federal funding and bankruptcy, was paying off. Ford had gotten lucky, to a degree, but mostly it had taken the tough decisions to make its own luck.

Throughout April and into early May, GM and the task force wrestled with the other b-word: *brands.* Harry Wilson's initial bias was for a streamlined GM with just two domestic brands: Chevrolet and Cadillac. That would leave GM with one mass-market brand and a separate elite marque that, between them, could cover every segment of the market, just like Toyota and Lexus.

Among the casualties, then, would be Saturn. Much had happened since its creation in 1985 to ensure, in Roger Smith's words, "GM's long-term competitiveness, survival, and success." Now Saturn was becoming a casualty, sadly, of GM's long-term failure. The special labor agreement, with its lofty language describing workers' desire to "care about their jobs and each other," had been scrapped years earlier. The factory in Spring Hill wasn't even building Saturns anymore but Chevrolets instead. And some Saturn cars were being imported—*imported!*—from Germany. Without a distinct identity,

Saturn's sales had dropped to just two-thirds of their peak level in 1995. GM had no choice but to let it go.

Adopting a two-brand lineup would also spell demise for Saab, Hummer, Pontiac, GMC, and Buick, which dated back to Billy Durant and the birth of General Motors in Flint. The luster had faded from Buick, which one auto-enthusiast website described that April as "an icon for retirement-home parking lots." As for GMC, its trucks were basically Chevrolets with steroidal styling. To Wilson and his task force colleagues, Buick and GMC had become distractions instead of assets.

Henderson and his team, however, fought to save them. Buick had quietly risen to near the top of the J.D. Power quality rankings, they argued, and the Buick Enclave SUV crossover was drawing buyers in their early fifties as opposed to those in their midsixties. (Besides, wasn't sixty supposed to be the new forty?) Buick also had become a top seller in China, where it was viewed, perhaps improbably, as a symbol of American luxury.

As for GMC, the dynamics of that debate spilled into the open in late April on an analysts' conference call with Henderson. One analyst asked why GMC shouldn't simply be folded into Chevy, since the trucks basically were the same.

"Okay," Henderson replied, "do you own a GMC?"

The answer was no.

Well, Henderson explained, GMC was "extremely profitable" because it carried more cachet than Chevrolet. "It wouldn't make good business sense," he added, "to try to collapse that into Chevrolet."

Put another way, a GMC truck adorned with a macho grille and marketed with country music commercials could be priced thousands of dollars higher than a nearly identical soccer-mom truck from Chevrolet. It was the sort of "badge engineering" that had blurred the differences among too many GM vehicles over the years, though it was reasonably more successful in GMC's case.

Buick and GMC created a dilemma for Wilson. He knew GM executives were adept at marshaling arguments for clinging to pieces of the company's past, and this might be more of the same. Then again, the company's numbers showed that GMC and Buick were profitable, and profits were something Wilson could understand.

Besides, he didn't want to step over the line between making suggestions and giving orders, at least not on the more refined aspects of brand strategy. Despite his initial misgivings, Wilson agreed to support a restructuring plan that included keeping both Buick and GMC.

GM's brand lineup was a little outside Wilson's comfort zone, but the company's capital structure was right in his sweet spot. He strongly believed that a structure similar to what the task force had arranged for Chrysler—with the union and Fiat taking 75 percent ownership—wouldn't work for General Motors.

There were all kinds of problems, really. Chrysler retained $17 billion of debt that it would have to repay. But that would be Fiat's problem, assuming its efforts with Chrysler succeeded. (If not, well, repayment would be moot anyway.) GM's debt burden would be its own.

Nor was it realistic for the UAW to take GM stock for its VEBA, as the union had done for Chrysler. GM's hourly workforce was several years older than Chrysler's, on average, so the union couldn't wait for stock in the restructured company to gain value.

But the biggest difference, which no one dared say publicly, was that the task force deemed GM too big to fail, while Chrysler had been a close call. Restructuring General Motors with a minimal debt burden, Wilson believed, would create a capital structure like those of Toyota, Honda, and Volkswagen and give GM the best chance for success. The catch was that minimal debt meant maximum equity, and people weren't lining up to get GM stock.

That was no surprise, because GM was running out of money for the third time in five months. The company's everyday expenses—paying salaries, purchasing parts, keeping the lights turned on—continued to outstrip its revenue, despite the previous cost cutting. On May 22 the Treasury loaned the company another $4 billion. That brought the total since December to $20 billion, if anyone was counting.

Four days later GM's debt-for-equity exchange offer expired. Not surprisingly, nowhere nearly enough debt-holders agreed to swap their notes for GM shares. The only thing left to do, aside from letting GM collapse, was for the government to step in.

So it was that fifty-six years after "Engine Charlie" Wilson said what was good for America was good for General Motors, young Harry Wilson (no relation) was about to make America the largest shareholder in General Motors. The U.S. government—by default, because there were no other takers—would get 60 percent of GM's stock in return for an additional $30 billion of financing. The Canadian government would get 12.5 percent, the UAW 17.5 percent, and the unsecured debt-holders 10 percent.

Just as with Chrysler, the UAW wanted cash for its VEBA instead of GM stock of dubious value, even though the task force offered the union $6.5 billion in preferred shares, which would pay dividends immediately. When Gettelfinger got the government's offer on the morning of May 20, he asked for time to think it over, and then walked the streets of Washington for two hours. Finally, he said yes.

As for GM's creditors, holders of the $6 billion in secured debt would be paid in full, in contrast to Jimmy Lee and the secured creditors at Chrysler. GM had enough assets to pay its secured creditors if the company was liquidated, which wasn't the case at Chrysler.

But GM's unsecured creditors, many of them small investors, would get just 12.5 cents on the dollar. There was no getting around the fact that GM's bankruptcy was going to hurt a lot of people—dealers, employees, creditors, stockholders—even though the U.S. taxpayers were investing $50 billion in direct aid to save the company. (There would be more indirect aid.) That amount alone, then, was double the $25 billion "loan" that Detroit's three car companies had sought from Congress, as a group, the previous November. Congressional skepticism about the $25 billion number was fully vindicated.

The GM rescue terms fell into place without most of the tortured negotiations that were required for the Chrysler-Fiat deal, but there were other complications. GM's financial structure was built on hundreds, even thousands, of transactions that had to be understood and in some cases unraveled.

Its vast debt structure included bonds issued through a paper company in Nova Scotia so they would be eligible for purchase by Canadian pension funds, under Canadian law. It turned out, however, that most of the Nova Scotia bonds were owned by New York hedge funds anyway. Likewise, GM had a joint-venture factory with Suzuki in Canada that had stopped making Suzuki vehicles years ago. But Suzuki remained a 50 percent owner anyway because that made the factory eligible for low-cost loans from Japanese banks.

Then there was Delphi, which GM had propped up with $12 billion in payments over the last three years—nearly double what Steve Miller had originally demanded—hastening GM's own demise. Now GM agreed to take back several big Delphi plants, undoing the reason it had spun off Delphi a decade earlier. The rest of Delphi would be sold with financial assistance from GM—that is, from the U.S. taxpayers.

Meanwhile GM's Opel subsidiary in Europe was failing as well and seeking assistance from the German government. Sergio Marchionne tried to sweep in with a no-cash purchase, just as he had engineered with Chrysler. The German government rebuffed him, however, determined to steer Opel into other hands.

On top of all this, GM had more than 800,000 contracts worldwide with companies that supplied everything from advertising to windshield wipers. There wasn't nearly enough time to review all of them, but thousands would have to be "diligenced" to get a sense of the company's financial commitments. The analysts and financiers poring over GM's books now grasped why the finance people instead of the "car guys" had run General Motors for so long. They were the only people who could understand the place.

The task force was so swamped, sorting through all this, that it asked GM and the UAW, on their own, to negotiate new work rules that would save the company money. Without adult supervision (or even young adult supervision), the company and union negotiators quickly reverted to old form. While they agreed to abolish the Jobs Bank, as at Chrysler, the contract's "new attendance procedure" still allowed an employee to have six unexcused absences without getting fired. Harry Wilson wouldn't even know about that until he read it in the newspapers, a week or two later.

GM's countdown to bankruptcy began on Friday, May 29, with two days of board meetings at the GM Building in New York. Henderson, Ray Young, and a small army of lawyers reviewed the company's planned Chapter 11 filing, the proposed structure of the new company, and myriad other issues. The marathon meetings were surreal, in a way, because the Treasury's task force was the real power at General Motors, not the company's board of directors. But legally, just as only GM's board could accept Rick Wagoner's resignation, only the board could officially approve a bankruptcy filing.

On Saturday night an exhausted Young left the GM Building about ten P.M. He walked down to Mickey Mantle's, where he grabbed a burger and a beer and sat alone watching the Red Wings Stanley Cup playoff game. He had gone from being afraid of bankruptcy to being almost relieved that it was about to happen. The next day—Sunday, May 31—GM's board convened again at eight P.M.; most of the directors dialed in by phone. By eight-forty-five P.M. they formally authorized a bankruptcy filing for the next morning.

During more than a century of existence, the company of Billy Durant, Alfred Sloan, and Harley Earl—and, yes, of Roger Smith and Rick Wagoner too—had made history. It had defined American corporate power, with everything from manufacturing might to muscle cars. Now just seven months after celebrating its hundredth birthday, General Motors was about to make history of a different sort.

At six A.M. on Monday, June 1, thirty-six-year-old David Markowitz boarded an Amtrak train in New York for Washington. The young task force member had been working three days without sleep while reviewing thousands of GM documents. But sleep could wait. He was invited to attend Obama's speech that day and wasn't about to miss meeting the president.

At 6:03 A.M. a small army of lawyers began hauling documents into U.S. Bankruptcy Court in lower Manhattan. The first one they filed was a bankruptcy petition for Chevrolet-Saturn of Harlem, Inc. The dealership was owned by General Motors, and its filing established jurisdiction for the parent company's case to be heard in New York. For a host of logistical reasons, nobody wanted to file this case in Detroit.

The main filing, at 7:57 A.M., stated that GM's $172 billion of liabilities overwhelmed its $82 billion of assets. And that the company's $59.5 billion in stock market value in April 2000—two months before Wagoner became CEO—had been all but wiped out. "There are no realistic alternatives" to bankruptcy, the filing added. "There are no merger partners, acquirers or investors willing and able to acquire GM's business . . . The transaction [bankruptcy] is the only realistic alternative for the company to avoid liquidation that would severely undermine the automotive industry." It was all sadly and horribly true.

The company would be split into "New GM"—Cadillac, Chevrolet, Buick, GMC, and other viable assets—and "Old GM," the discards. Those included Saturn, Saab, Hummer, Pontiac, and a bunch of other stuff, which would be sold if buyers could be found, or else liquidated. GM's restructuring plan called for closing up to fourteen more factories and lopping off another twenty thousand employees by the end of 2011.

As it happened, Jerry York's warning in January 2006, that GM could go under in a thousand days, had been only thirty days off. GM had tumbled over the waterfall, though the government tugboat was standing by to salvage part of the wreckage and to pick up survivors.

At eleven-thirty young Markowitz was walking into the White House, where the president would speak, when he suddenly felt faint, his legs started to wobble, and he realized he wasn't going to make it. Wilson propped him up and walked him over to the White House doctor's office. It looked like he wouldn't meet the president after all.

Nine minutes before noon Obama began his speech by announcing some good news. In the wee hours of the morning, even before GM's crack-of-dawn filing had begun, the bankruptcy court had approved Chrysler's restructuring plan. Chrysler had sped through bankruptcy court like a hot rod, handing Obama and the task force a major victory.

The president couldn't resist crowing a little, even though the bankruptcy court's decision faced an appeal to higher courts by disgruntled Chrysler creditors. "Keep in mind," the president said, "many experts said that a quick, surgical bankruptcy was impossible. They were wrong."

He went on: "Earlier today, GM did what Chrysler has successfully done and filed for Chapter 11 bankruptcy with the support of its key stakeholders and the United States government. In all likelihood, this process will take more time for GM than it did for Chrysler because GM is a bigger, more complex company. But Chrysler's extraordinary success reaffirms my confidence that GM will emerge from its bankruptcy process quickly, and as a stronger and more competitive company."

After he finished, Obama walked down to his doctor's office to get a couple Tylenol pills. Markowitz, still in a blur, sensed a sudden commotion around him, but he wasn't sure what was happening. A few minutes later he found himself shaking hands, groggily, with the president of the United States.

The handshake, though happenstance, was well deserved. Markowitz and the other automotive neophytes on the task force had brought more common sense to GM than the company had seen in decades. The Jobs Bank was ridiculous. So were mountains of debt, crippling work rules, eight different brands, and dozens of different "look-share" cars that were almost alike. They were like GM's dirty family secrets, known by all but never publicly acknowledged, much less resolved.

Shortly after Obama spoke, Henderson convened a press conference in New York and tinged his remarks with contrition that would have shocked his predecessors from GM's glory years. "Give us another chance," he implored those watching on TV. "The GM that many of you knew, the GM that in fact had let too many of you down, is history." His words suggested that the company had learned some hard lessons, though only time would tell.

"From here on, we move up," Henderson added. "This is not the end of General Motors but the start of a new and better chapter, one that needed to happen and one that begins today." The chapter would be new, all right, but almost certainly not better than GM's dominant days of yore—which in retrospect had been too good for the company, blinding it to the need to keep the customer first. General Motors was going to be just another company now. It would be big and important, but not like "Microsoft and Apple and Toyota all rolled into one," as the next day's *Wall Street Journal* described the company's glory days.

The Economist marked GM's bankruptcy with a cover story illustrated with a metallic dinosaur, made of car parts, dripping oil from its mouth. The headline said, appropriately: "Detroitosaurus Wrecks."

General Motors had virtually invented the modern corporation, with professional managers, as opposed to family founders, presiding over decentralized operations that were governed by central financial control. It had pioneered modern marketing, public relations, and the hierarchy of brands that made automobiles vehicles for social as well as physical mobility. It had set standards for everything from style and design to corporate healthcare plans.

The company had come through two world wars and the Depression and had stood as the defining corporation of America's economic hegemony after World War II. But that very success had bred complacency, arrogance, and hubris. It had fostered the isolation of executives who never had to shop for a car, and a union's transformation from protecting workers' rights to protecting their "right" to be paid indefinitely for not working.

Had GM's filing occurred a few years earlier, stock markets around the world would have collapsed in panic. But the day that it really did happen—June 1, 2009—the Dow Jones Industrial Average actually jumped 221 points. America, just like Ray Young, was almost relieved. So were many people in Detroit itself, now that the anxious waiting was over.

Approval wasn't universal, of course, for spending $50 billion from the public purse to rescue the fallen industrial colossus. The bailout signaled an "America poised to transform into Euro-Flop Social-Marxism, as we juggle open-ended bankruptcy," said one letter-writer to *The Patriot Ledger* in Quincy, Massachusetts. "What's next?" Similar, if less colorful, talk abounded around the country about creeping socialism, bureaucrats designing cars, and the like.

It was all understandable from a bailout-weary nation, especially because of the contrast with Ford. After careening from one disastrous decision to another between 1999 and 2006, the company had come to grips with its fundamental need to change. In 2009 Ford was reducing its debt, shedding dealers, and changing factory work rules without getting billions in federal funding. With the U.S. economy still depressed, Ford was still losing money, but its progress provided plain evidence that GM and Chrysler could have avoided bankruptcy too with better leadership and with a willingness to act decisively before it was too late.

As events had actually unfolded, however, the alternative to saving Chrysler and especially GM was . . . what? Maybe their outright collapse wouldn't have deepened America's worst economic crisis since the Great Depression. But it would have been foolhardy to find out.

Right after entering bankruptcy, GM aired a television commercial that pretty much said it all. "Let's be completely honest, no company wants to go through this," the commercial began. "There was a time when eight different brands made sense. Not anymore. There was a time when our cost structure could compete worldwide. Not anymore. Reinvention is the only way we can fix this." Ironically, those were the very same arguments that GM's critics had been making, and that the company had been denying, for years.

Only time would tell whether the commercial was simply a PR stunt, or whether GM had finally learned that problems left to fester will result in a reckoning, and the longer the festering, the more painful the reckoning. That was the broad lesson of General Motors—a lesson as old as the Bible, and as fresh as the epic collapse of Wall Street less than a year earlier.

The task of the new GM would be to prove another biblical lesson: that reform and redemption are possible.

ANOTHER CHANCE

S*uccess nearly destroyed Detroit.* Can failure save it? That's not a sure thing, even though Chrysler and GM made it through bankruptcy with startling speed.

Chrysler took just forty-two days; its appeal went to the U.S. Supreme Court but was quickly denied. General Motors took all of forty days, despite being the second-largest bankruptcy in American history. (The biggest was WorldCom, a fraud-ridden telecom company that tanked in 2002.) Experts had expected both GM's and Chrysler's cases to take years, not weeks. It was a clear victory for President Obama, though not a cheap one.

Both companies' cases were lubricated by the political capital of a popular new president, and by his decision to commit copious amounts of cash from the American taxpayers. Besides $50 billion in direct aid for GM and nearly $16 billion for Chrysler, more than $40 billion went to GMAC, Chrysler Financial, parts suppliers, Delphi pension guarantees, and GM tax credits.

The total amount would top $100 billion, enough to buy 5 million cars, more than every car sold in America in the first half of 2009. The Canadian and German governments provided additional billions in bailout funds for the Chrysler and GM operations in their countries. Some of the money might be repaid to the various governments over time, but probably no more than half.

All the money spent couldn't prevent enormous pain and dislocation that, while centered in Detroit, had spread across America. After closing twenty-two factories between 2004 and 2008, GM and Chrysler were scheduled to shutter another sixteen by 2011. More than three thousand dealerships were eliminated, or scheduled for elimination, by Detroit's three car companies. In every factory and dealership were people whose lives were disrupted and who were scrambling to adjust.

In Belvidere, Gene Young got a $75,000 severance package from Chrysler—$48,000 after taxes—plus a $25,000 voucher to buy a new Chrysler vehicle. He chose a small SUV, the Jeep Liberty. Young was taking a part-time job as a school bus driver and also planning to open a small business installing antennas and satellite dishes for homes and small businesses. His income would drop significantly, at least for a while. Young was worried about his family's future but was determined to cope. "I didn't raise him to sit around and feel sorry for himself," said his father, Fred.

Fred Young, for his part, would keep receiving his full pension and thus avoided his nightmare of having to return to work at his age. But he would have to pay more for prescription drugs and other medical benefits, such as dental care, which for years had been virtually free.

In South Paris, Maine, Gene Benner's dealership returned to profitability, thanks to his timely cost cutting. Sales got a boost in the summer of 2009 from the government's "cash for clunkers" program, which offered a tax rebate of up to $4,500 to a buyer who traded in an old car for a new, fuel-efficient model. The initial $1 billion for the program was exhausted in a week, and Congress rushed to appropriate more money.

The speed with which Chrysler and GM went through Chapter 11 seemed to banish the fear that nobody would buy a car from a company that declared bankruptcy. Everybody at Bessey Motor Sales, including Benner himself, had made sacrifices. But at least Chrysler was still in business, and they were still employed.

The experiences of the two Youngs and Benner were shared by many—the result of Detroit's problems being allowed to linger for years, even though many smart people had recognized them all along. Detroit's disaster didn't have to happen. It occurred because the solutions were painful, requiring not just brains but courage. For too long neither UAW officials nor company executives had been able to muster that courage. As a result, many good people were caught in a bad system, and couldn't escape its consequences.

For many GM and Chrysler executives, the consequences included retirements far less comfortable than they had once planned. Those who had worked for decades to accumulate stock options and stock grants found that their nest eggs were wiped out. GM executives were losing part of their pensions. So were Chrysler executives, along with the two free lease cars they had received every year for life. They were notified to turn in their cars within ten days.

UAW members were told their prescription drug insurance no longer would cover Viagra. Thousands who took buyout packages, like Gene Young, wouldn't be replaced. And when replacements were hired, they would be making only half the pay of their predecessors, under the two-tier wage system the UAW had accepted in 2007.

For both workers and executives, in short, some sacrifices were serious, while others were testament to the excesses that had produced the crisis.

Steve Rattner and Harry Wilson left the task force to return to private life soon after GM emerged from bankruptcy, while Ron Bloom and some others stayed on to handle the cleanup work. They fended off congressmen who tried to reverse the closings of factories and dealerships in their districts—predictably, some of the same congressmen who had railed against Detroit's bloated cost structure. Their attitude toward Detroit's cutbacks was a classic case of NIMBY—Not In My Back Yard.

At the cost of tremendous expense and sacrifice, Chrysler and General Motors both are getting another chance—which is a precious gift, as anyone who has survived a serious illness knows. The two companies restarted their assembly lines in July, after two-month shutdowns to reduce inventories. They face challenges that are similar in some ways but much different in others.

Chrysler will have to make an intercontinental merger work—no easy matter, as the company learned from its deal with Daimler. Fortunately, there were no early fights with Fiat about the size of the business cards or about putting the company logo on paper napkins, as there had been with the Germans.

Fiat's big challenges are overcoming a legacy of failure in America, and taking over a company whose product pipeline is running on empty. But the company has a great brand in Jeep, and a proven CEO in Sergio Marchionne. He has to get some compelling new cars into Chrysler's showrooms, quickly.

GM, being much bigger, is more complicated. In trimming down to four brands from eight, the company agreed to sell Saab to a little Swedish company called Koenigsegg that makes less than twenty cars a year—though they are high-tech sports cars that cost more than $1 million apiece. A Chinese company agreed to buy Hummer, but Pontiac, once a legend, appeared destined to disappear.

GM agreed to sell Saturn to Roger Penske, a former race driver turned automotive entrepreneur, who planned to make it sort of an automotive Costco. Automakers manufacture cars and distribute them through independent dealerships. But Penske planned to make Saturn a distributorship, procuring cars from various manufacturers and providing them to Saturn dealers.

In late September, though, the plan fell apart when Penske couldn't get a procurement pact in place. Barring another long-shot rescue effort, Saturn would die, a monument to noble intentions derailed by bitter reality. Spring Hill still has a street named for Don Ephlin, the visionary UAW leader who was committed to making Saturn a success. Ironically, the town also has a street named for Steve Yokich, the UAW president who was determined to destroy Saturn, and succeeded. Both Ephlin and Yokich have passed away.

Also scheduled for closure, sadly, was Nummi, the GM-Toyota joint venture in California. It had once been GM's worst factory, and the scene of nonstop labor-management strife. Under Toyota it had been transformed into a model of efficiency and quality, using cooperative methods that GM and the UAW, unfortunately, were reluctant to adopt. In 2009 both GM and Toyota were saddled with excess factory capacity, sealing Nummi's fate.

After prolonged wrangling, GM decided to keep Opel and its other European operations instead of selling them, thus remaining a global company but adding to its turnaround challenge.

GM emerged from bankruptcy with just $17.6 billion in debt, only one-third of its previous financial burden. The company's U.S. employment stood at about 70,000 people at the end of 2009, less than 12 percent of the peak level reached thirty years earlier, when GM was America's largest private employer. A downsized company should have a smaller executive suite, said Fritz Henderson, who promised to cut GM's executive ranks by 35 percent.

Henderson also pledged to lead a transformation of GM's culture, though his first executive appointees were GM lifers, like himself, which wasn't the most promising start for a company needing a cultural overhaul. But Henderson publicly acknowledged that GM wasn't going to get a third chance. That message was reinforced by the White House, which said Detroit's car companies wouldn't get more government money if they foundered again. Nor should they.

Besides changing its culture, GM's other big test will be making Cadillac and Chevrolet hot again—cars that people *want* to buy, as opposed to cars that they settle for because of deep discounts. And the company needs workers who will rush to repair a broken machine on the assembly line, instead of hanging around until the guy with the right job classification happens to show up. The UAW needs a cultural revolution just as much as the company.

As for the chances that any of this will happen, predictions are perilous. Even though the auto industry has huge companies and product-development cycles that take years, the speed of momentum changes can be breathtaking. Few people predicted Chrysler would survive in 1980, or that Nissan would recover in 2000, or that Fiat would mount a turnaround in 2005. Or that Ford would stumble so badly in 2000 through 2006, only to emerge in 2009 as the strongest car company in Detroit.

One encouraging sign for Detroit came from the blunt-spoken Mike Jackson at AutoNation. After years of buying import-brand dealerships and shunning domestic marques, he started looking for Chevrolet and Ford dealerships to acquire. Those were the two strongest Detroit brands, he figured, and he expected their fortunes to improve. Dodge and Jeep franchises, however, weren't on his shopping list, at least not yet.

New dynamics are certain to transform the long-running rivalry between Ford and General Motors. Ford has the disadvantage of retaining a full debt load. But GM has the offsetting disadvantage of being "Government Motors," a stigma sure to hurt.

The result might be that Ford supplants General Motors as the largest U.S. car company for the first time in more than eighty years. But being the largest U.S. car company won't mean what it once did.

No automaker will be like the GM of yore, with half the market to itself while others were left to divide the rest.

Instead, five or six car companies—Ford, GM, Toyota, Honda, Nissan, and maybe Chrysler—each will have between 10 and 20 percent of the market, mirroring the structure that Europe's auto industry has had for decades. Instead of the Big Three, America will have a Medium Six. All the companies will have to keep abreast of rapid technological change, making more gas-electric hybrids and perhaps eventually using hydrogen fuel cells.

Amid all this upheaval, however, one thing is certain: Americans will still love their cars—be they Hondas or hybrids, GMs or Jeeps—as they have for more than a century.

That much will not change.

Acknowledgments

I have many people to thank for their help and encouragement with this book—many more, in fact, than it is practical to name. Moreover, some of those who helped the most requested anonymity, and of course I will honor their wish. Of those I can name, Scott Moyers and Andrew Wylie of the Wylie Agency deserve heartfelt thanks, along with my terrific editors at Random House—Susan Mercandetti, Millicent Bennett, and their capable assistant, Ben Steinberg. Thank you to Mit Spears, also. Many dear friends in Detroit opened their homes and hearts during my regular research visits: Logan and Edrie Robinson, Joe and Jan McMillan, Gary and Leslie Miller, Al and Cathy Rutledge, and others. Susan Insley and Scott Whitlock provided invaluable perspective on Honda's critical early years in the U.S. Jim Fitzpatrick and his wife, Jan, provided keen insight—and appropriate critiques of my thinking—from Jim's years at General Motors. Fred and Gene Young in Belvidere, Illinois, and Gene Benner in South Paris, Maine, provided ground-level views of Detroit's drama of 2008–2009.

I owe much thanks for friendship and encouragement to two fellow authors, James B. Stewart and Jonathan Knee. And special appreciation goes to a host of friends and former colleagues from *The Wall Street Journal* and Dow Jones, including John Stoll, Joe White, Peter Kann, Irv Hockaday, Leslie Hill, Tunku Varadarajan, Neal Lipshutz, Howard Dickman, Rob Pollock, and Paul Gigot. Many good friends at the Morris County Golf Club in New Jersey provided welcome company when I needed to breathe some fresh air, hit something (hopefully 220 yards and straight), and take a break from writing.

Most valued was the support from my family, including my wife, Susie, our three dear sons, and my brother, Larry, the business editor of *The New York Times*—truly the top journalistic talent in our family.

One: Where the Weak Are Killed and Eaten

5   "We have done all we can do": Kevin Krolicki and Soyoung Kim, "SUVs at Altar," Reuters, December 7, 2008.

9   recommended that new bulletin boards be installed: GM Bulletin Board Study Committee, memo, November 23, 1988.

9   "Maybe instead of getting mad": Retired GM executive, interview by author, March 2009.

10   "We didn't undergo fundamental change": Robert A. Lutz, *Guts: 8 Laws of Business from One of the Most Innovative Business Leaders of Our Time* (1998; New York: John Wiley & Sons, 2003), p. 12, emphasis in original.

11   The cycle reached its peak: Jeffrey McCracken et al., "Delphi Bankruptcy Filing Expected," *The Wall Street Journal,* October 8, 2005.

Two: Dynasty and Destiny

15–16   "I will build a car for the great": David L. Lewis, *The Public Image of Henry Ford* (Detroit: Wayne State University Press, 1987), p. 43.

17   "the extra pay went only for better": "Labor: Model T Tycoon," *Time* (cover story), March 17, 1941.

17   "has in his social endeavor committed": Editorial, *The Wall Street Journal,* January 7, 1914.

17   "If an employer does not share prosperity": Henry Ford and Samuel Crowther, *Today and Tomorrow* (Garden City, N.Y.: Doubleday Page & Co., 1926), p. 141.

20   "There won't be any trouble": Bernard A. Weisberger, *The Dream Maker* (Boston: Little, Brown, 1979), p. 188.

22   "dressed just as he did in New York City": David Farber, *Sloan Rules* (Chicago: University of Chicago Press, 2002), p. 67.

26   "served a new demand on GM": *International News Service,* December 31, 1936.

28   "Mr. Ford, I don't think what": Arthur Railton, *The Beetle: A Most Unlikely Story* (Verlagsgesellschaft Eurotax AG, 1985) p. 109.

Three: Glory Days of Ponies and Goats

32   "If Ford makes success": Zora Arkus-Duntov memo to Chevrolet management, National Corvette Museum, Bowling Green, Kentucky.

33   "to settle for no more than": "First Among Equals," *Time,* January 2, 1956.

33   "If you stand still": Ibid.

33   cars should provide "visual entertainment": "The Design History of General Motors," GM press release, May 2006.

39   "like putting falsies on grandma": Lee Iacocca and William Novak, *Iacocca* (New York: Bantam Dell, 2007), p. 71.

Four: Crummy Cars and CAFE Society

45–46   "was thus by definition inflationary": Jerry Flint, "General Motors and Union Reach Terms for Pact," *The New York Times,* November 12, 1970, p. 1.

49   happened to fall on Ash Wednesday: General Motors executive, interview by author, May 13, 2009.

50   "I frankly don't see how": Jerry Flint, "Henry Ford Pessimistic on Foreign Autos; Doubts Detroit Can Compete," *The New York Times,* May 14, 1971.

50   "holding the industry's feet": Ibid.

51   Chairman James M. Roche: J. Patrick Wright, *On a Clear Day You Can See General Motors* (London: Sidgwick & Jackson, 1979), p. 158.

51   Meanwhile the Vega failed to meet: Ibid.

52   "Autos regularly roll off": "Labor Sabotage at Lordstown?" *Time,* February 17, 1972.

55   "I Would Have Rather Bought": Deborah Arnesen, interview by author, February 2009.

56   By 1975 GM's pension costs for UAW members: Roger Lowenstein, *While America Aged* (New York: Penguin Press, 2008), p. 42.

56   "Pension costs have substantially exceeded": Ibid.

56   "We were aware that the trend": Raymond Boryczka, *Archives of Labor and Urban Affairs: A UAW Chronology, 1935–1990,* Reuther Labor Library, Wayne State University.

56–57   "Our members have the best contract": Jeff Bickerstaff, assistant to marketing executive Buzz Hammer, interview by author, April 2009; Bickerstaff recalled this conversation between Woodcock and Hammer in the fall of 1978.

57   Between 1971 and 1974 the price of a typical Vega: Robert Spinello, "Complete Vega History 1970–1977 Including Yearly Changes, Virtues & Vices, Cosworth, '71 Press," online at http://H-body.org.

57   The Olds owner complained to the Illinois: "End of the Great Engine Flap," *Time,* January 2, 1978.

59   "It was like a large napalm bomb": "Fire Came from Fuel Tank Area," Associated Press article in *The Globe and Mail,* January 18, 1980.

59   "the tube leading to the gas-tank cap": Mark Dowie, "Pinto Madness," *Mother Jones,* September/October 1977.

59   "Burning Pintos have become": Ibid.

59   mainstream publications: "Ford Pinto Scored in Coast Magazine on Peril from Fire," Associated Press article in *The New York Times,* August 11, 1977.

60   Ford won a $19.2 million federal contract: Dow Jones News Service, May 6, 1980.

61   "The conventional case for a bailout": *The Washington Post,* August 2, 1979.

Five: Honda Comes to the Cornfields

64   But when the Americans asked for detailed: Shige Yoshida, retired Honda executive, interview by author, January 8, 2009.

64	"is going to have a Jap engine": Op. cit. Iacocca with Novak, *Iacocca,* p. 108.
65	"just a four-wheeled motorcycle": Masaaki Sato, *The Honda Myth* (New York: Vertical, 2006).
67	Improbably, a Japanese boy: Yoshida interview.
68	"Hippies," he said. "Blue jeans": Ibid.
69	"We're going tomorrow": Jim Duerk, interview by author, November 5, 2008.
69	The entire trip lasted just four and a half days: Ibid.
70	One of the first to apply: Al Kinzer, interview by author, March 2009.
71	Kinzer protested that Honda was ignoring: Ibid.
71	"I thought I had made a mistake": Brad Alty, Honda worker and later manager, interview by author, October 2008.
72	"It was all about speed, crazy speed": Toshi Amino, interview by author, October 2008.
72	"Where is the airport in Columbus": Yoshida interview.
73	The union viewed the nonunion plant in Marysville: Rev. Peter Laarman, former director of public affairs, United Auto Workers, interview by author, January 9, 2009.
74	Certainly they expected Honda's "associates": Ed Buker, former Honda factory manager, interview by author, January 14, 2009.
75	"I think we fight": Chan Cochran, Honda consultant, interview by author, October 2008.
114	Yoshida, who bore the brunt: Yoshida interview.

Six: Repentance, Rebirth, and Relapse

78	No one dared reveal: Op. cit. Iacocca with Novak, *Iacocca,* p. 102.
83	"birthday parties, benefits and bar mitzvahs": Urban C. Lehner, *The Wall Street Journal,* January 4, 1985.
83	"Are you saying we've been fucked": Retired Chrysler executive, interview by author, 2009.
85	"identified over 400 of the best": Ford sales brochure, 1986, National Automotive History Collection, Detroit Public Library.
87–88	"more secure than ever in history": Jeffrey McCracken, "Idle Hands," *The Wall Street Journal,* March 1, 2006.
89	CEO of the Year: *Financial World,* April 1985.
89	"cherubic chairman of General Motors": William J. Hampton and Marilyn Edid, *BusinessWeek,* June 17, 1985.
89	"Chrysler is diversifying": Lee Iacocca, chairman's letter, Chrysler annual report, 1985, National Automotive History Collection, Detroit Public Library.
91	Other automation-software malfunctions: Amal Nag, "Auto Makers Discover 'Factory of Future' Is Headache Just Now," *The Wall Street Journal,* May 13, 1986.
91	"Roger Smith works on everything": H. Ross Perot, interview by Doron Levin and Paul Ingrassia, Dallas, May 1986.
91	"The first EDSer who sees a snake": "Ross Perot's Crusade," *BusinessWeek,* October 6, 1986.
92	"What's Plan B?": Former GM executive, interview by author, 2009.
93	It was all perfectly legal: Gary Hector, "Cute Tricks on the Bottom Line," *Fortune,* April 24, 1989.

93   "reflect the company's renewed commitment:" Lee Iacocca, letter to sharehold-
          ers, Chrysler Annual Report, 1989, National Automotive History Collection, De-
          troit Public Library.

96   "I see it's three against one": Robert Stempel, interview by author, 1990.

98   "We realize the urgency of change": John F. Smith, Jr., letter to shareholders,
          General Motors Annual Report, 1992, National Automotive History Collection,
          Detroit Public Library.

Seven: "Car Jesus" and the Rise of the SUV

100   Honda executives told each other: Former Honda executive, interview by au-
          thor, 2009.

101   "has given Jeep's renowned Cherokee": Dennis Cauchon et al., "What's Hot,
          What's Not," *USA Today,* December 24, 1990.

102   "People from Ford prefer Chevy trucks": Joane Lipman, "Feud Revs Up Over
          Chevy's 'Ford' Ads," *The Wall Street Journal,* January 11, 1990.

103   "Nobody really loves you but your momma": Lindsay Chappell, "Billmyer Sen-
          tence Satisfied Ex-Dealer," *Automotive News,* October 9, 1995.

103   He threw Billmyer out: Ibid.

103   "kissing the ring": *United States v. John W. Billmyer,* U.S. Court of Appeals, First
          Circuit, No. 95-2147.

104   "Rolex conventions": Holman Jenkins, " 'Tis the Season of Sin at Honda," *The
          Wall Street Journal Europe,* December 18, 1996.

104   "Car Jesus": Scott Higham, "Bribe Case Steers Honda to Court," Baltimore *Sun,*
          July 21, 1996.

104   Cardiges made it happen: Ibid.

104   Another dealer who contributed: Bill Krueger, "Auto Tycoon Hendrick In-
          dicted," *Raleigh (NC) News and Observer,* December 5, 1996.

104   One New England dealer: Jenkins, " 'Tis the Season."

105   "mutual agreement": *United States v. John W. Billmyer.*

105   "could well be accused of being negligent": James Bennett, "Four Former
          Honda Employees Sentenced in Kickback Case," *The New York Times,* August 26,
          1995.

107   "It's a case of damage limitation": Seth Sutel, "Japan Carmakers Losing U.S.
          Sales," *Seattle Post-Intelligencer,* March 17, 1994.

108   The new Ram pickup: Keith Bradsher, *High and Mighty: The Dangerous Rise of the
          SUV* (New York: Public Affairs, 2004), p. 95.

109   But by 1995 that ratio was reversed: *Ward's Automotive Yearbook,* 1996.

112   "We wish we could just shrink-wrap": Former Chrysler executive, interview by
          author, 2009.

112   "We started jumping for joy": Ibid.

113   "We'll have the size, the profitability": Another former Chrysler executive, inter-
          view by author, April 21, 2009.

114   When the cover was pulled off the new vehicle: Former Ford executive, inter-
          view by author, 2009.

115   "It's wonderful to be in this industry": Gregory L. White et al., "Bumper Crop,"
          The Wall Street Journal, January 8, 1999.

Eight: Potholes and Missed Opportunities

116   "the largest auto show exhibit ever": "General Motors Begins Construction of Largest Auto Show Exhibit in North America," *PR Newswire,* November 12, 1999.

117   At the "line-off" ceremony: Former Toyota executive, interview by author, 2009.

119   "Don read books—and let the other guys know": Retired UAW staff member, interview by author, 2009.

120   "Our job was to prevent management": Mike Bennett, interview by author, March 13, 2009.

120   "the greatest threat to our livelihoods": Ibid.

121   "like heaven; a nice, clean new plant": Ann Fox, interview by J. Halpert, March 2009.

121   "You felt more loyal," she would explain: Ibid.

121–122 "People would shoot back: 'You Saturn guys' ": Former Saturn executive, interview by author, 2009.

122   "Where does that put the rest of what GM builds?": Kathleen Kerwin, "Saturn: GM Finally Has a Real Winner," *BusinessWeek,* August 17, 1992.

122   One senior executive: Elmer Johnson, former GM executive vice president, interviews by author, 2009.

122   "The UAW thanks Brother Ephlin": UAW convention brochure, July 20, 1989, Walter Reuther Labor Library, Wayne State University.

123   "Can America Still Compete?": S. C. Gwynne, "Can America Still Compete?" *Time,* October 29, 1990.

123   "scares the liver out of": Ibid.

124   *"Shinjirarenai"* ("Unbelievable"): Former Honda executive, interview by author, 2009.

124   Dealers were equally enthusiastic: Tom Zimbrick, interview by J. Halpert, March 2009.

126   In these decisions Mike Bennett tried to play: Bennett interview.

127   He was Stephen P. Yokich, the child: Terril Yue Jones, "Stephen P. Yokich, 66, Former President of UAW," *Los Angeles Times,* August 17, 2002.

127   "The cardinal's a fucking prick!": Stephen P. Yokich, interview by Jacob Schlesinger and Paul Ingrassia, Detroit, 1988.

129   It was the sort of utter craziness: James R. Healey and Micheline Maynard, "The Uncivil War," *USA Today,* June 29, 1998.

129   The strike's impact caused the entire: *Associated Press Financial News,* July 16, 1998.

130   "I mean it's nuts," Yokich told reporters: Healey and Maynard, "The Uncivil War."

131   fill out an internal "score sheet": Micheline Maynard, "Toasting New Harmony," *USA Today,* December 16, 1998.

131   "building 'lean and agile' plants too quickly": Thomas Donlan, "Now a Strike of Capital," *Barron's,* August 10, 1998.

132   a peace parley with Yokich: Maynard, "Toasting New Harmony."

133   "I'm optimistic . . . I think we'll make it work": David Sedgwick, "GM Plan to Reinvent Factory Gets Cautious OK from UAW," *Automotive News,* January 18, 1999.

133   "I haven't been involved": Jennifer Bott and Ted Evanoff, "President of Auto

Workers Union Undecided on General Motors' Car Plan," *Detroit Free Press,* January 13, 1999.

133   "put a muzzle" on Mark Hogan: David Sedgwick, "GM Comments on Yellowstone Get Frosty Response from UAW," *Automotive News,* May 17, 1999.

134   "So, I hear you've just been fired": Mark Hogan, interview by author, February 10, 2009.

134   "I've got to go dark": Ted Evanoff, "To Please Union, General Motors Quiets Talk on New Manufacturing Plans," *Detroit Free Press,* May 27, 1999.

134   regarded Yokich as a bully: Art Baker, interview by author, March 11, 2009.

135   "I wake up at night sick": Bennett interview.

Nine: From Riches to Rags

137   The Germans did get to drive Vipers: Gregory L. White, "Test Drives and Presents Help Lubricate a Car Merger," *The Wall Street Journal,* September 18, 1998.

137   "See you later, boys": Bill Vlasic and Bradley A. Stertz, *Taken for a Ride* (New York: HarperBusiness, 2001), p. 292.

137   the size of the business cards: Former DaimlerChrysler executive, interview by author, 2009.

137   another squabble: Ibid.

140   "get back to doing what we're really good at": James Holden, interview by author, October 23, 2009.

140   "the biggest business mistake of my life": Another former DaimlerChrysler executive, interview by author, 2003.

141   "If this business plan was a movie": Holden interview.

143   "It had to be done": Tim Burt and Richard Lambert, "The Schrempp Gambit," *The Financial Times,* October 30, 2000.

143   "Occupied Chrysler": Jerry Flint, "Occupied Chrysler," *Ward's Auto World,* November 1999.

143   "getting butts into seats": Justin Hyde, "Focus on 'Getting Butts into Seats' at Chrysler," Reuters, March 28, 2001.

145   "So now you have your monarchy back": Alex Taylor III, "The Fight at Ford: Behind Bill's Boardroom Struggle," *Fortune,* April 3, 2000.

145   He hired an "executive coach": Former Ford executive, interview by author, 2009.

145   So Nasser commissioned an internal Ford study: Another former Ford executive, interview by author, 2009.

146   "I see too many white male faces": Retired Ford manager, interview by author, 2009.

146   "Australian blue": Current and former Ford executives, interviews by author, 2009.

146   "be in a fight almost every day": Betsy Morris, "Idealist on Board: This Ford Is Different," *Fortune,* April 3, 2000.

148   "a cross between Al Gore": Alex Taylor III, "Jac Nasser's Big Test," *Fortune,* September 18, 2000.

148   A high-powered Washington consultant prepped him: Former Ford executive, interview by author, 2009.

148   "It's like tying two cats by the tails": Stephen Power and Clare Ansberry, "Bridge-

stone/Firestone Says It Made 'Bad Tires,' " *The Wall Street Journal,* September 13, 2000.

148   "nobody could have done a better": Robert L. Simison, "Behind the Wheel: For Ford CEO Nasser, Damage Control Is the New Job One," *The Wall Street Journal,* September 11, 2000.

149   "This decision is a painful one for me personally": Joseph B. White et al., "Ford Intends to Replace Millions of Tires," *The Wall Street Journal,* April 23, 2001.

150   "Jack Welch has 10 guys around him": Alex Taylor III, "Crunch Time for Jac," *Fortune,* June 25, 2001.

151   In October he tried to recruit Jim Holden: Holden interview.

151   "Gee, it's like the Lions won a game": Terril Yue Jones, "Bill Ford Takes Reins," *Los Angeles Times,* October 31, 2001.

151   "The question shouldn't be about me keeping the job": Jim Mateja, "Taking a Spin with GM's CEO-in-Waiting," *Chicago Tribune,* February 18, 2000.

152   "Rick's older brother": Former Fiat executive, interview by author, 2009.

152   Wagoner balked at the "put" provision: Ibid.

153   Around midnight on Sunday: Kathleen Kerwin et al., "For GM, Once Again, Little Ventured, Little Gained," *BusinessWeek,* March 27, 2000.

154   A *Forbes* headline declared: Jerry Flint, "Time to Praise GM," *Forbes,* December 10, 2001.

154   "Expected to operate as a play-it-safe": Alex Taylor III, "Finally GM Is Looking Good," *Fortune,* April 1, 2002.

155   But when the recommendations were presented: Former GM executive, interview by author, 2009.

156   a cover story titled "The End of Cheap Oil": Another former GM executive, interview by author, 2009.

157   "When the going gets tough": Chris Reiter, "DaimlerChrysler Won't Back Away from Global Plan," *Dow Jones Newswires,* April 8, 2004.

159   "I don't like saber rattling . . . a surprise": Danny Hakim, "A UAW Chief Awaits a GM Showdown," *The New York Times,* June 23, 2005.

160   "We strongly believe the auto business": GM press release, January 19, 2005.

Ten: The Hurricane That Hit Detroit

162   The company's healthcare expenses: David Welch, "GM Is Losing Traction," *BusinessWeek,* February 7, 2005.

164   In March 2005 crude oil hit a then-record price: Jeffrey Ball and Joseph B. White, "Rising Gasoline Prices Threaten Viability of Biggest SUVs," *The Wall Street Journal,* March 22, 2005.

165   "a significant full-year loss": GM press release, March 16, 2005.

165   "GM's big retiree handicap": Welch, "GM Is Losing Traction."

169   "We have a problem": Steve Miller, interview by author, January 10, 2009.

170   "Nobody wants to be the guy": Justin Fox, "A CEO Puts His Job on the Line," *Fortune,* May 2, 2005.

171   "Once again, we see the disgusting": UAW press release, October 8, 2005.

172   "Behind all this financial drama": Steve Miller, interview by author, October 12, 2005.

172   "Beyond Delphi, things are going": Ibid.

172   "Our people are irate about the approach": Joseph B. White and Jeffrey Mc-Cracken, "GM Presses UAW for Health-Care Deal," *The Wall Street Journal*, October 15, 2005.

173   "Our plans do not include anything": Joseph B. White and Lee Hawkins, Jr., "GM Cuts Deeper," *The Wall Street Journal*, November 22, 2005.

173   "It started out bad": Peter Brown et al., "Wagoner: 2005 Began Poorly, Then Worsened," *Automotive News*, December 19, 2005.

173   "Do you have to shoot yourself in the foot": David Gow, "DaimlerChrysler Shareholders Rebel," *The Guardian*, April 7, 2005.

174   "I am, and always will be, a Chrysler man": Brett Clanton and Christine Tierney, "How Zetsche Won Top DCX Job," *Detroit News*, July 31, 2005.

180   "in the best interest of GM right now": Monica Langley, "Pre-emptive Strike," *The Wall Street Journal*, June 5, 2006.

180   "I wouldn't be in this job": Ibid.

180   "While I will not offer excuses": Rick Wagoner to GM shareholders, April 28, 2006.

184   "Who does this guy from Las Vegas": Monica Langley et al., "Road Warriors," *The Wall Street Journal*, October 7, 2006.

184   "It's not logical or responsible": *Automotive News*, September 27, 2006.

185   "The company has made excellent progress": Jerome York to GM, resignation letter, October 6, 2006.

186   "We're profitable this year": Peter Brown and Amy Wilson, "Bill Ford: Company Is in Crisis, Not Chaos," *Automotive News*, December 5, 2005.

Eleven: Chapter 11?

192   "My next project may be called": Mark Phelan, "Charged Up," *Detroit Free Press*, January 8, 2007.

193   "I don't care what junior analyst": "BreakingViews," *GM Quotes*, booklet, June 1, 2008.

194   "Our entire GM team": GM 2006 Annual Report.

196   Cerberus's founder: Andrew Ross Sorkin, "A Recluse Lifts the Veil a Little," *The New York Times*, April 15, 2008.

202   "We've done a lot of things": Micheline Maynard, "73,000 UAW Members Go on Strike Against GM," *The New York Times*, September 25, 2007.

202   "bold gamble that it could get": NPR.org, September 25, 2007.

210   "not impossible": David Shepardson, "Wagoner Seeks to Quell GM Bankruptcy Speculation," *The Detroit News*, July 11, 2008.

213   "The stunning series of events": Andrew Ross Sorkin, "Lehman Files for Bankruptcy; Merrill Is Sold," *The New York Times*, September 15, 2008.

214   "I don't think it'd be a very smart move": "Memorable Quotations of 2008," *Automotive News*, December 29, 2008.

Twelve: As the Precipice Approaches

The preponderance of the material in this chapter came from confidential interviews with individuals directly involved, in a wide range of capacities, in the efforts to rescue General Motors and Chrysler. For simplicity's sake, these interviews aren't individually cited here; only material obtained from other sources is cited.

227   "Quite frankly, the White House": David Shephardson, "In Unlikely Role, Bush Is Last Hope for Detroit," *The Detroit News,* Decmber 15, 2008.

228   "We need these loans": Steven Mufson, "White House Moves Toward Auto Bailout," *The Washington Post,* December 13, 2008.

228   "I am so proud of Rick": George Fisher, interview by John Stoll, December 2008.

228   Deese was going to Washington: David E. Sanger, "The 31-Year-Old in Charge of Dismantling GM," *The New York Times,* June 1, 2009.

231   "that new-car smell": CBS, *Late Late Show,* June 5, 2005.

237   "strategic reviews—including their potential sale": "General Motors Corporation, 2009–2014 Restructuring Plan," February 17, 2009.

Thirteen: Bailouts, Bankruptcies, and Beyond

The preponderance of the material in this chapter came from confidential interviews with individuals directly involved, in a wide range of capacities, in the efforts to rescue General Motors and Chrysler. For simplicity's sake, these interviews aren't individually cited here; only material obtained from other sources is cited.

248   "I guess the UST is running it!": Neil King, Jr., and Jeffrey McCracken, "U.S. Pushed Fiat Deal on Chrysler," *The Wall Street Journal,* June 6, 2009.

251   "Uncle Sam wasn't going to be Uncle Sucker": Micheline Maynard and Michael J. de la Merced, "Will GM's Story Have a Hero?" *The New York Times,* July 26, 2009.

260   One eighty-one-year-old man in suburban Chicago: Kim Mikus, "GM Fallout," *Chicago Daily Herald,* June 5, 2009.

260   "We prefer to restructure outside of bankruptcy": Bill Vlasic and Nick Bunkley, "GM, Leaking Cash, Faces Bigger Chance of Bankruptcy," *The New York Times,* May 8, 2009.

263   "more than I can handle right now": Nick Bunkley, "GM Tells 1,100 Dealers It Plans to Drop Them," *The New York Times,* May 15, 2009.

266   "an icon for retirement-home parking lots": Adrian Imonti, "GM's Death Watch 172: Buick's Enclave," Thetruthaboutcars.com, April 15, 2009.

267   The U.S. government—by default: Maynard and de la Merced, "Will GM's Story."

272   "Microsoft and Apple and Toyota all rolled": John D. Stoll et al., "A Saga of Decline and Denial," *The Wall Street Journal,* June 2, 2009.

Afterword: Another Chance

275   After closing twenty-two factories between 2004 and 2008: Bill Vlasic and Nick Bunkley, "Scars of an Ailing Industry," *The New York Times,* July 31, 2009.

278   less than 12 percent of the peak level: Michael McKee, "GM's Long Decline May Make Bankruptcy 'Irrelevant' to Economy," Bloomburg News, June 1, 2009.

PAUL J. INGRASSIA is an award-winning financial journalist and author with nearly a quarter century of experience in writing about the automotive industry in America and around the world. In 1993 he won the Pulitzer Prize along with his colleague Joseph B. White for their reporting on the management crisis and boardroom revolt at General Motors. Ingrassia and White coauthored *Comeback: The Fall and Rise of the American Automobile Industry.* Ingrassia has chronicled the car industry's successes and epic failures over the past twenty-five years in the pages of *The Wall Street Journal.* As a former executive of Dow Jones, he is one of the few authors who has been trained as a journalist and has direct experience in running a business. He and his wife live in New Jersey and have three grown sons.

This book was set in Monotype Dante, a typeface designed by Giovanni Mardersteig (1892–1977). Conceived as a private type for the Officina Bodoni in Verona, Italy, Dante was originally cut only for hand composition by Charles Malin, the famous Parisian punch cutter, between 1946 and 1952. Its first use was in an edition of Boccaccio's *Trattatello in laude di Dante* that appeared in 1954. The Monotype Corporation's version of Dante followed in 1957. Though modeled on the Aldine type used for Pietro Cardinal Bembo's treatise *De Aetna* in 1495, Dante is a thoroughly modern interpretation of that venerable face.